Conducting Tours

THIRD EDITION

Conducting Tours

THIRD EDITION

Marc Mancini, Ph.D.

Professor
Department of Travel
West Los Angeles College

DELMAR
CENGAGE Learning

Australia • Brazil • Japan • Korea • Mexico • Singapore • Spain • United Kingdom • United States

Conducting Tours, Third Edition
Marc Mancini

Business Unit Director: Susan L. Simpfenderfer

Executive Editor: Marlene McHugh Pratt

Acquisitions Editor: Erin O'Connor Traylor

Editorial Assistant: Alexis Ferraro

Executive Marketing Manager: Donna J. Lewis

Channel Managers: Nigar Hale, Wendy Mapstone

Executive Production Manager: Wendy A. Troeger

Production Editor: Elaine Scull

Cover Design: Joseph Villanova

© 2001 Delmar, Cengage Learning

For product information and technology assistance, contact us at
Cengage Learning Customer & Sales Support, 1-800-354-9706
For permission to use material from this text or product,
submit all requests online at **www.cengage.com/permissions**
Further permissions questions can be emailed to
permissionrequest@cengage.com

Library of Congress Control Number: 00-043132

ISBN-13: 978-0-7668-1419-6

ISBN-10: 0-7668-1419-X

Delmar
Executive Woods
5 Maxwell Drive
Clifton Park, NY 12065
USA

Cengage Learning is a leading provider of customized learning solutions with office locations around the globe, including Singapore, the United Kingdom, Australia, Mexico, Brazil, and Japan. Locate your local office at **www.cengage.com/global**

Cengage Learning products are represented in Canada by Nelson Education, Ltd.

To learn more about Delmar, visit **www.cengage.com/delmar**

Purchase any of our products at your local bookstore or at our preferred online store **www.cengagebrain.com**

Notice to the Reader

Printed in the United States of America
12 13 14 15 16   19 18 17 16 15

Contents

Preface

To the Reader

Everyone, at one time or another, has considered what it would be like to be a tour guide. Tour escorting, specifically, has become one of the most attractive and sought-after jobs in the travel industry. It's easy to see why. A good tour conductor has the self-assurance and tact of a diplomat, the knowledge of a scholar, the performance skills of an entertainer, and the organizational abilities of a time management expert. Furthermore, a tour manager travels the world and is paid to do so. Indeed, tour conducting is a seductive profession.

But leading a tour is no easy job. And, sadly, many of the strategies for dealing with its challenges are learned most often on the job, sometimes when it's too late. Equally challenging is how to plan group departures. This skill, too, often comes only after years of practice.

Conducting Tours will be useful to you, whether you're contemplating a tour-escorting career or you're already managing groups of tourists or students on a study tour. It will serve as a guide for those of you who wish to go into other positions in the tour industry, especially tour planning. It will also give those of you in other segments of the travel industry—hotel personnel, city guides, travel agents, tourist bureau representatives, and the like—an intimate glimpse of the tour operations with which you so regularly deal.

Conducting Tours starts with useful, basic information about guiding, escorting, and tour planning and moves quickly to more subtle topics:

▼ What is the peculiar psychology of group behavior?

▼ What cross-cultural forces affect tour management?

▼ What are the ethical challenges to tour leaders?

▼ What are the "tricks" that can make guide commentary more effective?

▼ What makes an itinerary successful?

▼ How does one get a tour-escorting job and keep it?

▼ What other positions in the tour industry are available to you?

These are just some of the lively questions, explored in only a limited fashion elsewhere, that *Conducting Tours* answers.

To guide you through this subject matter, *Conducting Tours* relies on several handy organizational features.

▼ Each of the ten chapters begins with an overview of the knowledge you'll gain while reading.

▼ Headings and subheadings serve to clarify and organize what you read.

▼ The prose is in a magazine-like style, both simple and entertaining, so that *Conducting Tours* will be fun for you to study.

▼ Numerous photographs, graphics, and quotes from industry leaders illustrate key points.

▼ Profiles of working guides, tour managers, and tour-related personnel make the issues come alive.

▼ A summary at each chapter's end pulls together what you've learned.

▼ Following each summary are questions for you to consider and over thirty unique, creative, and entertaining activities that will enable you to apply information from your readings or to learn a little bit more about yourself.

▼ Glossary terms are highlighted in the text by bold type.

▼ At the book's end is an appendix containing a list of useful addresses, a glossary, a bibliography, addresses and phone numbers of major tour companies, and an index.

You can be sure of one thing: after reading *Conducting Tours* you'll be as well informed as a tour director, guide, or planner can be. The information is drawn from my experiences in conducting over 150 domestic and international tours, teaching courses in tour management for many years, and holding consulting positions with many of the industry's leading tour companies.

I wish you luck in your career. I hope that reading this text will be an enjoyable and educational experience for you.

To the Teacher or Trainer

This third edition of *Conducting Tours* and its accompanying *Instructor's Guide* have been designed so that a course, seminar, or unit on tour escorting and/or tour planning can be "plugged into" your curriculum with a minimum of hassle. We have retained and updated most of the features that made *Conducting Tours* the most widely used and recommended text in the field, while incorporating substantial new content on tour operations and planning to each chapter. Also, the number of activities, one of the most praised features in previous editions, has been increased.

The *Instructor's Guide* provides detailed chapter outlines (to help you design your course outlines), suggested teaching strategies, supplemental activities, answers to the text's questions and activities, a certificate of completion, video suggestions, and a test bank of thirty quizzes with accompanying answer keys.

The *Instructor's Guide* can be obtained through your local Delmar Publishers sales representative or directly from the company. Please remember that no portion of the student text can be reproduced without the written permission of Delmar Publishers.

You'll find, as other instructors have, that *Conducting Tours* can be used out of sequence. Chapter 9, for example, can be taught after Chapter 3. This versatility should permit you to deliver your course in whatever sequence you prefer.

Acknowledgments

My very deepest gratitude goes to my original reviewers: Marilyn Kern-Ladner, Maria McConnell, Talulah Gunter, John Kesler, and Jeanie Harris; Isabelle Ebert, my production assistant on the first edition; Karen Fukushima, my production assistant on the second and third editions; Sandy Hanlon and Micah Edwards, NTA; Robert Whitley, USTOA; Terry Lee, Marriott International; and to all those who provided me with information and advice. And to all the seminar participants, colleagues, tour participants, and students who contributed much through their questions, advice, and enthusiasm, my sincere thanks.

Finally, I wish to express my appreciation to my parents—who met on a tour, no less—and who have provided me with countless ideas and unlimited inspiration for this book.

Marc Mancini

PROFILE

Recent statistics indicate that the average American switches careers six times during his or her lifetime. "If that's so," says Thomasine Rogas, "then I'm breaking away from the norm. Tour management is my third career and I can't imagine doing anything else. I love it."

Thomasine entered the industry as a travel agent in Boston. Her second life change was when she became a mother. "Believe me," she says, "bringing up kids *is* a profession." As her children approached adulthood, however, Thomasine began looking for a career that would be challenging yet flexible. "I spotted a newspaper article about a tour conducting class at a nearby college. I was intrigued. I cut it out and filed it away. Four years later, no less, I contacted the instructor to find out if the class was still being offered. It was, and I was on my way."

Thomasine began to call and write to a number of companies. "It was discouraging at first," she admits. "The only experience I could point to was my familiarity with geography, via travel agenting, and planning field trips for my children's school."

Yet Tauck World Discovery saw something special in Thomasine's application. They interviewed her, and she was quickly on the road. "I believe that each tour conductor, to succeed, must play to his or her strengths," she says. "Mine are the willingness to do in-depth research on the places I go to and to do those little things that make a trip extra special for the clients."

Among those little things is a very unique service Thomasine provides. "Sometimes, the night before I leave on a tour, I bake bread or cookies. I then offer them to my clients during the first day on the road. It makes them feel appreciated, personalizes the tour experience for them, and certainly cements that all-important escort-client relationship."

What Is Tour Conducting?

Chapter Objectives

After reading this chapter, you should be able to:

▼ Define key terms commonly used in the tour industry.

▼ Explain why people take a tour.

▼ Identify for whom tour guides and tour managers generally work.

▼ Appraise the attraction of tour conducting as a career.

▼ Identify the disadvantages of a tour-conducting career.

▼ Explain what roles others play in a tour company's operation.

▼ Profile the "typical" tour manager sought by tour operators.

▼ Discuss which personality traits can undermine a tour conductor's success.

"I DON'T HAVE ANY RECORD OF A GROUP RESERVATION BUT THEY DO LOOK LIKE THEY QUALIFY"

Tour conducting"—to some the term inspires visions of glamour and adventure. To others it suggests a unique way to see the world, and get paid to do it. That old 1969 movie, *If It's Tuesday This Must Be Belgium*, gathers together many of the more appealing preconceptions: it depicts a dashing, charming escort who, calmly and easily, guides a congenial, slightly eccentric group of tourists across the face of Europe.

The mental image that most people have of tour conductors is quite similar to the picture the movie industry typically paints. Yet just a little more thought suggests that there can be a downside, too: lost luggage, overbooked planes, overwrought clients. To lead a tour can be a delight, but it can occasionally become a trying experience. It is often a well-paying job, yet at the same time it is a demanding career. Without question, though, to be a tour conductor is to be in one of the most exhilarating, potentially rewarding, and intensely sought-after positions in the travel industry, and to work in any capacity at a tour company often leads to genuinely creative and satisfying experiences.

The Tour Industry

As we journey from place to place, it's easy to underestimate the complexity and scope of the travel industry. Yet in the United States alone, travel generates nearly $500 billion in revenues yearly. That's equal to the combined sales of Exxon, Ford, IBM, and Sears.

But what of touring itself? According to the National Tour Association (NTA), group travel represents about 4 percent of consumer travel. That may sound insignificant until you consider that travelers from the United States and Canada spend over $11 billion yearly on tours, and according to the U.S. Travel Data Center, one out of every five persons who takes a trip of five nights or more does so through a packaged tour. Expand these statistics to a worldwide perspective (group travel is often more popular abroad than in the United States), and you begin to perceive how vast an enterprise touring really is.

Furthermore, surveys indicate that group travel is accelerating at a pace that outstrips that of the general travel industry. According to the NTA, consumer spending on group tours is increasing at about 15 percent yearly. The NTA's roster of members has swelled to more than 600 tour companies, all of which anticipate even greater tour activity ahead. As the post-World War II baby boomers reach their middle years, the tradi-

tional tour consumer segment, those people over fifty, is increasing dramatically.

But is the vision of slow, absent-minded, polyester-clad, senior-citizen tour groups an appropriate one? Hardly. Today's seniors are often the most energetic and adventuresome of tourists. Although the view of a fifty-plus tour market is valid (about 75 percent of the NTA's customers are retired and over fifty), it's also a bit deceiving. Increasingly, the tour marketplace is diversifying. There are now student camping tours, 1,000-mile bicycle excursions, UFO tours out of Las Vegas (looking for them, not riding them . . .), and even nostalgic bus tours for aging hippies.

Why Take a Tour?

Not everyone is a candidate for a tour. In fact, some people don't like the notion of tours at all. They perceive touring as an unpleasant form of travel, with limited freedom, forced companionship, and uncomfortable bus rides. They prefer—indeed, enjoy—controlling their own travel experience rather than having someone else doing it for them.

Yet many others actively seek out a tour experience. Every year at least 11 million Americans choose group travel. Why do they favor tours?

The Freedom from Hassles and Decision Making

"When I'm on vacation I don't want to worry about anything," is a comment commonly heard from tour participants (also called tour members, passengers, or clients). Indeed, travel (which comes from the French word for work) can be an exhausting task. Tours help cushion clients from hassles. A good tour leader solves problems long before tour members can become aware of them. To the average tour participant, the feeling of being pampered and catered to more than offsets the regimentation of group travel.

The Desire to Save Time and Money

Everyone has experienced how a wrong turn on a highway or an ill-chosen hotel can spoil a vacation. A well-designed and conducted tour minimizes wasted time; it ensures that the client sees all the essentials in a convenient, efficient manner. Furthermore, the

Early tour buses were a far cry from today's plush coaches.
Courtesy of the National Tour Association

group purchasing power of a tour company yields substantial savings on hotels, meals, and attractions. Part of this savings is absorbed into the tour operator's profit, but much of it is passed on to the consumer. The result: tour members enjoy a more upscale travel experience (better hotels, for example) than they could usually afford. And because the price of a tour includes most travel components, clients know and pay for most of their vacation costs before they even leave home.

Don't conclude, however, that just because tour clients seek value, they are a low-income group. In fact, quite the opposite is true: overall, escorted tour clients possess a higher yearly income, spend more on each trip, and take more trips than their counterparts who do not take tours.

The Companionship of People with Similar Interests

Several surveys have indicated that people who avoid tours sometimes fear they will have little in common with their fellow travelers. As those who frequent tours know, this is rarely the case. Most often, the price of a tour, its destination and its activities will automatically predetermine the socioeconomic level and interests of group members. It's no accident that long and deep friendships are often forged among the participants in a tour.

People with plenty in common are certainly found on those tours that are custom-designed for clients with special interests (for instance, skiing, shopping, wine tasting, ecotourism, astronomy, ballooning, bird watching) or even for specific clubs, schools, religious groups, or corporations (often called *affinity tours*). Some of the most intriguing successes in the tour business today are tours that are highly specialized and that target "niche" or specialty markets. One Los Angeles company, for instance, creates tours for insomniacs: the group sightsees all night and sleeps during the day. Another pulls together geologists on a moment's notice to visit erupting volcanoes. In fact, the modern touring phenomenon has its roots in affinity travel. Thomas Cook, a British travel pioneer of the mid-nineteenth century, organized his first group departures for prohibitionists who wished to attend faraway temperance meetings.

The Educational Nature of Touring

Without a guide (or at least a guidebook) the Forum in Rome is little more than an accumulation of pillars, stones, and rubble. On a tour, however, it becomes a place alive with the imagined footsteps of Caesars, senators, and centurions. A well-trained tour guide or escort can comment on almost anything: history, geography, architecture, trees, bushes, birds—whatever merits the kind of insight that the average tourist craves but can seldom achieve on his or her own. Indeed, one recent poll indicates that 84 percent of tour travelers rated "learning" as the most important component of a tour, and nearly half of those polled expressed an eagerness to share what they learned with their family and friends upon returning.

Tours can be custom designed for those with special interests. *Courtesy of the National Tour Association*

The Lack of Alternatives

In rare situations, *all* travelers perceive a tour as the most appropriate choice. For example, tour operators sometimes corner all hotel space close to some special event, such as Mardi Gras, a world's fair, or the Rose Bowl. The only way for the average consumer to obtain lodging is to book a tour. Such strategies pay off doubly for the tour company. It profits financially, and tourists who were previously reluctant to take a tour are often pleasantly surprised and become converts to group travel.

A traveler who perceives a destination as especially strange, foreign, unfriendly, or even dangerous will also find comfort in the notion of a tour. The great majority of tourists who visit Kenya, China, or Russia, for example, do so as part of organized groups. Those who are physically challenged often travel as groups, too,

knowing that the specialized tour company that planned their trip has already thought out wheelchair obstacles, elevator access, and the like.

How People Buy Tours

Tour operators make their product available to the public in two distinct ways. They may advertise a series of tours, with departures occurring on a regularly scheduled basis. For example, a company may schedule weekly, seven-day motorcoach tours of New England, departing from Boston every Sunday from late May to late October. The consumer finds out about it from the company's brochures, catalogues, Web site or newspaper advertisements, and then books the date he or she wants. Tickets are purchased either through a travel agent (who may even have recommended the company and tour in the first place) or by communicating with the company directly. Of course, if the tour doesn't fill, the company may cancel that departure and try to shift the client to another departure.

Tours offered to the public in this manner are often called **public** or **per-capita** tours. On the other hand, tour companies also sell tours to preformed affinity groups. One option is to set aside one of their regularly scheduled departures for a specific group. The tour operator may also create a customized itinerary for them, at a special price. Such tours are usually called **customized** or **charter tours**.

A customized tour is rarely advertised outside the group. Instead, potential tour participants find out about it via flyers, a meeting, word-of-mouth, or an organization's newsletter. They can then buy the tour in a number of ways. They may call the tour company and identify themselves as members of the group, book it directly through their organization, or sign up directly through the person in the organization who has spearheaded the trip (a teacher at a school, for example).

Types of Tour Guides

To the public, the generic term "tour guide" suggests almost any person who leads an organized group of people, whether for an hour through the halls of the Taj Mahal, for a week on a boat down the Amazon River, or for a month on a motorcoach tour across the United States. In the travel industry, however, the term "tour guide" has a very precise meaning: a **tour guide** is someone who takes people on sightseeing excursions of limited duration. There are many kinds of tour guides.

Specifically, an **on-site guide** conducts tours of one or several hours at a specific building (such as St. Peter's in Rome), attraction (such as Disneyland), or limited area (such as the Kennedy Space Center in Florida). In the travel industry, all such sites are often referred to as **attractions**. The tour may be given on foot or in some sort of vehicle (e.g., the trams at Universal Studios).

On-site guides rarely make much above minimum wage. At museums they often work free of charge. These volunteer (and usually well-informed) museum guides are called **docents**. Two kinds of on-site guides often do make fairly good salaries: those employed by the government (e.g., park ranger guides) or by corporations (e.g., those who give a tour of a factory).

A **city guide** points out and comments on the highlights of a city, usually from a motorcoach, minibus, or van, but sometimes as part of a walking tour. A city guide who does double duty by driving the vehicle while narrating is often called a **driver-guide**. Another type of city guide is the **personal** or **private guide**. Common in developing countries, where these services may be available at a reasonable price, private guides take a small number of individuals on their own exclusive tour. These guides often are taxi drivers and use their taxis as sightseeing vehicles.

Though they rarely spend more than a day with any group, city guides often need to have a considerable amount of accurate information about the municipality in which they work. For this reason, they're sometimes tested and licensed by a local government agency.

A **specialized guide** is someone whose expertise or skills are highly unique. For instance, adventure guides lead unusual, physically demanding tour experiences (e.g., diving, white-water rafting, safari, or trekking). Another example is Egyptologists on Nile cruises, who have highly specialized knowledge of the history, art, and culture of that country.

Guides can work for large local tour companies (such as Gray Line), for cruise lines (on a type of tour called a **shore excursion**), or for **ground operators** (also called **land operators** or **receptive operators**), which provide vehicles and other limited services to outside tour companies. Many guides, however, operate independently. Tour groups visiting from other regions hire them as freelance "specialists" who come aboard their motorcoaches to give an informed overview of the city to be toured. Such freelance guides are usually called **step-on guides**. City guides, adventure guides, and personal guides tend to be better paid than on-site guides, though their salaries can vary considerably from place to place, company to company, or situation to situation.

A docent takes a group through the Kennedy Library in Boston.
Courtesy of the National Tour Association

Tour Managers

Tour guides are a little like good teachers: they deliver information in an accurate and engaging fashion. On the other hand, a **tour manager**—a person who manages a group's movements over a multi-day tour—is part psychologist, ombudsman, diplomat, scout leader, flight attendant, entertainer, news reporter, restaurant critic, efficiency expert, and orator. In certain situations, tour managers may even be expected to be translators, detectives, mind readers, and miracle workers. To be successful at this job is no easy achievement. The rewards, however—both personal and financial—can be sizable.

Not too long ago, tour managers were more commonly called "**tour escorts**." The term is still in use, but not greatly in favor—the fear being that confusion could arise in the public's mind between these travel professionals and those working for dubiously named "escort services." Among the other terms used to describe a tour manager are **tour leader, tour director, tour conductor**, and, in Europe, **tour courier**. We will be using these terms interchangeably throughout the book. Note that a few companies, such as Collette Tours, even prefer to call their tour managers "tour guides" to stress their employees' sightseeing commentary skills.

Employers of Tour Managers

Tour-manager employment is even more diversified than that of tour guides. Tour conductors can be attached to any of the following.

Tour Operators

Tour managers are most commonly employed by **tour operators** (also called **tour companies, tour packagers, tour brokers**, or **wholesalers**). Tour operators contract with hotels, restaurants, attractions, airlines, motorcoach operators, and other transportation companies (or **carriers**) to create a multi-day tour "package." They then sell the tour to the public, either directly or through travel agents.

Travel agencies especially like to sell tours, since they can make a commission on most of a client's vacation activities (even meals) with minimal arrangement has-

sles. In some cases, travel agencies promote and plan their own group departures, becoming tour operators as well.

Inbound and Outbound Operators. An **inbound tour operator** is a subcategory of tour operator who specializes mostly in groups arriving in a specific city, area, or country. For example, Allied Tours, American Tours International, and GoAmerica Tours are all United States companies that sell tours abroad through their own branches or through those of other companies. Once a group from, say, Argentina arrives, all of its needs in the United States are serviced by the inbound operator (who in turn often works with a local ground operator). Inbound operators favor tour conductors who are fluent in a foreign language.

An **outbound operator**, another subcategory of tour operator, takes groups from a given city or country to another city or country. For example, Donna Franca Tours of Boston regularly transports groups of Americans to Italy. Occasionally, its tour managers accompany the groups from Boston to Rome. More typically, Donna Franca has bilingual tour conductors stationed in Italy who greet the group upon arrival.

Outbound tour operator practices vary enormously. Some companies send escorts with the groups, others station them at the destination, and still others contract with inbound operators at the destination and rely on the inbound company's tour leaders.

Motorcoach and Intermodal Operators. Another way to slice the tour operator pie is into motorcoach and intermodal companies. **Motorcoach operators** create tours, usually of about a week's duration, that transport group members via motorcoach to their destination and back. Well-known motorcoach tour companies, such as Tauck World Discovery of Westport, Connecticut, operate their North American packages primarily as motorcoach tours. Clients might meet up with their group in New York City, for example, from which Tauck's chartered motorcoach will take them on through scenic Connecticut, Massachusetts, and Vermont, and on up to Montreal and Quebec City. For other North American destinations, Tauck will use such "gateway" cities as Calgary, Honolulu, New Orleans, and Salt Lake City as the start points for their tours. Although Tauck does include flights on some of its itineraries (e.g., to Europe or Hawaii), more typically it is left to the client or travel agent to book a flight to the "gateway" departure city.

Since motorcoach tours sometimes involve long stretches of travel, operators who specialize in them

A motorcoach group visits the Rockies. *Courtesy of the National Tour Association*

favor tour leaders with considerable entertainment skills. In Europe, where motorcoach tours are especially popular, escorts who also act as tour guides are quite common.

Intermodal operators combine several forms of transportation, such as plane, motorcoach, ship, and rail, to create a diversified and efficient tour package. Increasingly popular, these kinds of tours appeal to the desire of a traveler to "get there." Intermodal operators tend to downplay the role of motorcoaches in their packaging. Several studies have shown that an aversion to bus transportation is the single most important factor that prevents clients from taking a group tour, despite the comparative luxury of modern motorcoaches.

Other Employers of Tour Managers and Guides

Tour operators aren't the only type of travel-related operation to employ guides and tour managers. Among the fastest growing employers of tour leaders are **incentive houses**. An incentive house (which is, in effect, a specialized tour company or is a division of a large travel agency) will approach a corporation with an overall strategy to boost sales, service, or efficiency by providing some sort of reward or incentive to the corporation's most productive employees. The most popular type of reward is travel, since it can be shaped into

group departures that reinforce company spirit and networking.

A national insurance company, for example, might fly all its agents who reach a certain predetermined sales level to Hawaii for a week, at company expense. (In reality, the increased sales that the incentive program has generated pay for the trip, provide the incentive house's profits, and generate higher revenues for, in this case, the insurance company.) Several people, of course, have to coordinate and host these group movements. For this purpose, incentive houses sometimes use their own planning staff. But, increasingly, they are hiring **trip directors** to do the job. A trip director is a sort of "super escort" who not only deals with traveling clients, but also is an essential player on the incentive company's pre-trip planning team. American Express Incentive Services is one of the largest incentive houses.

Tour conductors can also find employment with receptive operators and all sorts of specialized tour companies, including those who offer **student-study educational tours** or **adventure tours** (such as raft trips, hiking expeditions, and the like). Tour leaders for specialized affinity groups are often professionals in other fields—teachers, members of the clergy, or activity experts—who conduct the group for pleasure and a free trip. In some cases, a teacher will organize and escort a group departure for his or her students.

Banks—especially those in the South and Midwest United States—also frequently organize tours for their

A special kind of tour, the independent or *freelance tour*, bears examination, despite the fact that no escort is involved. In this type of package, a client purchases air, hotel, and attraction admissions and, typically, a car rental, for one price. The client does not travel with any group. (This kind of tour is also sometimes called an FIT. No one seems to agree, however, on what those three letters stand for—only that it means a custom-designed, prepaid travel package with individualized arrangements.)

For instance, a traveler who wishes to visit Hawaii can buy a seven-day package from Pleasant Holidays that includes six nights at the Sheraton Waikiki, air transportation to and from Honolulu, transportation between airport and hotel (called a *transfer*), a one-day car rental, and miscellaneous services (such as a lei airport greeting) for one reasonable price. The independent tour appeals especially to travelers who wish to have minimal regimentation yet want access to the efficient, bargain-priced packages that powerful volume group operators can offer. The introduction of this form of travel represents a major marketing success. In Canada and the United States, independent tours outsell escorted tours four to one.

It's common today for a tour operator to offer all three forms of group-generated travel to consumers. This strategy enables a company to reach several major segments of the traveling public: those who enjoy the leisurely, scenic pace of motorcoach tours; those who enjoy the group travel experience but find motoring to a destination via bus to be a dull waste of time; and those who don't like group travel at all but seek the volume prices and preplanning that tour companies can provide to independent travelers.

customers. In some cases, the bank staff member who is in charge of its travel program will escort the group. In other cases, the bank will contract with a tour operator to run its group departures. In such a situation, the tour company's tour conductor will manage the group, with a bank employee helping out.

Meet-and-greet companies may hire guides, escorts, or other "greeters" to be on hand when individuals or small groups of travelers arrive at an airport. The meet-and-greet person will help the visitors get their luggage and may even accompany or drive them to their hotel. (The meet-and-greet service is purchased in advance by the travelers.) **Convention** or **meeting planners** also sometimes hire guides and tour managers to operate pre- or post-convention tours for them.

Other Tour-Related Job Opportunities

Tour members often perceive the driver, escort, and guide as the tour company. But behind the scenes is a virtual army of individuals who ensure that the tour and company function well. Who are these people and what do they do?

▼ *Reservationists* deal with travel agents and the public via the telephone.

▼ *Sales representatives* serve as contact persons between travel agencies and the tour operator.

▼ *Marketing personnel* choreograph the company's advertising and generally facilitate the design and distribution of the tour product.

▼ *Operations staff members* ensure that the tours are well-planned and function smoothly. Many subcategories of tour operations exist, including itinerary planning, escort assignment and training, and company-supplier communications.

▼ *Executives* have ultimate responsibility for the company's success and for the performance of its workers.

It should be noted that during "slow" seasons, some tour leaders and guides serve their company in other capacities—for instance, as sales representatives or itinerary planners. Very common, too, is for tour managers to retire from their escorting careers in order to work in one of the above-described jobs. Indeed, most tour executives once served as tour conductors or guides.

The Appeal of Tour Conducting

The position of tour manager is one of the most attractive and sought-after in the travel industry. A recent poll of major tour operators indicates that the average company receives nearly 300 inquiries per year for escort employment. Some of the larger tour operators report more than 500 applicants yearly. Why do so many people want to be tour directors?

Glamour

Tour escorting is a high-profile, glamorous job. First, a tour conductor is paid to travel to the world's most exotic places, stay in splendid hotels (sometimes in a suite), and enjoy fine cuisine. Second, since the escorts are frequently hired as independent contractors, they often choose when and where to work. Tour conducting certainly is not a nine-to-five job.

Smartly dressed, the focus of attention for as many as fifty people, a master of a variety of skills, an escort becomes an instant celebrity to a tour group. Indeed, a good tour manager entertains and controls people in ways that are fascinating, dramatic, and heady.

Challenge

Tour escorting builds character and challenges one's skills. Why are good tour conductors so patient? Perhaps, in part, because the job made them that way. To succeed in the profession, a tour manager must have certain well-defined personality traits that are further refined through experience—having to make the right decision instantly, calm an irate passenger, break through to an obstinate hotel clerk, or improvise entertainment when a motorcoach breaks down. Jim Penler, retired chairman of the board of Paragon Tours, remarks, "It's amazing how many ex-escorts of ours are now lawyers, doctors, college professors, and leaders of the travel industry. One even became the mayor of the city where our corporate headquarters is located. I'd like to think that we spotted this energy and ambition when we hired these escorts. But I suspect that the job itself molded much of what later has served these people well."

A tour conductor becomes an instant celebrity to the group.
Courtesy of the National Tour Association

Salary and Benefits

Tour directors are paid well to see the world. Although this commonly held perception is largely true, a few caveats are in order. A tour operator often limits escorts to certain destinations. It's often true that escorts sample a narrow range of international attractions, at least in the early stages of employment, since companies assign novice escorts to less popular tours. Tour operators expect escorts to be fully available during high seasons. They may treat escorts as freelance independents, yet frown on their working for competing companies. And they'll certainly stop offering tours to an escort who turns down too many trips.

The financial rewards *can* be substantial. The typical tour operator pays a tour conductor a set amount per day (**per diem salary**), although some pay an hourly wage. A recent survey indicated that the average beginning tour director in the United States earned $50 per day; a veteran escort, $75 per day. Motorcoach companies tended to pay the least, with a starting average of about $40 daily. Inbound operators pay the most: veteran tour managers make as much as $150 daily, in large part because of the foreign language skills required for the job. Companies located in large cities, such as New York or Los Angeles, generally pay far more than those in smaller cities or towns. Incentive companies also pay a rather high per diem salary, if only because the trip director is less likely to receive tips or commissions.

Internationally, tour manager salaries can be quite high in relation to the standard of living. "In Ireland," observes James Murphy, chairman of Brendan Tours, "tour escorts are among the country's highest-paid people. And this is despite the fact that they basically work only from April to October."

When assessing the profitability of tour conducting, one must go beyond mere salary and examine the "perks" of the field:

▼ Transportation, accommodations, and most meals are provided free of charge to tour leaders. (Such free items are called **comps**, short for **complimentary**.) Most of their other expenses are picked up by the tour company.

▼ Tipping is an important revenue source. A good tour director makes about $400 to $600 in gratuities from passengers on a week-long trip, or about $2 to $3 per person per day. (It should be noted that a few companies disapprove of tips for tour conductors. Also, groups from certain countries,

such as Japan, aren't culturally accustomed to tipping.)

▼ Sales commission on **optionals** (also called **add-ons**) provide important income to tour managers at certain companies. An optional is a tour component that is not included in the tour price. The client can purchase this optional excursion during the tour. Optionals often appeal only to some passengers: a nightclub tour of Paris, a sightseeing plane flight over the Grand Canyon, a shopping excursion in Hong Kong. (This narrower interest in part accounts for its being optional.) The tour conductor typically gets 10 to 20 percent of what the client pays for the optional. This serves as a reward for their on-tour sales skills.

▼ Commissions on certain other extras must also be factored in. When a tour conductor "steers" a group to a gem factory, souvenir store, or extra nightclub tour, he or she often receives a **commission** or **kickback**. (Many tour companies and most incentive houses ban the practice; others ask the tour director to give half of the commission back to the company; and still others see it as an accepted means of supplementing the tour managers' incomes and allow them to keep it all.) It's not unusual for a tour leader to double his or her income in this manner.

▼ About half of all tour conductors and over two-thirds of those who work for inbound operators are treated by their companies as "independent contractors." Since they're self-employed, they're able to take a large number of tax deductions. Those who are considered employees usually receive company insurance and other benefits. (The government has put pressure on tour operators to classify tour managers as employees.)

▼ Many companies give their tour leaders a per diem expense allowance (not to be confused with per diem salary). This allowance, intended to cover such things as meals and laundry, is given whether the escort incurs the expenses or not. Typically it amounts to somewhere between $10 and $30 per day.

▼ A few companies place tour directors on a list that qualifies them for reduced airfares when they travel on their own. Tour managers for intermodal companies also accumulate substantial frequent-flyer miles, as long as their tour air tickets aren't free or at special industry fares.

In summary, a tour manager—or at least those veterans who work thirty to forty weeks a year—can make about as much as an airline pilot or a major travel industry executive.

The Downside of Tour Management

To many people, tour conducting seems to be a dream career. But unrealistic expectations can quickly transform that dream into a nightmare. Escorting is a tough, demanding job. Its rewards, though considerable, are hard-earned.

For instance, tour conductors live out of a suitcase. Any semblance of a normal life evaporates. Home becomes a place where you repack your luggage. No wonder that many tour managers are unmarried. Those who are married must adjust to long periods of absence from their families. Furthermore, the timing and number of tours made available to a tour conductor is thoroughly unpredictable, which makes it even more difficult to maintain a normal family life.

Once on the road, a tour leader faces considerable stress. He or she is responsible for dozens of people, some of whom may be difficult or demanding. The hours can be long. If someone calls at 3 A.M. with a problem, the groggy escort must respond immediately. In reality, a tour conductor is on duty twenty-four hours a day. Since they are "celebrities" to their group, they have very little privacy. As far as touring is concerned, Murphy's Law is very much in effect: if something can go wrong, it will.

Yet good training and practiced strategies can transform the stresses of tour conducting into a bracing set of challenges. It also helps to have the right personality.

The Tour Manager Personality

Does the perfect escort personality type exist? Probably not. Some tour conductors have achieved success by being intensely outgoing, others by perfecting their ability to deliver information, and still others by juggling a thousand concerns in a calm, low-key manner. Furthermore, each tour operator has its own favored personality type for tour managers. Many com-

In many cases, escorting or guiding is a second career.

panies seek out individuals who have strong entertainment skills—who can lead sing-alongs, tell jokes, and organize games. Others prefer escorts who can weave cultured and informed narration. For them, the ability to entertain is useful but not fundamental to the job.

In general, tour managers must love people, no matter how cranky or demanding they get. They must love travel—individuals who dislike its inconveniences and who rarely voyage far from home are poor candidates for escort work. They must love places—no trait impresses a tour member more than an escort's obvious affection for the destination to be visited.

There also seem to be specific character traits that predispose tour leaders to success in almost every context. Dozens of these traits exist. For simplicity's sake, they can be grouped into six general categories.

An Outgoing Personality

Tour managers have a positive, energetic, and open approach to both people and tasks. They're often instantly likeable, or at least grow on people quite quickly, and have good appearance, health, and grooming. They usually are quite articulate, with a well-developed sense of humor, solid conversational skills, and the ability to entertain people with their stories and anecdotes. Timid or withdrawn "wallflowers" rarely succeed as escorts although, with time, somewhat shy people have often blossomed as tour managers.

Decisiveness

"Your luggage is stolen. You're five thousand miles from home. What do you do? WHAT DO YOU DO?!!" So went the familiar American Express commercial. But tour conductors always seem to know what to do. Natural leaders who command respect, they are emotionally controlled, alert at all times, calm in the face of a challenge, and able to anticipate a problem before it arises or be doggedly persistent until it is solved. Tour leaders translate experience and common sense into firm, quick action. They think on their feet.

People Skills

Courteous, patient, sensitive, caring, unselfish, diplomatic, even-tempered, tactful yet firm—a tour director is expected to be all these things toward both clients and associates. Escorting is a consummate service job, one in which the tour leader carries on an extraordinarily subtle and extended relationship with each tour group served. It's no surprise that the ranks of tour management are filled with former nurses, social workers, and therapists. Tour conductors are types who genuinely care about people, listen to what clients have to say, and are ready to go beyond a nine-to-five mentality to a twenty-four-hour concern for a group's welfare.

Organizational Skills

In a 1930s movie, W.C. Fields approaches his desk, looking for an important paper. An "efficiency expert" has apparently reorganized the mess that was on his desk into neat little piles. Fields throws everything into the air and exclaims, "Ah, here it is!" He then easily plucks the wanted document from the newly created disarray.

W.C. Fields would hardly have made a first-rate tour conductor (for many reasons). A good tour manager must be a good time manager. Reports, schedules, deadlines, and money management are all integral parts of the job. Tour directors are conscious of details (one missed reconfirming phone call can spell disaster), punctual (a tour leader who is always late will rapidly lose control of a tour), and thoroughly responsible. They cannot, though, become obsessive about it all. On a tour, flexibility is as productive as accuracy.

Research Skills

Though knowledgeable tour guides usually supplement escorts at each destination, tour managers must nonetheless keep up on all sorts of facts, including such minutiae as postage and phone costs, tipping practices, foreign exchange rates, and the next day's weather—the kinds of things that loom large during a tour. Some companies even expect tour directors to do double duty as guides, in which case they have to study the history, geography, botany, and zoology of the visited area.

Intelligence and education, of course, are significant to escort success. But more important is a curious, inquisitive approach to things, a dedication to gathering accurate and up-to-date information, and a knowledge of where and how to find that information. Successful tour managers are the kind of people who have broad interests, skim the newspaper daily, enjoy watching *The Discovery Channel*, have at least some knowledge of a foreign language or two, and aren't so jaded that they stay on the motorcoach while their group visits some breathtaking attraction.

A tour conductor must also be able to communicate information in a clear, concise, and diverting manner. For this reason, tour operators often recruit escorts from among teachers, professional speakers, and actors.

A Sense of Ethics

Not too long ago, a *Time* magazine cover story warned that unfocused ethical standards have become a major threat to business. Nowhere is the problem more critical than in tour conducting. The tour conductor must balance fairness to the client with loyalty to the company. Both passenger and tour operator must depend on the honesty and integrity of a tour leader. Tour managers—with the power, perks, and independence they enjoy on the road—must be well-situated ethically.

Final Considerations

A few decades ago it was common to hear that women carried too little authority to succeed as tour directors and that tour managers who were middle-aged or older had too little energy. Though traces of this sort of stereotyping remain, modern employers understand that sex, race, religion, and age are poor predictors of escort success. Indeed, the majority of all tour conductors today are women. A job that was once the province of students looking for something interesting to do during the summer or of young adults

6. Explain three reasons tour conducting appeals to many people.

7. Discuss how tour managers are financially compensated.

8. What are the disadvantages of a career in tour conducting?

9. Name six specific personality traits that are common among tour conductors.

10. Why are escort careers often short?

■ ■ ■

ACTIVITY 1

▼ Read the following very carefully:

Mr. and Mrs. Jones wish to arrange a vacation through Getaway Travel, a neighborhood agency where they usually book their travel. Ramon, a Getaway employee who regularly counsels the Joneses on their needs, recommends that they take an escorted tour. Specifically, Ramon favors Blossom Tours, an American company that sends many people to Asia and with which other clients of Ramon have been very pleased.

Two months later the Joneses arrive at the airport and are met by a woman in a red blazer. She introduces herself as Lynette, the tour conductor for Blossom Tours who will accompany the Joneses and their fellow travelers for the tour's fifteen-day duration. Most of the other group members have already gathered near the airline counter.

After a long overnight flight, the group arrives at its first stop, Tokyo. A small transfer bus transports the group to their hotel. Their luggage is loaded onto a separate truck. The next day, a large motorcoach marked "Japan Excursions" picks up the group. Lynette explains that Blossom Tours works with Japan Excursions on all American tours visiting Japan. She introduces Yuki, who works for Japan Excursions and will be their guide for the day. (Each day a different guide will narrate their tour.)

Yuki's English is excellent. She explains the passing sights of Tokyo with great precision and flair. Upon arrival at a Buddhist temple, however, Yuki turns over the sightseeing chores to Saburo, who works there and knows the shrine area in depth. The same thing happens at the Tokyo Museum of Art, where a volunteer guide, Keiko, takes the group through the museum's halls.

Lynette accompanies the group back to the United States and bids them farewell at the airport.

▼ Now complete the following sentences with the items below. No item can be used more than once. Two items will not be used at all.

a tour escort	a travel agency	a meet-and-greeter
a docent	a personal guide	an inbound operator
a site guide	a travel agent	
an outbound operator	a city guide	

1. Getaway Travel is probably

2. Ramon is probably

3. Blossom Tours is

4. Lynette is

5. Japan Excursions is

6. Yuki is

7. Saburo is

8. Keiko is probably

■ ■ ■

ACTIVITY 2

▼ Select a famous person—past or present, real or fictitious (from a book, play, movie, etc.)—whom you could imagine as being a highly successful tour manager. Explain your choice:

The famous person:

Those traits that would make him or her successful as a tour manager:

ACTIVITY 3

▼ A person who is organized and able to handle stress probably has a better chance of being a successful tour director or, for that matter, successful in any capacity at a tour company than one who is not. Complete the following questionnaire, answering only "yes" or "no" to each item. If you have trouble fitting your answer into a yes or no category, choose the one closest to your usual behavior. Several questions assume you own a car; if you do not, answer these questions according to what you think you would do if you owned a car. Your instructor or trainer will then help you score and interpret the results. If they show that you are not well-organized or do not handle stress well, you will have to concentrate more on your sense of organization and your stress-coping skills. If you score well, you are already on the road to escort success! But remember, this is an indication of only two of the many skills that a tour manager should have.

TIME-MANAGEMENT QUESTIONNAIRE

Yes No

☐ ☐ 1. Are you often upset when the other line at the supermarket moves faster than yours?

☐ ☐ 2. At home, do you have a monthly calendar (one that shows an entire month on one page, with space to write things in)?

☐ ☐ 3. Do you occasionally incur finance charges unintentionally by paying your bills late?

☐ ☐ 4. As a student, do you or did you ever consider handing in the same assignment for different classes?

☐ ☐ 5. Do you have a personal organizer—either paper-based or electronic—that you carry with you?

☐ ☐ 6. Assume it's a weekend and you have absolutely no chores or work to do. Will doing nothing make you feel guilty?

☐ ☐ 7. Are you a morning person?

☐ ☐ 8. Do you usually try to arrive exactly on time (neither late nor early) for appointments?

☐ ☐ 9. Do you usually make a copy of documents you write or sign?

☐ ☐ 10. Do you have maps in your car?

☐ ☐ 11. Do you usually reconfirm appointments that were made some time in advance?

☐ ☐ 12. Do you try to return a phone call within 24 hours?

☐ ☐ 13. In your home, do you have a customary place for your keys?

☐ ☐ 14. Do red traffic lights upset you when you drive?

☐ ☐ 15. While in school, do you or did you usually cram before a test?

☐ ☐ 16. If you went home right now, would there be a pad and pencil next to the phone you use most?

☐ ☐ 17. Do you often put off returning a call to someone you don't like, even if it's important?

☐ ☐ 18. Are you frequently tired, even after a good night's sleep?

Yes No

☐ ☐   19. Do you generally have your car tuned up on a regular basis?

☐ ☐   20. Do you ever throw away, unopened, mail that is obviously junk mail?

☐ ☐   21. Is lunch usually the most substantial meal of your day?

☐ ☐   22. Do you wait until you have dental problems to see your dentist?

☐ ☐   23. Do you frequently skip breakfast?

☐ ☐   24. Do you have a filing system at home for your personal papers?

☐ ☐   25. Do you lose your temper more often than you would like?

☐ ☐   26. Do slips of paper with phone numbers, addresses, etc., tend to pile up in your purse or wallet, on your desk, or in your pockets?

☐ ☐   27. Do you get frequent headaches or backaches?

☐ ☐   28. If the light bulb in the main lighting fixture of your bedroom were to burn out tonight, would you have another bulb in storage to replace it?

☐ ☐   29. Do you ever take material to read with you while waiting to see a doctor?

☐ ☐   30. When you're alone at home, do you almost always pick up the phone when it rings, even if you are busy?

☐ ☐   31. Do you respond to your e-mail and other messages in a timely manner?

☐ ☐   32. Is there something in your home that has been broken for months?

■ ■ ■

PROFILE

Ecotourism has become a powerful force in today's world. That explains why the tiny, off-the-beaten-path but ecologically rich island of Dominica is an increasingly popular destination. That's also why Cheryl Mason has become a tour guide.

"Growing up on this island, I couldn't help but be fascinated by its flora and fauna. But I never realized that my knowledge would ever be very useful." Indeed, the Dominica of Cheryl's youth had very little tourism. Even today, it is dominated not by big hotels, fast-food outlets, or crowds of tourists, but by steep mountains, moist jungle, and lofty waterfalls. "When I take people into the island's interior, they become fascinated by just about everything: our odd little land crabs and lizards, the papayas growing wild, and the poinsettias that add color everywhere. Through visitors to our island, I can re-appreciate Dominica's wonders."

Though Dominica is modestly sized, it has a clear and strong philosophy about how tourism should develop. And part of that philosophy is its attitude about tour guides. "Our government wants us to be true professionals, to be ambassadors of our culture, to promote our island and, above all, to be accurate and informed. Many tourists have gone through a lot of trouble to come to our island. They deserve a great experience."

Cheryl, like other guides, underwent weeks of classroom training, as well as numerous field trips and even courses in first aid. As her "final exam," she was obliged to give a tour for a veteran guide, who graded her performance.

Now that she's a veteran guide herself, Cheryl—who speaks both English and French fluently—has heard just about every question imaginable. But many center on her remarkable heritage. Cheryl is a descendant of the original Carib Indians who populate the area when Columbus "discovered" them. Only a few thousand Caribs are left, and most live on Dominica. "It's tragic what happened to my ancestors," says Cheryl. "So many died, either from disease or conflict, and so quickly. They eventually withdrew into the deeper recesses of this island. That's the only way they could survive."

"In many ways, tourism is the same," Cheryl concludes. "It's fragile. It's like this precious egg. And it's the responsibility of a tour guide to protect it in every way."

2

City and Site Guiding

Chapter Objectives

After reading this chapter, you should be able to:

▼ List the advantages and disadvantages of being a guide.

▼ Explain what "guidespeak" commentary shares with conventional public speaking.

▼ List five strategies for overcoming fear of public speaking.

▼ Enumerate the peculiarities of guidespeak, both for city guiding and for on-site guiding.

▼ Describe the motorcoach environment and how it affects tour guiding.

▼ Discuss strategies for keeping performance fresh.

"DON'T WORRY. THE CAVE LIGHTS WILL COME BACK ON SOON. THEN YOU'LL BE ABLE TO SEE THE AWESOME STALACTITES THAT NATURE FORMED OVER MILLIONS OF YEARS."

Have you ever taken a city bus tour? Or followed a guided excursion through a noteworthy building? If you have, you know that a good tour guide can bring a place alive for visitors. To do so in an entertaining and enlightening fashion, though, is no easy matter. Good tour guides are a rare and, some say, vanishing breed.

Very little attention has been given to the mechanics of effective tour guiding. Although this book focuses on tour *conducting* rather than tour *guiding*, a side excursion into the subject of guide work is quite relevant. A tour conductor needs many of the same skills as a guide, is often called upon to do double duty as a guide, and most certainly will work with numerous guides while managing a tour. Furthermore, many tour managers enter the travel industry by first becoming city, area, or on-site guides. Escort employers see guide experience as an excellent qualifying step on the road to the broader responsibilities of tour conducting.

The Advantages of Guiding

Although tour conducting holds a more glamorous place in the travel industry, many find tour guiding to be a most satisfying occupation. The demands of the job rarely require a person to be uprooted from his or her home in the way that escorting does. The stress is also far less. Though guiding is a people-oriented activity, a guide isn't responsible for the around-the-clock needs of a group as is a tour leader. And though the job is somewhat limited, it does offer two especially appealing opportunities: to be a center-of-attention "performer" and to be an "authority" who is deeply informed on a particular place.

The practical advantages of guiding are, in some circumstances, also attractive. Though city or area guides who work for local sightseeing companies often make only minimum wage, tips may increase their profits. Those guides who also drive the touring vehicle usually make a good salary, since their responsibilities are greater. Step-on guides—freelancers hired by an arriving tour company to come aboard its motorcoach—generally earn about as much daily as the average tour manager. Step-on freelancers also have the advantage of being able to work seasonally, at times of their own choosing. In those areas where summer months constitute prime tourist season, it's quite common for teachers, for example, to work as step-on guides to supplement their regular fall-to-spring assignments.

On-site guide salaries tend to be at or just above minimum wage. For this reason, attractions frequently hire high school or college students to fill these seasonal positions. On-site guides can earn more than minimum wage if they're government employees. For example, full-time United States Park or State Rangers

An on-site guide explains the history of Boston's "Old Ironsides," The *USS Constitution*. *Courtesy of the National Tour Association*

are the tour guides at Hearst Castle (San Simeon, California), Yellowstone National Park, Alcatraz Prison (San Francisco), and Kitty Hawk (North Carolina). Outside of North America, guides at historic buildings, churches, or other important attractions are often mature scholars who, though low salaried, sometimes receive tips for their services.

The Disadvantages of Guiding

Both site and city guiding carry certain liabilities. The potential for boredom is very high. Guides must repeat the same information, often several times a day. The questions they hear are predictable. They must feign surprise at what a visitor may feel is a most original question. (Indeed, many guides remark that they welcome the challenge of a question they have never heard before.) If they're vehicle-driving sightseeing guides, they must concentrate on their narration and driving simultaneously. (In Japan, to offset potential safety problems with this sort of arrangement, *three* employees often accompany each tour bus—a guide-narrator, a driver, and an aide, whose responsibility is to help passengers on and off the bus and to assist the driver when parking in tight spots.)

Finally, in many cases technology is making guides obsolete. At some attractions visitors may rent a portable audio player. They then move through the site while listening to a taped commentary through earphones or a cell phone-like handset. At other attractions the visitor's presence in a room will automatically trip a taped audio narration or video monitor. City guides aren't irreplaceable either. A driver can now simply push a button on a dashboard cassette or CD player to activate a prerecorded commentary.

Tour guides, though, will never disappear entirely, for they personalize a visit in a way no machine can. You can't, after all, ask a tape recorder a question. But there's little doubt that technology will continue to threaten the job security of tour guides.

Guidespeak

Guide and escort applicants often forget that the job is, in fact, a form of public speaking. They arrive armed with facts, familiar with company procedures, well-versed in group management logistics, and then the

hard reality hits. They must now speak to an audience of forty people. Their palms sweat, their hands tremble, and their upper lip begins to twitch annoyingly.

Have you found yourself in a similar situation? You're not alone. Surveys report that public speaking is what people fear most—more than heights, spiders, confined spaces, and even death.

That no one has ever died of public speaking (though there have been some rather deadly speeches given) is irrelevant. The fear of speaking before a group is a phobia with no connection to reality, an anxiety that, to at least some degree, afflicts 85 percent of us.

Fear-Dampening Strategies

In some ways **guidespeak** (many tour companies call it **tour commentary** or **narration**) is a very different form of public oration, one that is less fear provoking than traditional speaking. Yet there are just enough similarities to warrant a set of general, proven strategies to combat nervousness. These strategies may be useful to you as a guide, as a tour director, or in just about any situation where you must communicate to a group of people.

Focus on One Person. Good speakers often pick out one individual in the audience who seems especially sympathetic. They talk to that person, then expand their attention to others so as not to seem oblivious to everyone else. Other common strategies—especially if having everyone looking at you at once bothers you—are to unfocus your eyes, look at an area just above your audience's head, or even imagine your audience in their underwear.

Accept an Audience's Desire to Like You. People rarely show up for a speech in order to hate the speaker. People almost never take a tour in order to hate the guide—they're on vacation to have a good time. Exploit that good will. Know that they'll be happy with even a modestly successful performance.

View Nervousness As an Ally. Adrenalin may make you nervous, but it also energizes you, makes you alert, and helps sharpen your commentary. Furthermore, the people who surround you at a site, or especially, who accompany you on a motorcoach will probably be totally unaware of the nervousness that looms so large in your consciousness. Your tour participants would need a magnifying glass to see that twitch that feels to you like an earthquake.

Know That Experience Lessens Fear. Most guides and tour managers report that fear diminishes dramatically after one or two tours and that after a week or two it disappears altogether. In fact, some guides miss the edge that the initial adrenalin-provoked excitement gave them.

Take Strength in the Fact That You Know More Than Your Audience. Fear of public speaking is usually based on a dread of saying something wrong or stupid. Yet a guide almost always knows more than the tourists to whom he or she is speaking. Why else would they be there? Study and organize the points you want to make, the facts you wish to convey, and the anecdotes you want to relate. Once that's done, there will be no valid reason for fear. If someone should ask a question for which you don't have the answer, simply say so and promise to look it up.

What You Say

Paying careful attention to *what* you say will not only help you control your anxieties but, more importantly, will also ensure the quality of your commentary. The following points should guide your tour narration.

Be Specific. It's not enough to simply say that Calcutta's Howrah Bridge is always filled with people and traffic. It's far more effective to say that the Howrath Bridge is 1,500 feet long, 72 feet wide, carries 60,000 vehicles a day, and, considering the incalculable number of pedestrians who teem across its span, is widely believed to be the busiest bridge in the world.

This sort of precision piques a listener's interest and reinforces confidence in a guide's expertise. Tom Gorman, a licensed Washington, D.C., driver-guide, confides, "Very early on in any tour I make a point of giving the exact height (555 feet 5 1/8 inches) and exact cost ($1,187,710.31) of the Washington Monument, just to make sure that my passengers know that I know what I'm talking about. From then on, I ease off on the facts. The point has been made."

Also effective is to pepper one's commentary with entertaining trivia. That some of Waikiki's sand was imported from California, that the now century-old Eiffel Tower was built as a temporary world's fair attraction, and that the first person to go over Niagara Falls in a barrel was a woman (Annie Taylor) aren't earth-shaking facts, but they do enliven otherwise dry subjects.

Be Accurate. Where's the world's largest shopping mall? To listen to certain guides, it could be almost anywhere. One of the inside jokes of the industry is that every guide claims that his or her city has the biggest mall. (Depending on how you calculate, it could be either the Mall of America outside Minneapolis or the West Edmonton Mall in Alberta, Canada.)

Guides are, among other things, scholars, and scholars take great pains to ensure that their knowledge is factual and up-to-date. They know where to find information, and they know better than to take someone else's word for anything. For nothing undermines a guide's credibility more quickly than when a passenger discovers that a bit of information or an anecdote, told because it makes for an interesting story, is false. Remember: 68 percent of your passengers, according to a NTA study, "spend a lot of time reading about an area before traveling there." If you say something really inaccurate, someone in your group is likely to know.

To protect sightseers from dubious information or sloppy research, such cities as New York, New Orleans, San Francisco, Montreal, and Niagara Falls put would-be guides through a rigorous licensing procedure. (To be a tour guide in these cities without a license is illegal.) Washington, D.C., applies an especially rigorous accreditation procedure to its guides. A licensed Washington guide probably knows more about the United States capital than most professional historians. London's **Beefeaters**, perhaps the world's most famous site guides, are world-class authorities on the intriguing history of the Tower of London. In Russia, tour guides have to take a two-year course at Moscow University that includes special courses in history, art, architecture, and foreign languages.

Know Your Audience. The guide who fails to tailor delivery and information to each particular group is an ineffective communicator. A commentary that would work for a group of Wisconsin dairy farmers might be inappropriate for a tour of New York City doctors. A charter group from St. Mary's Catholic Church will definitely expect their city guide to point out the local cathedral. A tour made up of teenage girls will be thrilled when their Beverly Hills sightseeing van drives by the mansion of their latest rock star hero. And a tour group of foreign visitors will appreciate it if you give distances in kilometers, rather than miles.

A more subtle exercise in empathy would be for you to predict, then point out, sights that are exotic to visitors but to which you've become accustomed. American visitors to Eastern Canada, for instance, are often startled by that region's squirrels: they're jet black and, at first glance, appear to be skunks running through the streets. The number of people on bicycles always astonishes visitors to Beijing, no matter how prepared they are for the sight. Scandinavians arriving in Miami will immediately rivet their attention on its palm trees. Identify and comment upon such sights in your city and you'll be sure to enrich the experience of your tour groups.

Once you've found all the information you need, remember the following two things:

▼ Clients often like their information delivered as a story. San Antonio's Alamo is most fascinating when a guide retells its story in a dramatic and engaging way. If the guide talked only about the Alamo's architectural significance or merely recited dates and statistics, the tourist "audience" would soon fall asleep.

▼ Passengers find extra meaning in a tour if you can connect information given at one point in the tour with some other bit of knowledge given later. On a Los Angeles tour, the story of the city's development as an oil-producing center, explained as the motorcoach passed near an old oil field, becomes even more concrete and meaningful later in the tour when clients see the opulent mansion of oilman Edward Doheny.

An unusual step-on guide addresses the group.
Courtesy of the National Tour Association

Keep It Light. Nothing is more deadly than a too-serious guide. People travel for enjoyment. A guide who adds to their pleasure, who lightens the factual burden with humor and wit, will seem abler than an earnest, unsmiling colleague. Of course, don't force the laughs. You're not expected to be a stand-up comedian, just a guide who doesn't take himself or herself too seriously.

Keep It Positive. How would you feel if a city guide spent all his time telling you about what's wrong with his city? You'd probably come away with a sour feeling about the tour you just experienced.

Of course, someone taking a tour of Los Angeles, for example, wants to know a little about the earthquakes, riots, and brushfires. But clients will feel better about their visit if the guide counterbalances his or her commentary with what's *good* about L.A.—why so many people still choose to live there and how most Los

Angelenos move past a crisis and find ways to make their lives even better.

Personalize Your Information. Andy Warhol once said, "In the future everybody will be famous for fifteen minutes." For tour leaders and guides, that extends to a few hours or days. It's not surprising, then, that tour members are curious about their guide's personal and professional life. To be a guide is to be an instant, if only temporary, celebrity.

Guides can turn tourists' inquisitiveness to their advantage. A few unpretentious personal observations or revelations can humanize a tour. One sightseeing driver regularly pointed out his modest home as he drove his groups by it. The sight elicited one of the strongest reactions during the tour. A guide, of course, shouldn't get carried away with self-praise or preaching personal causes. Nothing irritates more than commentators who place themselves on a pedestal, in a pulpit, or on a soap box.

Where should you go for detailed information on a destination?

- Established guidebook series (e.g., Access, Fodor, Frommer, and Rough Guide) contain information on accommodations and dining, in addition to sightseeing and other background information. Some also have Web sites.

- Travel-specific Web sites (e.g., Travelocity) offer (among other details) current information on destinations, accommodations, and transportation.

- Local publications, obtained at the site or city in question, provide a wealth of useful information. (Many tourist bureaus also offer this information on-line.)

- Encyclopedias and almanacs are reliable sources for the history and background of a destination.

- Travel videos (e.g., *Video Visits*, *Travelview*, and *Fodor*) enable you to see the destinations that you'll be visiting.

- The *Guiness Book of World Records* is a trustworthy reference for more offbeat facts.

How You Say It

In ancient Greece, a group of poets and public speakers concluded that effective, persuasive expression was an art form in itself. They began to study the elements and structures of speaking styles, to find ways to please the eye, ear, and mind. Their science became that of **rhetoric**. Their overriding belief was that how you say things is as important as what you say.

There's a rhetoric to guidespeak that is distinctive and critical to a successful presentation. A few of its tenets are basic to all speechmaking: vary your pace, speak distinctly yet naturally, be aware that time passes more quickly for the speaker than for the audience, and avoid overusing a particular word or phrase. Guidespeak, though, has certain peculiarities of presentation that bear special discussion.

Walking Tours

Walking tours present a very unusual speaking context. Here are some of the factors you must consider when you deliver a walking tour:

▼ **An on-site guide moves from place to place during the course of his or her presentation, as does the audience.** There's less chance for group boredom or lethargy to set in as the group strolls down paths or corridors, up or down staircases, through outdoor gardens, or into majestic rooms. Fatigue, though, can be a factor, both for the guide and the group. An on-site guide must walk quite slowly. Some group members may be slow, while others, looking around, may lose track of the group's movement. A common occurrence is for a guide to lead a group in a leisurely manner yet find that those bringing up the rear are racing to keep up.

▼ **An on-site guide profits from very dramatic "audiovisual aids"—the actual sights that surround the group.** A tour of an attraction has far more immediacy than any conventional speaking event could ever have—even one supported by slides or films. Indeed, the environment's impact is so great that a guide must constantly vie for the group's attention through voice and positioning. (One solution is to speak from the top of a set of steps.)

▼ **An on-site guide must learn to project his or her voice.** An on-site guide has to forever compete with distracting voices and the sound-diffusing nature of a large space. A guide must, for example, repeat questions before answering them. The inquiry almost certainly will not have been heard by many group members. Another important strategy is to herd the group into a semicircle. This configuration maximizes the visitor's ability to hear and concentrate on commentary. Above all, guides must learn the from-the-diaphragm speaking skills that professional orators use to project their voices. Certain attractions provide guides with small, portable public address systems, which can help offset weak voices.

▼ **On-site guides must avoid memorizing their "guidespeak."** Memorization or detailed notes seem to be just the sort of tool you need to protect yourself from public-speaking anxieties. Not so. What happens when you lose your place in a rote-learned spiel? What will it look like if you must forever refer to your notes? The effect will undermine your professionalism. A few reminders or a brief outline on an index card would be acceptable for a first-time on-site guide. After that the information should be fully absorbed and then delivered in a natural, unstructured way.

On-Coach Speaking

Because they work from motorcoaches, step-on guides, tour managers, and those on-site guides who operate from trams or buses encounter peculiar public-speaking conditions. In such a situation, eye contact with an audience is difficult or impossible. One of the first questions that faces novices is where to position themselves while speaking through a motorcoach's public address (**P.A.**) system. Do you stand next to the driver, facing forward? Do you face the group, with your back to the passing sights? Perhaps you should sit in the front row behind the driver or on a step or portable chair in the aisle between the two front seats.

There's no easy answer. Standing is a precarious, often dangerous practice. Standing in front of the white line that marks the beginning of the passenger section is usually illegal, though standing behind the line, in the passenger aisle area, is generally permissible. Sitting on the dashboard, as some guides do, is far worse—it blocks the driver's view of the road and side mirror and promises instant injury in a collision or rapid braking maneuver.

A common solution is to sit in the seat directly behind the driver or, if available, on a well-anchored drop seat that folds down in the aisle, next to the first passenger row. Of course, the guide will now lose eye contact with his or her audience, and client attention may easily drift away from the disembodied voice of the guide. In addition, to appropriate part of the first row deprives a client of prime seating.

On the other hand, a front row seat enables the guide or tour director to spot attractions easily and converse with the driver when necessary. If group attention begins to wander (a great deal of chatter usually signals this), a guide can momentarily rise to stand in the aisle in order to reestablish eye contact with the group.

It may be comforting to note that the minimal eye contact between group and guide on a motorcoach tour makes this form of speechmaking less intimidating than more conventional forms of public speaking.

Another prime consideration on a motorcoach sightseeing tour is the audience's energy level. That level varies according to the time of day. Groups are most alert in the morning and least alert just after lunch. (A guide will often look back at a group that has just finished a meal and find their heads bobbing and mouths agape. The most exciting commentary cannot offset the effects of a heavy repast.)

Experienced guides and tour leaders deploy an arsenal of tactics to energize a drowsy group:

▼ Make occasional photo-taking and bathroom stops. The *maximum* amount of time a group should remain on a city sightseeing bus without stops is about forty-five minutes.

▼ Give the group time for shopping after lunch. Hunting for bargains and souvenirs does wonders to pep people up.

▼ Rather than show a group something from the motorcoach, take them off the bus to see it. Many Toronto guides enliven their tours by taking groups out of their motorcoaches to see the city's famed, odd City Hall. In the midst of the building's forecourt (Nathan Phillips Square), they describe its curving forms and startling, saucer-shaped City Council Building. They point out the numerous lofty skyscrapers that surround the square, then remark, "Had you been here thirty years ago not one of these skyscrapers would have been here." That comment, delivered out-of-doors, powerfully and directly underscores Toronto's explosive growth.

A guide or tour conductor must also be alert to weather conditions. If the gardens and fountains of Italy's Villa d'Este are on the afternoon's agenda and the weather forecast isn't favorable, perhaps shifting that visit to the morning or to another day is a good idea. Museums and other indoor attractions are best kept for inclement days. A common joke among Washington, D.C., guides is that if it's raining, it's time for the Smithsonian.

Guides must be especially adept at using a P.A. system.
Courtesy of the National Tour Association

One final on-coach speaking consideration: a city guide must always be mindful that passing attractions dictate delivery and pacing. A cardinal guiding error is to point out something by saying, "And over there . . ." you must be *specific*, since your passengers are looking at the sights, not at you. Use precise directions ("to your left," "to your right") and indications ("The tan building to your left is . . ."). Time yourself carefully by *leading* your comments. A little before you arrive at a point of interest, begin talking about it ("And coming up on your right is . . ."). By the time your group has redirected its attention, the attraction will be outside the motorcoach window. You can also use leading to build anticipation ("In a few minutes, after we round this bend, you'll see the renowned Sphinx of Egypt. It's 240 feet long . . .").

Leading sounds simple, but it's not. Beginners often mention a sight too early—by the time the vehicle gets there, they're on to something else—or too late, when it's already passed by. With practice, though, it becomes second nature.

Two other related challenges confront every novice city guide. First, the speed of the motorcoach, not the amount of information, must determine pacing. Traffic, road width, and driver habits all have an impact on a guide's delivery. You must be prepared to pare down or stretch out your remarks according to the vehicle's movement. Remember: you don't have to say everything you know. Second, your route may include long stretches with absolutely nothing of real interest. Generalized discussions—of cultural uniqueness, major industries, leisure activities, and the like—are best saved for these times. Your ability to conjure images where none exist may also prove useful. Guides assigned to the Gettysburg National Monument, with its rolling but featureless plains, do a remarkable job, through words alone, of eliciting in the mind's eye the sights and sounds of the great Civil War conflict that took place there. Here is where storytelling really works.

Two final considerations deserve attention. First, should a guide speak constantly through a city or on-site tour? Probably not. Speaking about 80 to 90 percent of the time is best. Constant, unpaused commentary will soon overwhelm your listeners. They'll stop paying attention to half of what you say. If you talk less than 80 percent, though, you will lose their attention. They'll begin to rely on the comments of their seating companions rather than on yours.

Second, should a city guide put information on note cards, to be consulted as the motorcoach progresses on its route? Never. More than one beginner has dropped cards on the motorcoach floor or looked up to find that he or she has totally lost track of what was going by.

Tour guides must become adept at using a motorcoach's public address system. P.A. systems are finicky pieces of technology. The ones in motorcoaches are especially temperamental, as they are rarely of high quality. To make matters worse, the guide must compete with engine and air-conditioning noises.

You must allow the P.A. system to work for you. Holding a microphone a foot away from your face and speaking loudly is pointless. Keep the microphone close to your mouth and let the system amplify your voice. Be sensitive to how your voice carries through the motorcoach and adjust the volume control accordingly. Beware of *feedback*, the irritating whine that occurs when a microphone is in direct line with a loudspeaker. Angle your mike (often abbreviated as mic) so it never directly faces an overhead bus speaker. Consider purchasing your own quality microphone. Make sure that the one you buy has a lengthy extension cord and a plug that is compatible with a motorcoach P.A. outlet.

You might consider getting a clip-on mike or a head-set, like singers use. Such microphones allow you to talk without having to keep a button pressed, as hand-held versions require. Another possibility is a wireless mike. If you do purchase your own mike (clip-on, wireless, or whatever) make sure that someone knowledgeable in microphones helps you. Some complicated adjustments may be required to make the mike you purchase compatible with the motorcoach's sound system.

The Motorcoach Environment

Though almost everyone has spent at least some time on buses, few people pay much attention to their layout, features, and idiosyncrasies. Guides and tour conductors, however, must be extremely aware of the motorcoach environment, for their group, even on an intermodal trip, will spend a great deal of time busing from place to place.

Types of Motorcoaches

The variety of motorcoaches is virtually endless. (The industry prefers the term "motorcoach," since it conveys the relative luxury of today's $275,000 vehicles.) These vehicles can be divided into five basic types: city buses, bare-boned commuting vehicles that are rarely used for tours; school buses, also seldom used for anything but school outings; minibuses or vans, downsized vehicles that accommodate small groups; sightseeing buses, large coaches with broad window areas expressly designed for local tours; and over-the-road coaches, large, well-powered vehicles that can transport groups and their luggage over long distances. The versatility of

A conventional motorcoach.
Courtesy of the National Tour Association

over-the-road motorcoaches makes them the preferred vehicle for escorted tours. They're often also used for local sightseeing, transporting charter groups, and regular intercity transportation.

In North America, motorcoaches have long been beefy, no-nonsense affairs that can accommodate anywhere from thirty-five to fifty-three passengers. Manufactured by Motorcoach Industries (MCI), General Motors, or Prevost of Canada, they're capable of high speeds and cushy rides and are usually equipped with lavatories and voluminous luggage space. (See Figure 2–1.) Westours even has a fleet of extra-long (60 foot) coaches that accommodate sixty or more passengers. (To permit going around corners, they "bend" in the middle. Such vehicles are labeled "articulated" coaches.)

Elsewhere in the world motorcoaches tend to be more luxurious, with huge windows, superb P.A. systems, plush interiors, and dramatic designs. This approach is often called "Eurostyling." Because many tour companies in the United States have begun to import their coaches from abroad, U.S. bus makers have increasingly taken a "Eurostyled" approach in newer models. Other rather astonishing vehicles exist: a double-decker German bus that has sleeping quarters, showers, and cooking facilities for its passengers; a Japanese motorcoach that boasts wall-to-wall carpeting and chandeliers; a "super bus" in which the driver rides in a truck cab up front while the passengers are towed behind in a 46 foot trailer (used for touring the twisting roads of Catalina Island, California); motorcoaches with small "lounge" areas in the back; and the French "Cityrama" double-decked behemoths from which nearly a hundred people can view Paris while listening to narration, via earphones, in any of several languages.

Guides and tour leaders must pay special attention to several unusual aspects of motorcoach touring. Though subtle, these factors can dramatically affect a client's enjoyment of a tour.

Line-of-Sight Difficulties

One great advantage of taking a motorcoach tour: because the vehicle is so big, passengers sit higher than they would in a car. As a result, they have a better view of things.

But certain necessary design elements do limit what a tourist can see from a motorcoach. Guides must adjust for these limitations. For example, passengers, except for those in the first few rows, can't see out the vehicle's front windshield. To point out something straight ahead is a futile action—you must wait until it's to the left or right of the coach. Tall objects close to the motorcoach's side are also a problem. If you're passing immediately by the Empire State Building, don't expect anyone to see its higher levels unless the vehicle is one with windows that wrap up and over the coach's roof. Wait until it can be viewed from a distance. Passengers sitting in the last two rows, to the left of a lavatory, will see nothing pointed out to the right—unless the lavatory has transparent walls (an unlikely feature). (See Figure 2–2.)

Experienced guides often solve such problems by designing a route that doubles back along important, sight-filled streets. This way clients on both sides of the vehicle get a clear view of significant attractions.

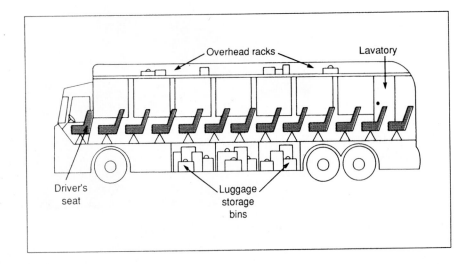

Figure 2–1   A standard motorcoach (cross-section)

***Figure 2–2*   A motorcoach floor plan**

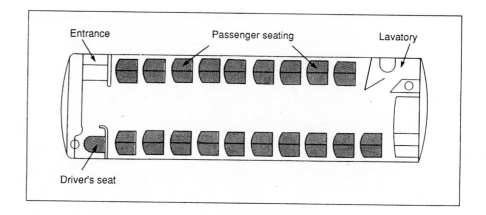

Air-Conditioning

No one ever seems satisfied with a motorcoach's temperature. Each client seems to have his or her own ideas as to what constitutes comfort. The front of a motorcoach tends to be cooler than the back. The vehicle's west side becomes hotter in the afternoon—the sun angles fiercely through all that glass.

To make matters worse, bus climatization systems are frequently primitive. The air-conditioning (**AC**) is either on or off, and the heat is either on or off—there's nothing in between. If both systems are shut down, the coach interior gets stuffy with alarming speed.

Though it's terribly manipulative, the best solution to a client complaint (unless the entire group is complaining) is to pretend to adjust a thermostat in the driver's area (there may even be one). This trick often has a placebo effect—the client *thinks* the temperature has improved.

Safety Considerations

From time to time, clients will wish to stand up and stretch in the aisle. This is generally permissible, as long as it doesn't go on for a long time. Although often legal,

An example of an "articulated" motorcoach. *Courtesy of the National Tour Association*

Some coaches have lounges for clients to relax.
Courtesy of the National Tour Association

standing in the aisle is perilous in the case of an accident or a sudden change of speed. You'll find yourself traveling the aisle often, especially on intercity trips. Fortunately, tour managers gain a motorcoach equivalent of "sea legs." With practice, they can adjust quite easily to the vehicle's constant little movements. Novices, though, should beware. A beginner hasn't yet learned how to brace quickly to a sudden movement. The constant motion takes a toll on the feet and legs.

A guide or tour leader must carefully guard passengers as they enter or exit the motorcoach. You must assist them by the arm or hand—a bus step is quite high for some people. For this reason, some drivers carry a step box with them to place in front of the coach door. Newer motorcoaches have a hydraulic step that extends when the door is opened. You must also direct clients away from traffic. Crossing the street in front of a motorcoach is a risky thing, since the vehicle's bulk obstructs the view of oncoming traffic.

Special safety considerations come into play when accommodating physically challenged passengers on a tour. The Americans with Disabilities Act stipulated that physically challenged clients must have full access in almost all situations, including motorcoach tours. Bus manufacturers are now equipping their coaches with wheelchair lifts. Some, to accommodate the disabled,

have created more space in the coach's first row. Both tour operators and guides have become increasingly sensitive to the fact that physically challenged clients have as much of a right to enjoy a tour as anyone else.

Logistical Matters

You should always board a motorcoach before clients arrive to check its condition. Are all seats upright? Is there any trash on the floor or the seats? What is the temperature like? Memorize the coach number and have your passengers learn it, too. The average person returning to a parking lot full of coaches may become totally confused. Take a head count of the passengers on board at the tour's beginning. You'll need to check during the tour to make sure no one is missing. Ask the driver if he or she will stay with the motorcoach at stops along the way or will lock the door while away from it. If not, counsel your passengers to take their belongings with them. At the end of the day (or at the end of a multi-day tour), remind passengers not to leave anything in their seats or in the racks above. When the coach is empty, check to make sure nothing has been left behind and fill out a motorcoach report form, if one is required (see Figure 2–3).

MOTORCOACH REPORT

TOUR: _____

DEPARTURE DATE: _____

ESCORT MAKING THIS REPORT: _____

ASSESSMENT OF COACH NO. _____ FROM_____BUS COMPANY

Item	Satisfactory	Not Satisfactory	Comment
Air Conditioning	☐	☐	_____
Cleanliness	☐	☐	_____
Heating System	☐	☐	_____
Lavatory	☐	☐	_____
P.A. System	☐	☐	_____
Seating	☐	☐	_____
Overall Rating	☐	☐	_____

ASSESSMENT OF DRIVER.   NAME: _____

Attribute	Excellent	Very Good	Good	Poor	Comment
Appearance	☐	☐	☐	☐	_____
Courtesy	☐	☐	☐	☐	_____
Driving Skill	☐	☐	☐	☐	_____
Personality	☐	☐	☐	☐	_____
Professionalism	☐	☐	☐	☐	_____
Overall Rating	☐	☐	☐	☐	_____

Figure 2–3   **Sample motorcoach report**

Keeping Your Commentary Fresh

So far we've focused primarily on those factors a novice tour guide needs to know. But what problems do veteran guides face? There's only one: keeping one's performance fresh.

Constantly repeating the same information can rapidly lead to boredom. Here are strategies that can help you maintain enthusiasm and keep your presentation lively:

▼ Keep researching your subject. New insights can give new energy to your commentary.

▼ Strive for constant improvement in your performance.

▼ View what you're sharing through the eyes of your "audience." Have you ever noticed how explaining something to a child often excites you, no matter how mundane it may be? It's because you see it again, fresh, through their eyes. The same can happen through your clients, who probably are experiencing what you show them for the first time.

▼ Draw your energy from the audience's reactions. This is precisely what a stage actor does. How else can a performer keep dong the same play right, day after day, sometimes for hundreds of performances? A guide is indeed a sort of actor. Think of yourself as one, and you may find renewed and invigorating tactics to make yourself not simply a good guide but a *great* one.

Summary

Compared to tour conducting, guiding has both advantages and disadvantages. Guides are public speakers and must rise above the fear of addressing groups. Like all speakers, guides must be specific, accurate, knowledgeable, organized, and adept at keeping their delivery light, positive, and personal. The kind of speaking a site or city guide practices is unique in several ways. Both city guides and tour managers must be especially aware of motorcoach design and how it affects the guide's performance and client satisfaction.

QUESTIONS FOR DISCUSSION

1. Why do some people prefer to be a guide rather than a tour director? What are some of guiding's liabilities?

2. Give five general strategies for coping with fear of public speaking.

3. List six ways you can ensure that what you say has clear, solid content.

4. Discuss four peculiarities of guidespeak when a person is giving a walking tour of a particular site.

5. List five ways in which the delivery of a city sightseeing bus tour is unique.

6. Discuss the physical positioning problems that face a guide delivering a motorcoach tour talk.

7. What tactics can help a site guide be heard by his or her group? What can a city guide do to keep up a group's energy level while on a tour?

8. Describe five types of buses or motorcoaches. Which one will an escort or guide encounter most often?

9. What line-of-sight difficulties face a guide giving a sightseeing tour from a motorcoach?

10. Define the following: AC, MCI, P.A., mic, Prevost.

■ ■ ■

ACTIVITY 1

▼ Tour guides are good speakers, but they must also be good listeners. Assess your listening ability by taking the test below. Your instructor will help you analyze the results.

▼ Answer each statement by circling the number that applies. At the end, count up your point total.

Never	Occasionally	Often	Usually	Always
1	2	3	4	5

1. When I'm listening to someone, I pay attention, rather than let myself drift off.

1	2	3	4	5

2. While listening to someone, I pick up on the feelings and attitudes of the speaker as well as the words.

1	2	3	4	5

3. I block out distractions when listening to somebody.

1	2	3	4	5

4. If I disagree with a person, I manage to avoid letting my own attitudes block out what is being said.

1	2	3	4	5

5. I pick up on "nonverbal" cues that may communicate what the person is saying over and above his or her words.

1	2	3	4	5

6. I try to avoid interrupting the person talking.

1	2	3	4	5

7. I succeed in paying attention to slow, rambling, or boring individuals.

1	2	3	4	5

8. I refrain from thinking of what I am going to say to someone before they are finished talking.

1	2	3	4	5

9. I keep eye contact with the person who is talking to me.

1	2	3	4	5

10. When the person is finished talking, I verbally indicate that I've understood (or not understood) what they've said.

1	2	3	4	5

Total: _____

■ ■ ■

ACTIVITY 2

Choose a notable building or other attraction with which you are acquainted or which is nearby. Pretend that you are a guide there and must give groups an introductory talk of about five minutes. Research your choice. Then outline your presentation below, citing at least one research source at the bottom of the outline. (Be prepared for your instructor to ask you to deliver your talk without notes or outline.)

ACTIVITY 3

▼ One of the best ways to do something right is to watch someone else do it first. If they do things well, you can model your own performance on theirs. If they do things poorly, you can learn from their mistakes.

▼ Seek out an opportunity to take an on-site or city tour. Observe the tour guide closely. Take notes if you can. Then fill out the following:

The tour I took:

What the guide did right:

How could the guide improve his or her performance?

■ ■ ■

ACTIVITY 4

▼ You've been hired to be a London city Blue Guide. Blue Guides are considered to be among the world's most knowledgeable tour guides. You're in the early research phase of your job—you haven't given a city tour yet. Using reference books and/or the Internet, answer the following questions regarding sights you'll have to be informed about.

1. Who designed St. Paul's Cathedral?

2. Where is the Rosetta Stone?

3. What is Piccadilly Circus?

4. Where is London Bridge?

5. Whose statue is in Trafalgar Square?

6. What is the London subway popularly called?

7. In front of which London palace does the Changing of the Guard take place?

8. Who lives at 10 Downing Street?

9. Where was Anne Boleyn beheaded?

10. Which river flows through London?

11. Where is Chaucer buried?

12. What is Harrods?

13. In which palace, begun by Cardinal Wolsey, is there a famous maze?

14. At what time of the year does the Wimbledon tennis tournament take place?

15. Where are England's crown jewels kept?

Your research sources:

■ ■ ■

PROFILE

Niche tours. They're one of the hottest new trends in the tour business. Yet Brenda James has been designing, promoting, operating and escorting niche departures for nearly 20 years.

"Specialization is the way to go," says Brenda, whose own specialty is ski tours. Currently the Executive Vice President of Ski Connections, a division of France Vacations, she had to overcome several tendencies within the ski market. "Skiers tend to be very independent in the way they think," explains Brenda, "so you must come up with a good reason for them to take a tour."

What were some of those reasons? "First, you must concentrate on a ski destination that's somewhat exotic, that seems a bit alien to skiers who usually just pack their skis into their SUV and take off for a nearby resort. By specializing in *European* ski packages, I was able to steer them toward tours—they feel more comfortable with going to, say, Switzerland as part of a packaged trip."

"Second, I promote other European opportunities that both the skier and his or her spouse could take advantage of, like a Christmas market or winter carnival. Third, many skiers are quite price-conscious, so I would take advantage of the leverage of group buying to get great prices."

Using such leverage, Brenda was able to package tours that included air to and from the West Coast, seven nights accommodation, some meals, taxes, gratuities, and transfers for as little as $989.

Brenda adds that volume isn't the only way to get great prices from suppliers: "It's always good to meet as many people as possible in this business, to make contacts wherever you go, because it's a lot easier dealing with an acquaintance or friend than with a total stranger. Also, I attend as many conferences as possible. It shows that I'm serious about my specialty."

Brenda has even begun to find niches within her niche. Her most current one: firefighters. She hopes to package an Olympics-like Firefighters' Winter Games to take place in which firefighters from across the world will compete in skiing (both downhill and cross-country), hockey, curling, snowboarding, bobsledding—all to be capped off with a fireworks display. "No one has thought of exactly doing this sort of event," says Brenda, "so my hope is high that it will turn out to be the biggest 'tour' event I've ever staged."

3

Multi-Day Tours

Chapter Objectives

After reading this chapter, you should be able to:

▼ List the materials you'll need to manage a multi-day tour.

▼ Explain the typical routines of a multi-day group trip.

▼ Read and analyze a tour itinerary.

▼ Discuss ways to keep a group entertained while a tour is in progress.

"DON'T YOU THINK THIS IS TAKING SERVICE TOO FAR?"

For city and on-site tours, guides must draw upon such resources as speaking ability, memorization skill, and the ability to pace performance to a group's movements. These aptitudes are modest, however, compared to those needed to conduct a multi-day tour. To manage a group's progress through many days and destinations, often on all types of vehicles, is fiercely challenging.

Most tour operators schedule training sessions just before the major tour season starts. For tour managers, it's the time to learn or review company procedures. These procedures are often summarized in a company **tour manual**—a compendium of facts, rules, and recommendations distributed to all tour leaders. Many companies also operate a **training tour**, composed entirely of new tour conductors, to demonstrate tour operations in a realistic setting. They may require a novice "intern" to go on a tour as an observer or assistant to a more seasoned tour conductor. The general industry term for tours that familiarize travel personnel with a particular destination or tour is **familiarization trip** or **fam trip**.

On-the-job experience is truly the ultimate teacher, but in-depth knowledge of exactly how a tour unfolds is also essential. For this reason, tour operators often brief escorts before every trip. These briefing sessions may also serve as a debriefing from the previous tour.

In briefing sessions, tour conductors review the itinerary for the upcoming trip and find out a little about the group's makeup. They're told when to report to the airport, the bus or train terminal, or the cruise ship. They're given all the materials they'll need to manage the trip. In very unusual situations—for example, when a tour director is hired in an emergency, last-minute situation—this briefing session may be the only training the tour director gets. In such cases, the tour manager may have to rely on the driver's knowledge to keep one step ahead of the passengers.

Materials

To understand how a tour operates, you must be familiar with the materials you'll need during the tour. Most of the materials will be provided by your company. However, you may have to obtain or create some of the materials yourself. Be prepared for a long list. It's amazing how much is needed to manage an escorted tour. You'll need a healthy-sized briefcase or travel bag in which to carry it all.

Forms

A considerable amount of the work a tour manager does remains completely invisible to his or her passengers. Telephone calls must be made, gratuities given, reservations reconfirmed, and expenses logged in. For company purposes, tour managers must track most of these activities on various forms. Throughout the inventory that follows, you'll be given samples of many of the forms discussed. Examine these illustrations carefully. No matter what area of the tour industry you work in, at one time or another you *will* have to deal with forms such as these.

Itinerary. An **itinerary** is a listing of a tour's day-to-day activities. Tour managers work with two different itineraries. The first is the one clients see, which often appears in the sales brochure. Sometimes a more detailed itinerary is sent to clients after booking. The second itinerary is a more extensive one for the tour manager's use. As a tour leader, you must be sure to read both very carefully before leaving. Are the sights, stops, hotels, etc., in both identical? If not, your copy may reflect changes made since the clients received their versions. If so, you must diplomatically explain why. If you leave anything out that the client expects or, for that matter, that the company expects, then you can be sure you'll hear about it.

Things-to-Do-List. Tour managers must remember dozens of little details. To keep track of these details, you may want to note "things to do" in red pen along the margins of your itinerary. An even better method is to use a checklist of reminders. Several sample checklists are included in this book.

List of Suppliers. Companies that provide tour operators with services are called **suppliers**. The most common suppliers include hotels, airlines, cruise lines, bus companies, restaurants, and attractions. For each tour, you should have a list of all suppliers that will service your particular trip, with addresses, phone numbers, and the names of contact persons. Some tour operators place this information at the end of the escort itinerary, or even within the body of the itinerary.

General Tour Report. On this form, a tour conductor reports delays, problems, or other unusual occurrences (see Figure 3–1). The tour conductor also profiles the group on this form. Did the group seem to enjoy themselves? Could something different have been done? Were there any problem clients? Finally, a

GENERAL TOUR REPORT

TOUR: _____   DEPARTURE DATE: _____

ESCORT: _____   NO. OF PASSENGERS: _____

Modes of transportation: ☐ Motorcoach   ☐ Ship   ☐ Other (Specify)
                            ☐ Plane   ☐ Train   _____

Specific comments on transport equipment and personnel: _____
_____
_____

Hotels used: Rating (A, B, C, D, F):

1. _____   ___ Front desk   ___ Rooms   ___ Services
2. _____   ___ Front desk   ___ Rooms   ___ Services
3. _____   ___ Front desk   ___ Rooms   ___ Services
4. _____   ___ Front desk   ___ Rooms   ___ Services

Special comments: _____
_____
_____
_____

Restaurants used (excluding breakfast); give rating of each (A, B, C, D, F):

1. _____   ___   6. _____   ___
2. _____   ___   7. _____   ___
3. _____   ___   8. _____   ___
4. _____   ___   9. _____   ___
5. _____   ___   10. _____   ___

Special comments: _____
_____
_____

Miscellaneous comments (including attractions, complaints, compliments, problems):
_____
_____

Copyright © Delmar Publishers

Figure 3–1   **Sample general tour report**

general tour report usually asks a tour director to evaluate service from the personnel at hotels, restaurants, airlines, cruise lines, and attractions.

Daily Tour Report. Some tour operators use such a form to report the daily experiences of a tour. Assembled together, the daily tour reports may eliminate the need for a general report, or they may serve as a comprehensive backup to the less detailed general report.

Time Sheets. A few companies, especially those that pay an hourly rate, will require you to log in your working hours for each day on a company time sheet.

Copies of Confirmations. Some tour operators provide tour managers with photocopies of confirmations,

with prices and dates agreed upon, from each supplier. The confirmations can be useful. For example, when a restaurant claims that your company never made reservations for your group, all you have to do is pull out the confirmation and, *voila!*, there's the proof. The burden of resolving the misunderstanding must then be assumed by the restaurant manager.

Expense Sheet. To be reimbursed for out-of-pocket expenses, you'll probably have to use a special form to list each expense. Occasionally, a special form for telephone expenses will also be required.

Rooming List. Several weeks before a tour begins, the tour operator must send a list of passengers for that tour to each hotel being used (see Figure 3–2).

ROOMING LIST

HOTEL: _____   NO. OF NIGHTS: _____

ARRIVES: _____   DEPARTS: _____

TOUR: _____   ESCORT: _____

DRIVER: _____   SPECIAL REQUESTS: _____

Room No.	Tag No.	Name(s)	Room No.	Tag No.	Name(s)

Figure 3–2   **Sample rooming list**

Information specific to the hotel is filled in at the top of the form. On its copy, the hotel adds room numbers next to the passengers' names. Upon arrival at the hotel, the tour manager receives a copy of the completed rooming list for reference purposes. (A completed rooming list is given in Activity 1 of Chapter 5.) The tour director should have several extra lists with passengers' names but without specific hotel information. These lists can be useful if, for instance, the hotel's copier is broken. The tour conductor can transfer the room numbers onto the blank version.

Many tour leaders also use rooming lists to track luggage, a procedure explained later in this chapter. Finally, the tour operator may give the tour conductor a final copy of the rooming list reflecting last-minute passenger changes. This list can then be shown to hotel front-desk personnel upon arrival.

Passenger List. This document lists vital information on each client. Information such as name, home address, and telephone number will be crucial in an emergency. The passenger list, which is usually in alphabetical order, may also list special requests, a client's VIP status, and perhaps personal information such as occupation and age. (Note that in the travel industry the word "passengers" is often abbreviated as **PAX**.)

Blank Seating Chart. On most tours, passengers are given assigned seats on aircraft, trains, and even motorcoaches. Normally you don't need a blank seating chart for an aircraft—airlines almost always assign seats themselves. When they don't, they'll give you block seating for your group before departure. For a motorcoach, however, you will need a seating chart (see Figure 3–3). Assigned seating and seat rotation are almost a necessity on a multi-day motorcoach or intermodal tour.

Optional Tour List.

Many tour companies offer extra side tours to clients at an additional cost. On this form, tour managers note which clients have signed up for extra cost services (see Figure 3–4).

Passenger Questionnaire.

Tour operators are interested in feedback from clients at a tour's end. Questionnaires are the best way to obtain this informa-tion. These surveys guide tour planners in redesigning tours and inform employers of how well the tour conductor is doing his or her job (see Figure 3–5).

Emergency Form.

For legal purposes, a tour opera-tor must receive a detailed report on any accident, sick-ness, or death that occurs on a tour. This form must be filled out carefully, with all circumstances clearly described.

Supplies

"Be prepared." That has long been the motto of scouting. It applies just as much to tour conducting. A tour manager must bring along an arsenal of miscella-

MOTORCOACH SEATING CHART

COACH TYPE:_____ DRIVER: _____

TOUR: _____ ESCORT: _____

DATE: _____ NO. OF PAX: _____

SPOT TIME AND FIRST PICK-UP LOCATION:

_____

ADDITIONAL CITIES TO PICK-UP:

_____

SEAT ROTATION TRACKING:

1	2	3	4	5	6	7	8	9	10	11	12	13
14	15	16	17	18	19	20	21	22	23	24	25	26

Row	City	Name	Row	City	Name
(13)		LAVATORY	13		
(12)		(OR 2 EXTRA ROWS)	12		
11			11		
10			10		
9			9		
8			8		
7			7		
6			6		
5			5		
4			4		
3			3		
2			2		
1			1		

DOOR ENTRANCE   DRIVER

Copyright © Delmar Publishers

Figure 3–3   **Sample motorcoach seating chart**

```
┌──────────────────────────────────────────────────────────────┐
│  OPTIONAL TOUR LIST                                            │
│                                                                │
│  TOUR NAME: _____   TOUR NO: _____       │
│  NO. OF PAX: _____   TOUR ESCORT: _____       │
│                                                                │
│              Optional Tour                   Optional Tour     │
│                                                                │
│  Price                        Price                            │
│  Name of Passenger            Name of Passenger                │
│   1.                           26.                             │
│   2.                           27.                             │
│   3.                           28.                             │
│   4.                           29.                             │
│   5.                           30.                             │
│   6.                           31.                             │
│   7.                           32.                             │
│   8.                           33.                             │
│   9.                           34.                             │
│  10.                           35.                             │
│  11.                           36.                             │
│  12.                           37.                             │
│  13.                           38.                             │
│  14.                           39.                             │
│  15.                           40.                             │
│  16.                           41.                             │
│  17.                           42.                             │
│  18.                           43.                             │
│  19.                           44.                             │
│  20.                           45.                             │
│  21.                           46.                             │
│  22.                           47.                             │
│  23.                           48.                             │
│  24.                           49.                             │
│  25.                           50.                             │
│         SUBTOTAL                      TOTAL                    │
│                Copyright © Delmar Publishers                   │
└──────────────────────────────────────────────────────────────┘
```

Figure 3–4   **Sample optional tour list**

neous supplies—some essential, others just useful—to keep things moving smoothly. Below is an inventory of tour operation supplies.

Vouchers and Tickets. Tour operators have to pay for services somehow. Tour conductors make many of these payments or bring proof that the service has been paid for in advance. When a tour company pays for a service in advance or makes arrangements to be billed, the escort is given a voucher. A **voucher** is a document indicating that a service has been prepaid. The tour manager then gives the voucher to the supplier (see Figure 3–6). Vouchers are often used for city tours, bus transfers between hotel and airport, meals, admissions, and, occasionally, hotels. Other terms for voucher are **exchange order**, **tour order**, and **coupon**.

Tour directors are occasionally given actual tickets instead of vouchers—for a New York musical, for example, or for admission to Disneyland. The clients' airline tickets may also be given to the tour manager in advance, to be distributed to the passengers before their first flight with the group. (Some companies mail the airline tickets to the tour members several weeks in advance.)

Lost vouchers can always be replaced, but tickets have real value. Zealously guard them during your trip.

Credit Cards and Checks. The tour operator may have a tour manager pay suppliers through company checks, traveler's checks, or company credit cards. Again, you must guard these important items carefully. You may also be given a small amount of cash to pay

WE HOPE YOU HAVE ENJOYED YOUR TOUR!

May we ask your cooperation in taking a moment of your time to fill out this questionnaire? Please return this form to your tour escort.

	Out-standing	Better than expected	As expected	Less than expected	Needs improvement
1. Your hotels	☐	☐	☐	☐	☐
2. Your meals	☐	☐	☐	☐	☐
3. Your motorcoach	☐	☐	☐	☐	☐
4. Your tour escort					
Speaking/ entertainment	☐	☐	☐	☐	☐
Information	☐	☐	☐	☐	☐
Courtesy	☐	☐	☐	☐	☐
Dress/appearance	☐	☐	☐	☐	☐
5. Your tour driver					
Skill	☐	☐	☐	☐	☐
Courtesy	☐	☐	☐	☐	☐
6. Air/cruise portions	☐	☐	☐	☐	☐

7. Please list (in order of preference) those things you liked most:

a._____

b._____

c._____

8. Was there anything about this tour you didn't like?

a._____

b._____

We are in the process of planning more tours for next year. We would like to have your ideas about the kind of tours you would like to take.

9. I prefer tours of the following number of days (please circle one):

1 2 3 4 5 6 7 8 9 10 11 12 13 14 15

10. Here are some of the places I would like to visit:

a._____

b._____

c._____

If there are any special comments you would like to make, use reverse side. Thanks!

Copyright © Delmar Publishers

Figure 3–5   **Sample passenger questionnaire**

for miscellaneous items like tips, or the company may instruct you to pay these charges with your own money and submit an expense report later.

Reference Materials. Could your driver get lost? Could a passenger ask you a question to which you do not know the answer? If so, where can you find the information you need quickly? Tour conductors must bring along at least one guidebook and a good map for each destination on their tour. You never know when you'll need a handy reference source. The tour operator may also give you airport layout maps before departure. These maps are usually photocopied from a standard industry reference called the *OAG Business Travel Planner* and can be helpful in navigating an airport that's new to you. Some tour managers bring notebook computers with them and tap into the Internet to research that especially tricky question and to easily send and receive e-mail.

Extra Passenger Supplies. Clients are usually sent one luggage tag for each piece of luggage allowed on the trip. A two-week trip to the Far East might merit two suitcases and, therefore, two luggage tags. A weekend tour to Atlantic City, on the other hand, would require only one piece of luggage and one tag. These tags are often brightly colored to permit the tour manager to spot them quickly.

Luggage tags often fall off or get lost. Hence, tour managers should bring several extra tags (see Figure 3–7). The tour company may provide clients with name tags to help the escort remember their names

```
                              TOUR: _____
                              CODE: _____
TO: _____ (Supplier)  ADDRESS: _____
                                          _____
                                          _____

Please provide the following service(s): _____

     NUMBER OF              PRICE PER PERSON          TOTAL

    _____   Adults   x  $ _____  = $ _____
    _____   Children x  $ _____  = $ _____
    _____   Comps    x  $ 0.00            = $ 0.00
                                     Total Cost = $ _____
OR

Total cost of service as contracted (not based on no. pax): $ _____

Date of service: _____

Supplier signature: _____

Escort signature: _____
```

Figure 3–6   **Sample voucher**

and help passengers get to know one another. The escort should also bring a few blank name tags.

Handouts. Tour members love getting free handouts such as maps, brochures, and promotional material. These handouts are often provided free by tourist bureaus. They can enhance a client's trip and serve as mementos on return. However, it can be awkward for the tour conductor to carry them around, especially on intermodal tours. One solution is to pick them up in each city or at each attraction.

Office Supplies. Tour leaders may sometimes feel like accountants or secretaries because there's so much paperwork to do. An escort's office is wherever he or she is at a particular time: the hotel room, onboard a 747, or in the back seat of a Greyhound. You'll need a large, well-organized briefcase. Your briefcase will become both your desk and filing cabinet. You'll also require some supplies: a pen, a pencil, a notepad, a clipboard, a calculator, some folders, a few rubber bands, and thumbtacks for posting schedules on hotel bulletin boards.

A portable traveler's office kit would also be a wise investment. This small, inexpensive case contains scissors, a ruler, and many other useful items.

Miscellaneous Items. Among the other useful things you might bring along:

▼ Luggage or duct tape to repair damaged items

▼ Birthday and anniversary cards for clients' special occasions

▼ Band-Aids to treat minor cuts (Remember that in most countries, aircraft, shops, trains, and motorcoaches are by law equipped with first-aid kits.)

▼ Plastic trash bags to help keep motorcoaches clean

▼ A small screwdriver or Swiss Army knife (You never know when it could come in handy.)

▼ A spare microphone, since the one that comes with the motorcoach could be inadequate or defective

▼ Refreshments or drinking water (Some coaches have a small galley in the back for storing and serving refreshments.)

▼ "Flag-on-a-stick" device, so clients can follow you easily in crowded areas.

Personal Supplies. Tour directors, too, can occasionally forget to bring things for a trip. Get a good packing list. Luggage stores often give them out for free. Remember to bring your own airline ticket and passport. Bring plenty of personal business cards along. (The tour operator usually supplies them to you.) Buy a quality personal organizer, either electronic or paper-based, to help you keep track of appointments, meetings, and other obligations. Also remember to bring throat lozenges, especially at the beginning of a tour season when your voice is not used to so much exercise.

Gadgets

Walk into your neighborhood electronics store. These days, it's filled with all types of electronic marvels, many of which are immensely useful to tour managers. When you consider buying such gadgets, though, ask yourself the following: Is the electronic device more efficient than the conventional alternative? If the answer is yes, then tell your friends you have a great idea for a Christmas gift!

Personal Digital Assistants. PDAs, as they're usually called, come in two primary types: handheld personal computers (HPCs), "mini-laptop computers," which have miniature keyboards and screens; and palm-size PCs, which don't have keyboards (e.g., a Palm Pilot). You instead use a little stylus and touchscreen. PDAs can be used to store contacts and calendars. They also can be used for word processing, Internet access, and e-mail communication.

The Electronic Translator. This device allows you to punch in any word in French, Spanish, or German and read or even hear an instant English translation (or vice versa).

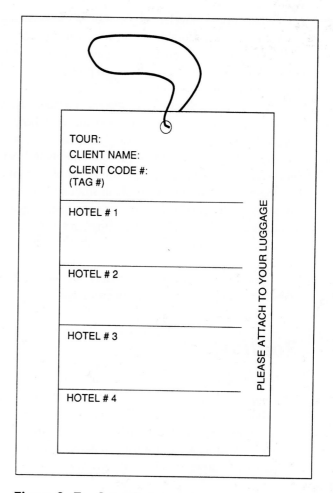

Figure 3-7   Sample luggage tag

The Briefcase Alarm. You place one part of the alarm in your briefcase and the other in your pocket. Stray more than twenty feet from your briefcase and the alarm will go off. This is a great gadget to discourage loss or theft of important tour company documents.

Cellular Phones and Personal Pagers. These essential tools can facilitate communication with suppliers (you can call ahead directly from the motorcoach), from motorcoach to motorcoach, or allow you to be paged by the tour operator when someone needs to contact you. They're especially useful in emergencies. However, either device can be useless if you are beyond the range of a transmission station. (Satellite-based systems will soon overcome this limitation.)

Luggage and Packing

In any given year, a full-time tour conductor may travel hundreds of thousands of miles. Quality luggage is essential. Some travelers argue that hard-sided suitcases are the most durable, while others maintain that soft-sided ones allow more packing and are acceptably strong. Most tour conductors seem to prefer hard-sided luggage. The choice is up to you.

Tour managers become proficient packers. They learn all the tricks: how to store socks in shoes, how to roll clothing to minimize wrinkles, and how to color-coordinate to company uniform requirements (62 percent of all tour operators require some sort of uniform). Free pamphlets on efficient packing strategies are usually available at travel-oriented stores or from luggage manufacturers. Remember two things: it's not necessary to cram so much into a suitcase that the pressure exceeds that which turns coal to diamonds. Your best-laid packing schemes will probably be completely undone by the first customs inspector anyway.

Routines

Certain general procedures are used on all tours; these are called **routines**. At first they seem rather overwhelming in number. With time and practice, though, they become second nature.

One way of looking at a tour manager's routines is to break them down into five categories: *Pre-trip routines* (to prepare for the trip); *first-day routines* (done early in a tour); *each-day routines* (repeated daily); *last-day routines* (to close off a group trip); and *post-trip routines* (done after the tour is over).

A short discussion of each routine follows. More detailed descriptions will appear in later chapters when we reexamine hotel, airline, train, and ship procedures.

Pre-Trip

Before a tour leaves, a tour manager usually:

▼ Finds out what tours have been assigned to him or her. Some companies assign tours months in advance, while others assign them on a week-by-week basis.

▼ Researches the tour if it is unfamiliar.

▼ Checks to see if any special holidays occur during the tour.

▼ Attends a briefing meeting and asks about anything that is unclear.

▼ Reviews the material given. A good tour leader will carefully review the passenger list and become familiar with passenger names and any special client information or requests.

To manage a large group, routines are a must.
Courtesy of the National Tour Association

First Day

On the tour's opening day, a tour manager reports to the place the tour will begin. Usually the **spot time** (the time at which the tour manager must report for duty) will be well in advance of the clients' arrival time. The tour director should determine whether all is running on schedule and check the terminal to find the location of restrooms, shops, restaurants, and other conveniences. On motorcoach tours, this procedure may have to be repeated several times, since clients are often picked up in more than one departure city.

When passengers arrive, the tour manager introduces himself or herself, checks luggage, hands out essential documents, and assigns seating. A tour director must be friendly and professional from the start. The first impression is invariably the most lasting one.

Very early on, the tour conductor will have to review with the group the general itinerary for the tour as well as the rules and regulations (such as the seat rotation policy). This is also the time to establish camaraderie with and among the group. Make it clear that everyone is about to embark on an adventure. If the tour begins on a motorcoach or train, this introduction will be easy. It can be done on the bus or in the train passenger compartment, if practical. If the tour starts on a cruise ship, you'll have to wait for your group's reception party later in the day. If the tour begins on an aircraft, you'll definitely have to wait until you get to your destination. You can then do the necessary introduction on the airport-hotel transfer bus or later at a group get-together at the hotel.

Each Day

You must carry out certain routines every day on the tour, especially on motorcoach tours.

▼ Inform the group of the day's times and events first thing in the morning.

▼ Find out about any special free activities (e.g., a parade, fireworks, or free concert) and tell your clients about it.

▼ Research times and places for those passengers who wish to attend religious services (especially on a Saturday or Sunday).

▼ Whenever clients leave the motorcoach, give them a precise time to return. It's more effective to give the return time as a specific clock time—for example, "It's now 2:15. Be back at 2:30." Do not say,

"Be back in fifteen minutes," since fifteen minutes feels different to each passenger.

▼ Be sure to get back to the motorcoach well before your clients do.

▼ When they return to the coach, take a careful head count to make sure everyone is back. Then tell them what will be happening next.

▼ Assist passengers as they enter and exit a coach to be sure they don't walk off a bus directly into traffic.

▼ Inform clients of when a seat rotation will occur.

▼ Circulate among the group and encourage general cordiality and information exchange.

▼ In spare moments, reconfirm all appointments that are about to come up, including those for the next morning.

▼ At day's end, give tour members a general outline of the next day's events and specific information about the next morning's first activities and departure times. Immediately after they disembark, check the motorcoach's seats and luggage racks to make sure nothing has been left behind.

Train yourself to do all of the above routines automatically. If you forget one of these routines, don't worry. Odds are that a passenger will remind you of your oversight.

One final point: a tour where clients have plenty of independence poses a communication problem. You may, for example, go for days on a cruise tour without seeing your clients together in one place. The solution is to ask hotel or cruise personnel to allow you to type up an information/reminder sheet each day, photocopy it, and place a copy each night under the passenger's hotel room or cabin door.

Last Day

A tour's last day is a peculiar one. "It's so easy to drop the energy level," says escort Pat Rodriguez. "The passengers are tired and so are you. But the last day leaves a strong impression. An escort should do everything possible to liven up the day."

If you're on a plane or train, make an effort to circulate as much as possible among your clients. On a ship, it will be easy—the cruise line usually holds a farewell extravaganza. On a motorcoach, carry out as many activities as possible to make the time go by quickly. This is also the time to review other tours your clients may wish to take. At the end of a successful trip, clients are most open to thinking about their next tour options.

Post-Trip

After the trip is over, the tour manager usually reports to the company, handing in required forms and describing any unusual events that occurred. Some companies wisely send follow-up notes to clients, thanking them for the business. This might be a good opportunity for you to "piggy-back" a note to a client who was particularly helpful or generous.

Itineraries

With a little practice, escort itineraries are quite easy to read. They usually include times, locations, precise notations of all activities, and contact phone numbers. This information either appears within the body of the itinerary or at the end.

Below is a sample escort itinerary for an eight-day motorcoach tour to Eastern Canada. The trip originates and ends in Boston, Massachusetts. Read it carefully. There will be questions on it in a later activity. The tour could just as easily have been an intermodal air tour, with the group departing for Montreal from, for instance, New Orleans and flying back to New Orleans from Toronto.

ITINERARY: EIGHT-DAY CANADA CLASSIC

Note: All meals and admissions included in tour price are indicated in parentheses.

SATURDAY

	7:45 A.M.	Spot time at Boston bus terminal; motorcoach from BONANZA BUS LINES (401) 751-8800
	8:30 A.M.	Clients will begin to arrive at terminal.
BOSTON TO MONTREAL	9:00 A.M.	Departure, bus terminal *Routing for day*: Rt 93 to Rt 89; Rt 15 to Montreal
	10:00 A.M.	Rest stop, Dunkin' Donuts at Exit 14, Manchester, New Hampshire
	10:30 A.M.	Leave Dunkin' Donuts
	11:45 A.M.	Lunch stop, White River Junction, Vermont (Exit 1) BEST WESTERN (802) 295-3015
	1:00 P.M.	Leave White River Junction *Note:* Extraordinary scenery on Route 89 through Vermont
	3:00 P.M.	Arrive for Canadian border inspection, at Highgate Springs. Have clients use restrooms at border inspection station.
	3:30 P.M.	Leave Highgate Springs

	5:30 P.M.	Arrival, Montreal LE CENTRE SHERATON 1201 Blvd. Rene-Levesque West (514) 878-2000
	7:00 P.M.	Dinner Welcome Reception; hotel function room (*dinner included*)

SUNDAY

MONTREAL	6:30–8:00 A.M.	Breakfast on own in hotel coffee shop, "Le Boulevard" (*breakfast included*). Tell clients to sign check and bill to their rooms (same procedure to be followed on all tour breakfasts).
	9:00 A.M.	Departure for full-day city tour aboard coach from GRAY LINE BUS CO. (514) 934-1222 Tour will visit Notre Dame Cathedral, old town area, St. Joseph's Oratory, Olympic area, and Mt. Royal. Lunch stop to be determined by driver. *Note:* Escort should not organize tip for driver. Tip driver for company out of petty cash ($40 Canadian). *Note:* Do not try to give tour yourself on Bonanza coach; city law requires local coach and driver-guide.
	4:00 P.M.	Return to hotel
	6:30 P.M.	Departure on Bonanza coach for dinner and entertainment at FESTIN DU GOUVERNEUR St. Helene's Island (just over J. Cartier bridge) (514) 879-1141 (*dinner included*)
	10:00 P.M.	Approximate return time to hotel

MONDAY

	6:30–8:00 A.M.	Breakfast on own in "Le Boulevard" (*breakfast included*)
MONTREAL TO QUEBEC CITY	8:30 A.M.	Departure for Quebec City day trip *Routing:* Rt 40 to and from Quebec City
	10:00 A.M.	Rest stop. Location in Trois Rivieres area at discretion of escort and driver
	10:30 A.M.	Leave rest stop

	Noon	Arrival, Quebec City. Lunch at L'AUBERGE RESTAURANT 30 rue Fleury (418) 436-7100
	1:00 P.M.	City and area tour begins. Step-on guide to meet escort at restaurant: BERNARD PETIT (418) 555-3060 Tour to feature city walls, Plains of Abraham, and excursion to Ste. Anne de Beaupre Church *Note:* Clients will be off and on bus frequently.
	6:00 P.M.	City tour ends at dinner location *Note:* Company will reimburse and tip Mr. Petit directly. Dinner at CHATEAU FRONTENAC HOTEL "Cafe De La Terrasse" 1 rue des Carrieres (418) 692-3861 *Note:* Limited tour menu (*dinner included*)
QUEBEC CITY TO MONTREAL	8:00 P.M. (approx.) 11:00 P.M. (approx.)	Leave Quebec City Arrival, Montreal

TUESDAY

	6:30–8:00 A.M.	Breakfast on own in "Le Boulevard" (*breakfast included*)
MONTREAL TO TORONTO	9:00 A.M.	Leave Montreal *Routing:* Rt 20, 401
	11:00 A.M.	Lunch at Lansdowne Rest Area restaurant (cafeteria)
	11:45 A.M.	Leave Lansdowne
	11:55 A.M.	Arrive for noon 1000 Islands cruise at Gananoque (*cost of cruise included*) GANANOQUE BOAT LINE 6 Water St. (613) 382-2144
	2:00 P.M.	Boat returns to Gananoque; departure for Toronto
	3:30 P.M.	Rest stop in rest area just past Trenton
	4:00 P.M.	Leave rest stop
	5:30 P.M.	Arrival, Toronto SHERATON CENTRE 123 Queen St. West (416) 361-1000

	7:30 P.M.	Dinner in hotel in the "Winter Palace" on 43rd floor (*dinner included*; limited-choice menu) *Note:* Tell clients that restaurant is somewhat formal.
	9:00 P.M.	Dinner ends *Note:* Suggest entertainment in the "Pinnacle," next to "Winter Palace."

WEDNESDAY

	6:30–8:30 A.M.	Breakfast on own in hotel facility the "Redwoods" *Note:* Buffet breakfast (*breakfast included*)
TORONTO	9:00 A.M.	Departure for city tour aboard coach from GRAY COACH SIGHTSEEING (416) 865-0329 *Note:* This is a special limited 3 1/2 hour city tour; includes admission to Casa Loma Castle. Tip driver from petty cash ($40 Canadian). No group collections. *Note:* Do not try to give tour yourself on Bonanza coach; local coach and guide required by city law.
	12:30 P.M.	Return to hotel. Rest of day free for sightseeing, shopping, etc. *Note:* Tell clients that major shopping center (Eaton's) is only two blocks from hotel. *Reminder:* Tell clients before end of city tour of following morning's activities.

THURSDAY

	6:30–8:30 A.M.	Breakfast on own in the "Redwoods" (*breakfast included*)
TORONTO TO NIAGARA	9:00 A.M.	Departure for Niagara Falls *Routing:* Queen Elizabeth Way (QEW) *Note:* Make stops along way at roadside farmers' fruit stands (large sign will indicate exit) and Welland Canal Locks (sign indicates). If practical, wait for ship to pass through locks in front of public viewing area.
	11:30 A.M.	Arrive, Niagara Falls (Ontario) SKYLINE FOXHEAD HOTEL 5875 Falls Ave. (905) 374-4444 *Note:* Hotel has guaranteed Falls View rooms for our guests; rooms may not be ready at 11:30

A.M. Take group directly to lunch in hotel in "Penthouse Room" (*lunch included*; buffet). Have bell captain deliver luggage in P.M. when rooms are ready. Explain to clients that early arrival means rooms aren't ready. They'll get their rooms after tour.

1:30 P.M.	Leave hotel for tour of Upper Rapids area, including Journey Behind the Falls (*admission included*). Step-on guide will be DON or KAREN ROBINSON (905) 555-8268 *Note:* Allow clients time to shop at Table Rock Souvenir Shop at exit of Journey Behind the Falls.
4:00 P.M.	Tour ends *Note:* Company will reimburse and tip Mr. or Mrs. Robinson directly. Evening free *Note:* Point out that hotel is adjacent to Clifton Hill Tourist Area.

FRIDAY

NIAGARA	7:00–8:30 A.M.	Buffet breakfast on own in "Penthouse" (*breakfast included*)
	9:00 A.M.	Departure for tour of Lower Rapids Area, including admission to Spanish Aerocar (*admission included*)
	Noon	Return to hotel. Afternoon free for shopping or for ride in *Maid of the Mist* boat (admission *not* included)
	8:00 P.M.	Departure for farewell dinner in revolving restaurant atop SKYLON TOWER 5200 Robinson St. Niagara Falls, Ont. (905) 356-2651 (*dinner included*) *Note:* Check in at desk for tickets for elevator to top (*admission included*). *Note:* Clients have full choice of menu for main entree. Appetizers limited to salad or soup; dessert, to pie or ice cream. All other orders (including alcoholic drinks) to be billed by waiter to client. *Note:* Allow clients time after meal to go to open-air observation tower one level below restaurant to see Falls illuminated.

| | 10:30 P.M. | Return to hotel |

SATURDAY

| | 6:30–7:30 A.M. | Breakfast in "Penthouse" (*breakfast included*) |

| NIAGARA TO BOSTON | 8:00 A.M. | Departure
Routing: Rt 190, 290, 90
Note: Cross border at Rainbow Bridge.
Prepare clients for possible luggage inspection. |

| | 10:45 A.M. | Rest stop just before Syracuse |

| | 1:00 P.M. | Lunch at AURIESVILLE SHRINE CAFETERIA
(exit at Route 30 exit; follow signs)
(518) 853-3033
Note: Allow group to walk grounds after lunch. |

| | 2:30 P.M. | Leave Auriesville |

| | 4:30 P.M. | Rest stop on highway just after Springfield area |

| | 6:00 P.M. | Arrival, Boston bus terminal |

END OF TOUR

Quebec City is a popular destination for multi-day tours.
Courtesy of the National Tour Association

Special Routines

Two escort routines bear special scrutiny. The first has to do with seat rotation. The second concerns tracking luggage.

Seat Rotation

Clients are terribly territorial. Given the chance, they'll latch on to a motorcoach seat for an entire trip, staking out their claim with sweaters, bags, and whatever else they can drape across the seat when leaving the vehicle. Left to this informal system, group members will surely begin to argue among themselves or complain to you, because for every client who gets a good seat, another client will not.

Therefore, a fair seat rotation system is necessary from the very start. There are exceptions. Incentive and charter groups like to decide seating on their own. Intermodal trips that rely mostly on planes, ships, or trains and minimally on motorcoaches can operate with no formal seat rotation policy. But for intermodal tours that make heavy use of motorcoaches or for purely motorcoach trips, seat rotation is usually essential.

The following steps should guide your seat rotation system:

Establish an Initial Seat Assignment the First Time a Client Gets on the Motorcoach. You must establish your authority in this matter right away. Work out your initial passenger seating assignments well in advance on your seating chart. If you have more seats than passengers, leave the back rows empty. Try to seat friends across from one another, and start them from the back of the bus (you'll see why soon).

As clients get on the coach for the first time, be precise when you give them their initial seat assignment. Say, "For now, you're in the fifth row on the driver's side," or, "For now, you're in the front row on the door side." Do not say "on the left" or "on the right," since that depends on which way the client is facing. Don't forget that in countries of British influence, the door and driver sides will be reversed. Some tour managers stick tapes with passenger names on them to the top of each seat, then change the tapes at each rotation. It's a lot of work, but it helps avoid confusion.

On Each Seat Rotation of a Typical-length Tour, Have the Client Move One Row Forward. If, for example, the rotation will happen after lunch, tell the clients to take their things and drop them off in the seat in front of them when they leave the coach for their meal. Front-row people will be going to the back (or whatever row is the last one filled) either on the same side or on the opposite side—it's your choice. Tell them to leave their things on the coach's front dashboard to pick up when they return. Since buses often have unequal numbers of rows on each side, people sitting across from one another will be separated when they rotate to the rear. If you use name stickers, move them forward after everyone leaves the coach or ask the clients to do it for you.

This system ensures that each passenger moves through all the rows during the course of a trip. The one exception: on a trip of two or three days clients may have to move two rows on each rotation in order to move through the full length of the motorcoach.

Other rotation systems do exist. One requires clients to move one row backward on each rotation. This system is awkward, though, and psychologically negative. Another has clients move through the motorcoach in a clockwise fashion. However, this system splits up friendly couples on the first rotation and is needlessly complicated.

Calculate Each Seat Rotation Based on the Time Clients Spend in a Given Row. It wouldn't be fair to rotate passengers out of the first row after a half-day morning tour in which they've been mostly out of the motorcoach, with almost no time spent in their seats. Explain to the group that you will rotate rows after two or three hours of *seat time.* On multi-week tours, you may wish to rotate only once every day. Of course, don't rotate passengers while the coach is in motion— the clients will tumble like bowling pins. Wait for a stop when clients exit the vehicle (for instance, at lunch), or tell them at the end of the day that they'll rotate the next morning.

Track the Number of Seat Rotations on Your Seating Chart. If you don't use the name-sticker system, clients will remember where they are seated according to who was in front of them. If that person gets confused, then the whole system may crumble. Expect clients to occasionally become uncertain about where to sit. By consulting your chart and checking the number of rotations up to that point, you can easily determine where they should be seated.

Tracking Luggage

Imagine yourself away from home with no toothbrush and no change of clothes. That's what happens to a client when luggage becomes lost. The tour director can't prevent an airline from misplacing a suitcase. He or she, though, is directly responsible for the safe transport of luggage at most other times. The following carefully thought-out routine can ensure that luggage will rarely be lost.

Don't Track Luggage According to Total Luggage Count.
Many tour managers count the total pieces of luggage a group has and then assume that this knowledge will be enough. It *is* important to know how many pieces of luggage your clients have. In some instances, however, such knowledge can give you a false sense of security. For example, let's say the group had forty-two pieces at the tour's beginning and the **bell captain** (the hotel employee in charge of luggage) at the first hotel checkout says that forty-two pieces have been loaded onto the motorcoach. Everything is fine, right? Wrong. Suppose one client's piece has been missed but another client has added a piece. The total count will still seem correct. Perhaps the bell captain didn't count the escort's and driver's suitcases and says that there are only forty pieces.

You'll then waste time looking for the two "missing" pieces.

Depend on a quick total luggage count only when things are so hectic—for example, at airport customs—that you have no other choice.

Track Luggage by Using a Blank Rooming List or a Passenger List.
As you check off a piece of luggage for the first time (the driver or reception operator may help you), put a slash (/) next to the client's name. (Sometimes tour operators use code numbers instead of names, or they use a combination of names and numbers.) This will give you an exact luggage count. The next time you check the luggage, cross the slash (/), making an X. At the end of the check, look for any slash that hasn't become an X. This will indicate a missing piece of luggage. If you have nothing but Xs, all pieces are accounted for. It's that simple.

What about the next luggage check? Cross each slash a second time, or start an entirely new list. You may wish to create many copies of the slash-marked list on the first tour night and use them for the remaining luggage checks (see Figures 3–8 and 3–9 for examples).

CHECKING OFF LUGGAGE ON A ROOMING LIST (FIRST COUNT)

Room No.	Tag No.	Name	Room No.	Tag No.	Name
//	101	O. Shawn Cruz C. Cruz	/	122	M/M Russ Traunt
/	102	Erin Tyre	//	121	Ray L. Rhode Rhonda Rhode

Figure 3–8   **Luggage check, using rooming list (first day)**

CHECKING OFF LUGGAGE ON A ROOMING LIST (THIRD CHECK)

Room No.	Tag No.	Name	Room No.	Tag No.	Name
X X	101	O. Shawn Cruz C. Cruz	X	122	M/M Russ Traunt
X	102	Erin Tyre	X X	121	Ray L. Rhode Rhonda Rhode

Figure 3–9   **Luggage check, using rooming list (after two hotel checkouts)**

Do Luggage Checks Whenever Possible and Necessary. You should do luggage checks in the following instances:

▼ When your clients first arrive for the tour to determine what luggage each client has.

▼ When your luggage is loaded onto a transfer vehicle or a motorcoach. There's no need to check luggage as it is being unloaded from the coach (for example, upon arrival at a hotel), since your previous loading check ensured that it was in the vehicle's storage compartments.

▼ In the baggage claim area of an air, ship, or railroad terminal. This may not always be possible, since baggage claiming can be among a trip's more frenzied moments. You could wait until you load the baggage onto the transfer coach. However, at that point the missing piece may be on the other side of customs. If your clients are pulling their suitcases off the luggage conveyor belt, they'll soon find out if something is missing. If all luggage moves through customs at once and is not carried by individual clients, the least you can do is take a quick total luggage count—not a full check of each individual piece—and make sure it matches your total baggage count. You should do a full and proper count later when this luggage is ready to be placed on the transfer bus.

Tell Clients Not to Add Extra Pieces of Luggage or Use Luggage Tags They Did Not Use on the First Day, Without Telling You in Advance. Explain that this will completely derail your suitcase tracking system. If they inform you that they want to add something, add a slash (/) beside their name on your checklist to increase the total count.

A few tour companies have clients take care of luggage themselves. The luggage is off-loaded from the motorcoach, the passengers claim their suitcases and then carry them to and from their hotel room. In such a case, it's highly unlikely that luggage will be lost.

One final note: In many countries, order often yields quickly to semi-chaos. You may find it impossible to maintain your routines. Just keep your fingers crossed.

Keeping a Group Occupied

Put down this book, stare at something uninteresting for one minute, and then come back to your reading. That minute seemed like an eternity, didn't it? Yet it pales in comparison to the long stretches of idleness that can occur on a tour. Thanks to the U.S. interstate highway system, for example, it's now possible to travel from New York to Los Angeles without seeing anything of great interest—just gas stations, exit signs, and trees. Especially on a motorcoach tour, there will be times when clients will have almost nothing to look at. As the tour manager, you have the obligation to keep them occupied during these hours. You must help make their time pass quickly. If they're bored, it'll be a form of criticism—criticism of your skills as a tour leader.

Luckily, your entertainment skills won't always be needed. Airlines provide a parade of drinks, meals, movies, and audio programming to break up the monotony of long flights. Ships stage a multitude of social events. The dramatic scenery that can sweep by your motorcoach or train window is often enough. Indeed, a tour manager would be foolish to keep up a constant patter while the grand panoramas of Canada's Rockies or California's Big Sur pass by.

At other times, though, on a long motorcoach ride, you may notice that many members of your group are dozing off. If they're tired from the previous day's tumult or an especially ample meal, you might just leave them alone, for a while. If boredom has spawned those catnaps, however, it's time for a tour director to find some way to enliven the proceedings.

Some of your ideas may be clever, and some may be corny. All, though, will probably be welcomed. One rule of thumb: on a long motorcoach ride, the tour manager should be on the mike about 50 percent of the time. As you can see, this is quite different from what is expected of a tour guide, who generally should be on the mike giving sightseeing commentary about 80 to 90 percent of the time.

Giving Information

Tourists are hungry to learn new things. It's one of the main reasons they travel. A tour conductor, then, should take the opportunity during long, tedious stretches to talk about the destination that lies ahead or the geographic area through which the group is passing. While crossing the Arizona desert, you could discuss the unusual saguaro cacti that dot the landscape. While rambling over New Zealand's hills, you could explain the importance of sheep to that country's economy. Crossing America's flat, featureless Midwest could prompt a review of how weather so profoundly affects what farmers can or cannot grow. There are always

Motorcoaches now often boast TV monitors and VCRs.

those individual sights that you can point out along the way: an unusual building, a notable mountain, a historical spot. One of the best ways to find out about interesting landmarks is from "Triptik" maps, provided free of charge to AAA members. (Triptiks will be discussed in more detail in Chapter 9.) CD-ROM and Web-based computer mapping programs can also be useful. For example, at www.escortnotes.com you can click on the route your coach will be taking and obtain detailed information on places along the way.

Commentary isn't the only way to convey information. A tour director could pick up free pamphlets from a nearby tourist bureau outlet and pass these out on the coach. Tour conductors might also consider playing comedy tapes or radio dramas to keep their groups occupied.

Modern motorcoaches sometimes come equipped with a TV monitor and a videotape player. Hundreds of fine tapes now exist (usually thirty to sixty minutes in length) that could be shown to prepare a group for a destination. Among the best series are the Video Visits, Travelview, and Fodor's series. Also useful: those from PBS, *The Discovery Channel,* and other learning-focused networks. Feature films would work, too. *Witness* would be a fine film to prepare travelers for Pennsylvania Dutch Country, and *National Lampoon's*

European Vacation, as silly as it is, would certainly enliven any voyage through the Continent. One warning, though: Showing a video, especially a feature film on a coach, without paying the distributor for "exhibition rights" is often interpreted as illegal.

Playing Games

Game playing on a motorcoach may be considered corny, but it's nonetheless a favored way of keeping a group occupied. A bored group will do almost anything to make the time fly. Bingo on tours is very popular. Game boards made especially for use on moving vehicles can be obtained from large toy stores or tour supply companies. The old game "telephone," in which one person tells a story to another, who then tells it to a third, and so on, works extremely well on a motorcoach. Groups find it hilarious to hear the tale passed from the tour director to the front row left, around through the coach, and back to the front right—completely mangled, of course.

Many tour managers purchase books of games designed to occupy children on long car rides. A few of these games are adult enough to be adapted to tour-group use. Some conductors sponsor a contest in which each client must guess the exact mileage for the entire tour. The figure is then tracked through the driver's odometer (which is often located on the hub of one of the coach's tire wheels). You can also adapt a popular game show to touring, though the necessary paraphernalia may be cumbersome.

Singing Along

New tour managers find it astonishing that companies may expect them to conduct sing-alongs or that groups would even want to do such a thing. Yet most groups delight in singing. You will need sing-along books, however. They're usually provided by the tour company and are filled with standard songs almost everyone knows.

What if you can't carry a tune? You could just start each song and let the group do the rest, or you might ask someone onboard to lead the song for you. There's always some client with a golden voice or—who knows—the driver might enjoy singing. However, you may discover that the group isn't interested in the sing-along. In that case, you should drop the idea after a while. Otherwise, you could end up sounding like a bad lounge singer.

Making Small Talk

No matter what tale-spinning skills you may have or how good a singer you may be, there comes a time in every tour when a tour leader should keep quiet. People need time to talk to friends, rest, or stare off into space. You'll need that time, too. Maybe there's paperwork to be done. Possibly you need to rest your voice. Perhaps this is the occasion to get to know individual passengers and assure them that you're there for them as individuals as well as a group.

This is *not* the time for *you* to nap, however. Except in unusual circumstances, a tour manager should never sleep on a motorcoach. (In an airplane on a long flight, it is acceptable.) Clients may consider your nap a sign of disinterest. After all, what would you think if you walked to the rear of the plane and saw all the flight attendants sleeping?

Telling Jokes

On United States motorcoach tours, especially, tour conductors are expected to be entertainers. This is less typical outside America, where the escort-as-commentator tradition is more ingrained. The ability to tell jokes well or to be generally funny seems to be an inborn talent. Actually, almost anyone can learn to be amusing. A few recommendations are in order, however.

Avoid Any Jokes Based on Race, Sex, or Ethnicity or That Are Vulgar in Any Way. Such crude comedy is below the dignity of a tour manager. Moreover, it's almost certain that out of forty people at least one will be offended and will write a complaint letter. Religious jokes are a delicate matter, too. Gentle ones are acceptable, but anything that belittles religious beliefs or particular groups should not be used.

You may be thinking, "But that doesn't leave anything!" True, humor is often based on the taboo subjects of a society. However, plenty of inoffensive jokes exist. You can often gather them by watching such TV programs as the "Tonight Show."

Don't Allow Your Passengers to Tell Jokes on the Microphone. There are many comedians in the world, but very few good ones. If someone asks to tell a joke to the group, tell him or her it's against company policy. Once you hand that microphone over to clients, there's no telling what they might say.

Try to Tie in Your Joke to a Passing or Relevant Attraction. Here's a joke that a Washington, D.C., guide used to tell: "Last week I had this client. He was a great guy, but he loved to interrupt me to brag about how quickly they could build things in his home town. We went by the Washington Monument and I said, 'The Washington Monument is 555 feet high and took about forty years to complete.' He said, 'In my city we built an obelisk almost that big and it took us only a year.' I then pointed out one of the Smithsonian buildings and mentioned that it was three years in construction. He chimed in, 'We built a giant museum in my town in only six months.' Finally we passed by the Pentagon, one of the world's biggest structures. He didn't recognize it, for all its size. So, all of a sudden, he yells out, 'Hey escort, what's that big building there?' 'I don't know,' I answered. 'Wasn't there yesterday . . .'"

Keep Your Jokes As Short As Possible. If the listener can't remember the beginning of a funny story when the punch line finally arrives, your joke is too long. Note also a peculiar fact about jokes: they're almost always structured in three parts. So don't use four parts—it's unnecessary. And don't use two parts—the joke will misfire.

Don't Exclude Corny Jokes. It's peculiar what forty people in a bus will find amusing. For years, one tour conductor got major laughs by telling groups that Canadian pennies had perfume in them. Clients would search through their pocket change and bring pennies to their noses. At that instant, the escort would ask, "What's the matter, don't you smell a cent?" It was an awful pun, but it always worked!

Draw on Personal Escorting Experiences for Humor.
Anecdotes about previous tours fascinate clients. Be careful not to demean previous groups or to bring up anything that might unduly worry your tour members. Here's one incident that actually happened to a tour conductor. He later regularly told this story to clients on the tour's last day, to great effect:

"Our bus was going along at full speed down the Massachusetts Turnpike. While I was talking to the group on the microphone, I noticed a lady go into the restroom. When she finished, she looked around for a flush button. There was none. She then opened a small door under the sink. That door is supposed to be kept locked, but on this trip someone had forgotten to lock it. When the bus is in the garage, a mechanic enters the lavatory, unlocks the door, pulls a device inside, and all twenty gallons of lavatory contents are unloaded from a holding tank into a sewer that the bus has been positioned over."

"Well, here we are, speeding along on a highway and this lady sees something under the sink that says TO FLUSH, PULL. She does. Meantime, I'm on the microphone. I see this sudden, vast cloud forming behind the bus. Cars are swerving. Windshield wipers are wiping. And the lady walks out of the lavatory, totally oblivious to the havoc she has just caused."

"Fortunately, no one behind the bus was hurt. But if there's a moral, it's this: 'Never, never follow a bus too closely.'"

Summary

To correctly manage a tour, a tour leader must make effective and careful use of forms and supplies. The tour director should also be aware of the gadgets and luggage-packing strategies that improve travel and job efficiency.

All tours have certain routine tasks that must be carried out, yet each tour presents its own set of procedures that must be followed. Most of these procedures are outlined in the escort's itinerary. Two routines deserve special scrutiny: seat rotation and luggage checking.

A tour manager must also keep a group occupied during a tour. Time-occupying strategies include giving information, playing games, conducting sing-alongs, making small talk, and telling jokes.

■ ■ ■

QUESTIONS FOR DISCUSSION

1. Describe what occurs during a briefing session.

2. Define the following: supplier, voucher, spot time, and escort's itinerary.

3. Give two possible uses for blank rooming lists.

4. Name five routines that are specific to the first day of a tour.

5. List eight routines that should be repeated each day of a tour.

6. What are four steps that should guide your seat rotation system?

7. Why will friends seated across the aisle from one another on a motorcoach eventually be separated in the seat rotation system described in this chapter? Why would saying "We'll rotate seats every half-day" not work?

8. Give four ways to ensure that a luggage tracking system will work.

9. What are five general activities that can be used to keep a group occupied?

10. List six concerns you should have when telling jokes to a tour group.

■ ■ ■

ACTIVITY 1

▼ Read the passenger itinerary below, taken from an actual brochure. Then answer the questions that follow the itinerary.

Singapore * Thailand * Indonesia * Hong Kong   **16 Days from $3,648**

THE ADVENTURE

Day 1 (Tue) LOS ANGELES/SINGAPORE. Your adventure begins as you wing across the Pacific aboard your Singapore Airlines jumbo jetliner, losing a day as you cross the International Date Line.   F

SINGAPORE

Day 2 (Wed) SINGAPORE. After completing brief entry formalities, you will be met and accompanied to the Grand Hyatt Hotel.   F

Day 3 (Thu) SINGAPORE. Your tour of this intriguing island republic combines the British tradition of Old Singapore with the more westernized culture of Modern Singapore. Retrace her history at the National Museum, housing jade pieces formerly found in the House of Jade. Stop at the nostalgia-filled Raffles Hotel, the 150-year-old Thian Hock Keng Temple, and Chinatown. From atop Mt. Faber view the city plus neighboring Malaysia and Indonesia, before admiring the orchids of the Botanic Gardens. The remainder of the day is open for optional tours of Sentosa Island, a harbor cruise, or the Jurong Bird Park, haven for over 350 species of birds. This evening is highlighted by a Chinese dinner.   B/D

Day 4 (Fri) SINGAPORE. Spend this free day as you please, perhaps enjoying one of the many optional tours available. B

THAILAND

Day 5 (Sat) SINGAPORE/BANGKOK. Your flight from Singapore brings you to the charming Oriental kingdom of Thailand. In the capital city of Bangkok, you will be escorted to the Royal Orchid Sheraton Hotel.   B/F

Day 6 (Sun) BANGKOK. An early morning cruise along the Chao Phraya River's tributaries affords you the spectacle of the famous floating market, where local farmers congregate on the klongs daily to market their produce in sampans. Next enter the Grand Palace, famed seat of the court of old Siam, and see Wat Phra Keo (Temple of the Emerald Buddha). The afternoon may be spent at your leisure.   B

Day 7 (Mon) BANGKOK. Today is open to indulge in your shopping or sightseeing pleasures. Take an optional trip to the Rose Gardens to see a Thai cultural show or ride an elephant. Tonight's treats include splendid Thai cuisine and the grace of traditional Thai classical dances.   B/D

INDONESIA

Day 8 (Tue) BANGKOK/DENPASAR (BALI). Fly onward to Bali, the Island of the Gods, and its capital city of Denpasar, where you will be transferred to the Bali Hyatt Hotel.   B/F

Day 9 (Wed) DENPASAR (BALI). Bask in Bali's magical beauty as you witness the vividly costumed Barong Dance this morning. Next see the temple of Tampaksiring, followed by lunch at a local restaurant. On your journey through the villages of Ubud, Celuk, Batuan, and Mas, experience the inspiring talent of the Balinese as they demonstrate their prowess in stone and wood carving, painting, weaving, and jewelry crafting. This evening see the Kecak or "monkey dance," where a chorus of 100 men depict the dramatic story of the Ramayana to their own chanting, followed by dinner at a local restaurant.   B/L/D

Day 10 (Thu) DENPASAR (BALI). This island paradise is yours to explore today. Take an optional trek to the Monkey Forest at Sangeh, where hundreds of sprite monkeys delight in perching on visitors' shoulders. Or relax amidst a striking sunset at the temple of Tanah Lot, suspended on a huge offshore rock.   B

HONG KONG

Day 11 (Fri) DENPASAR (BALI)/HONG KONG. Today marks the start of the final leg of your journey as you discover the vitality of Hong Kong.

From the green hills, rocky islands, and rice fields to the cosmopolitan bustle of Hong Kong Island and Kowloon, this vibrant city will inscribe its lasting impact. You will be met upon arrival, then settle into the Hyatt Regency Hotel.   B/F

Day 12 (Sat) HONG KONG.   Sightseeing of Hong Kong Island includes a visit to the market in the old fishing village of Stanley; Hong Kong's largest beach, Repulse Bay; Aberdeen, crowded with Chinese junks and their floating population; and lunch atop Victoria Peak at the Peak Cafe.   B/L

Day 13 (Sun) HONG KONG.   Today is set aside for you to partake in the bargains that exemplify Hong Kong as a commercial haven. Numerous optional tours are available to Guangzhou, Macau, or the islands of Lantau or Cheung Chau.   B

Day 14 (Mon) HONG KONG.   You may wish to spend this free day experiencing a taste of the past at the Sung Dynasty Village, a recreation of an era one thousand years ago featuring craftsmen garbed in period attire.

Or journey into the future at the Hong Kong Space Museum, one of the world's largest and most modern planetariums.   B

Day 15 (Tue) HONG KONG.   Fill your open schedule today with an optional cruise of Hong Kong Harbor or a visit to Ocean Park, featuring a highly advanced oceanarium with over 30,000 fish. Tonight you are hosted to a group farewell dinner to recount the exciting moments shared on your tour!   B/D

Day 16 (Wed) HONG KONG/WEST COAST.   You will have ample time to prepare before departing to enjoy the pampering of your Singapore Airlines flight. Bid farewell as you return to the West Coast.   B/F

DEPARTURES AND TOUR PRICES:

Includes round-trip airfare from West Coast

Tour No.	Departs	Returns	Tour Price
01AT-0126	Jan 26	Feb 10	$3,648
02AT-0301	Mar 01	Mar 16	$3,648
03AT-0329	Mar 29	Apr 13	$3,648
04AT-0426	Apr 26	May 11	$3,778
05AT-0517	May 17	Jun 01	$3,778
06AT-0531	May 31	Jun 15	$3,778
07AT-0614	Jun 14	Jun 29	$3,648
08AT-0628	Jun 28	Jul 13	$3,648
09AT-0726	Jul 26	Aug 10	$3,648
10AT-0823	Aug 23	Sep 07	$3,648
11AT-0913	Sep 13	Sep 28	$3,778
12AT-0927	Sep 27	Oct 12	$3,778
13AT-1011	Oct 11	Oct 26	$3,778
14AT-1018	Oct 18	Nov 02	$3,778
15AT-1025	Oct 25	Nov 09	$3,778
16AT-1101	Nov 01	Nov 16	$3,778
17AT-1108	Nov 08	Nov 23	$3,778
18AT-1122	Nov 22	Dec 07	$3,778
19AT-1213	Dec 13	Dec 28	$3,648

Next Year

20AT-0124	Jan 24	Feb 08	$3,648
21AT-0221	Feb 21	Mar 08	$3,648

Single Supplement $958

1.   How many flights does this tour feature?

2.   Which are the only flights that clearly will be on Singapore Airlines?

3. How many meals (including flight meals) are included? (*Note:* F indicates a meal while in flight.)

4. How many hotels will be used?

5. Indicate whether the following are included as part of the tour price (Y or N):

   a. Lodging at the Raffles Hotel

   b. Singapore Harbor Cruise

   c. Cruise in Bangkok

   d. Monkey Forest at Sangeh

   e. Visit to market in Stanley

6. How many days (out of sixteen) are entirely free for shopping, individual sightseeing, or whatever?

ACTIVITY 2

▼ Review the sample itinerary shown earlier in this chapter. Then answer the following questions that a client might have regarding that tour.

1. How many meals are included in the tour price?

2. Where will this trip's best scenery be?

3. Where will we cross the border into Canada?

4. How long will the Thousand Islands cruise be?

5. Is there any meal for which we will have to dress rather formally?

6. When will we have free time to shop?

7. Is a trip on the *Maid of the Mist* included?

8. When will we have a chance to get a view of the Falls illuminated at night?

■ ■ ■

ACTIVITY 3

▼ Respond to the following tour manager concerns regarding the sample itinerary shown earlier in the chapter.

1. Which days will we use a bus other than our own from Bonanza Bus Lines?

2. Why will we use another bus on those days?

3. This itinerary doesn't give all city routings. How could a driver or guide find out how to get from, say, the hotel to the Festin du Gouverneur?

4. Meal and admission costs aren't given here. How could the tour director obtain this information?

5. How many step-on guides are used?

6. Which bus trip will be the longest without stops?

7. What does the company's position on tips for step-on guides and for drivers from other companies seem to be?

8. If seats were rotated after every two to three hours of in-seat time, about how many rotations would this tour have? (Assume that on each city tour, clients will be in their seats at least two hours.)

■ ■ ■

PROFILE

Many people have noted the similarity between two professions—tour managing and acting. Anita Heiberg bridges both: for many years she performed in movies, on the stage, and in commercials. But surprisingly, Anita, who studied at the famous Lee Strasberg School of Acting as a scholarship student, feels that her talents were never fully put to the test until she took up tour conducting.

"Both professions," explains Anita, "require good speaking and entertaining skills, the ability to remember things, and the joy one gets from audience acceptance. But only tour management demands that you be 'on stage' for days, even weeks."

A native of Oslo, Norway, Anita began first as a local tour guide. She came to the United States in 1975 to act. In 1989, she decided it was time for a new career. She took travel classes at a nearby college "with only the vaguest idea of what jobs the travel industry might offer." A class in tour management pinpointed the niche that would work best for her. "It was immediately clear to me that tour conducting was exactly what I wanted to do. Here was a job where you're not stuck behind a desk from nine to five, yet can make good money."

That Anita speaks Norwegian, Swedish, French, and a little German and Spanish led to her immediate success among such inbound tour operators as American Express, Allied Tours, and Royal International. Lately she has also been conducting tours in Scandinavia in the middle of the summer. She conducts about fifteen two-week tours a year, leaving twenty-two weeks a year for other pursuits. One of her most interesting off-season activities was serving as a host for the Kodak Corporation at the 1994 Winter Olympics at Lillehammer, in her native Norway, and then again at the 1998 Winter Olympics in Nagano, Japan. "That came directly from an incentive trip I once worked on," explains Anita. "Some of the passengers were from the Norwegian Olympic Organizing Committee. I guess they liked what I did, so they recommended my work to the Olympic Sponsors."

Does Anita have any regrets about giving up acting? "Not at all," she responds. "Like many actors, I thrive on the love that an audience gives back to me. And tour groups do precisely that, in a more genuine way. Plus, as an independent contractor, you have the freedom to choose your own stage. And that stage includes some of the most beautiful and sought-after places on earth!"

chapter

4

Client and Escort Psychology

Chapter Objectives

After reading this chapter, you should be able to:

▼ Discuss strategies for managing group behavior.

▼ Explain why and how a tour leader can be culturally sensitive.

▼ Apply tactics for smooth interaction with flight attendants, motorcoach drivers, and step-on guides.

▼ Identify strategies for preventing escort burnout.

Special Exercise: Go directly to Activity 2 at the end of this chapter, and answer the twelve questions in the pretest. You'll complete the remainder of the activity later.

For the very first tour I conducted," explains Leo Lucas of Lucas Travel Management Associates, "I did massive research on the area I was to comment on, the Grand Canyon. I was prepared—or so I thought. What I wasn't ready for was the fact that the group seemed more concerned about golf stores, souvenirs, the safety of luggage, and seat rotation—I had a near riot over that—than about what I had to say about the Grand Canyon. Tour groups can behave quite strangely."

Managing Group Behavior

What Leo Lucas experienced is very familiar to anyone who has taken or conducted a tour. Powerful psychological forces shape group behavior. Understanding these curious but usually predictable forces can enable a tour manager to turn them to his or her advantage. Here are the three patterns you will probably encounter.

High Expectations

Tour participants bring with them high expectations. To purchase a tour is a decision of great consequence in the average person's life. Only buying a house or a car is more expensive. The dollars spent and the decisions made lead vacationers to expect a good time and a clear value.

Brochure descriptions, media ads, and their friends' positive experiences all serve to increase expectations. If the client has been on a previous tour, he or she will expect this trip, and your performance, to be as good as or better than what they experienced before. Passengers dream that every meal on the tour will be perfect, every flight on time, and every hotel an ideal home-away-from-home. This will be true even on a budget tour. The one exception—an adventure tour, where clients generally have more realistic expectations.

And what do tour members expect their tour manager to be? Why, a supremely knowledgeable, infinitely talented miracle worker, of course!

The Flock Factor

Tour participants quickly adapt to group thinking as they seek cues to "correct" behavior from those around them. Peer pressure becomes a very real factor. There's a desire to conform, even among those tour members

Tour clients discuss their expectations with their tour manager. *Courtesy of the National Tour Association*

who are mature and set in their ways. One amusing side effect can be a sort of herd instinct or "flock factor." If a tour manager leads a group into a building through a single door, all group members will probably try to pass through that one door, even if a dozen other entrances are available. Groups will dutifully follow a tour conductor across the street, even if the traffic signal has turned red. One tour director reports being followed into a men's room by an entire group, including its female members.

Apart from such odd phenomena, group cohesiveness carries significant advantages. Dominated by congenial individuals and a sensitive tour conductor, a group quickly takes on the kind of easy-going attitude that will help make the tour pleasant and successful. Because they see others doing it, clients will try an activity, a balloon ride, for example, that they would never do on their own.

A tour manager should encourage the "bonding" process by introducing passengers to one another (especially at a get-acquainted party, if scheduled), reserving large tables at restaurants so clients can interact, setting up a group photo, and using every other possible opportunity to break down the anonymity and transform forty strangers into a cohesive, cooperating family.

On the other hand, the flock factor and peer influence can lead to counterproductive behavior. A few disgruntled clients can quickly sour an entire tour. In a crisis, group conduct can even become dangerous. Through example and subtle management, a tour leader must reroute unsuitable behavior to more positive directions.

The Regression Syndrome

Tour directors often find it puzzling that mature adults on a tour can occasionally be cranky, argue over seating, compete for attention, be overly picky about food, take naps at almost any moment, and have tantrums. This juvenile behavior, however, can be expected. To free themselves of hassles and responsibilities, these adults have placed themselves in a situation where someone else, the tour manager, makes all the decisions for them: when to eat, sleep, and even go to the bathroom. It may be the first time since childhood that they've given up so much control to someone else.

It shouldn't come as a surprise, then, that touring adults could regress to childlike or childish behavior

and expect their tour director to become a surrogate parent, an authority figure who takes charge in a sensitive, fair, and firm manner. The group may be composed of senior citizens and the tour manager may be eighteen years old, but it doesn't matter. The tour conductor will still be both father and mother to forty adoring but occasionally unruly "kids."

Strategies for Managing a Tour Group

After reading about how clients dream, flock, and regress, you may wonder how a tour manager could possibly reshape such behavior into more sensitive and productive forms. Actually, the group-managing strategies required of a tour director aren't difficult to learn. They *are* subtle, however, since the context is so unexpected. (Tell a veteran tour conductor that he or she is a parent figure, and the first reaction will probably be one of amusement—until the similarities become stunningly obvious.) Good tour-managing tactics parallel good parenting tactics. They're solid adult leadership techniques as well.

A Tour Manager Must Be Fair

From birth, we all crave attention. As adults, we continue to enjoy the attention of others and to be disturbed by its absence. A tour director must parcel out attention equally to all tour members. Playing favorites leads to jealousies and "sibling rivalries" within the tour group family.

A tour leader who always sits with the same clients at group dinners, for example, will soon alienate others on the tour. Spread yourself around over the course of a tour or eat with the driver, not tour members.

Some tour managers, hoping to get a little free time, leave the group when a step-on guide takes over. Again, this sometimes provokes resentment. The group sees it as an unfair and uncaring act for a tour director to abandon his or her charges to an unfamiliar "babysitter." A tour conductor should remain with a group that is being led temporarily by someone else. If you *must* leave, then explain the reason clearly to your clients.

At the end of a motorcoach tour, don't drop off clients near their houses just because they live along the route to the tour's final destination. Others, expecting you to be consistent, will start asking for the same service. Soon you'll be making a dozen extra stops, and those who haven't asked for this favor will be steaming.

If you discover that it's someone's birthday or anniversary, a cake and a round of song are thoughtful gestures. Just don't overlook someone else's birthday that falls during the tour.

Be sure to apply the seat rotation system described in Chapter 3 with great care. Nothing upsets tour members more than inequitable seating assignments. The issue can easily turn into the tour equivalent of deciding which child gets stuck in the back seat of the car.

A Tour Manager Must Praise a Tour Group's Behavior

Kenneth Blanchard and Spencer Johnson, in their best-selling *The One Minute Manager*, argue that "to help people reach their full potential, catch them doing something right." So, too, must you acknowledge, praise, and reward appropriate client behavior in order for a tour to reach its full potential for success.

The most obvious quality to be praised is punctuality. A tour runs on finely tuned gears. If a few tour members are repeatedly late, those gears will start to grind badly.

One way tour conductors sometimes discourage tardiness is by embarrassing latecomers (for example, having the group "boo" them when they arrive on the motorcoach late or forcing them to contribute a dime to a "demerit" box). A more gentle, effective, and adult tactic is to warmly thank a group the first time all its members are punctual (which is often the first or second announced departure). A pattern will be set, useful habits will be reinforced, and peer-group pressure will discourage those who otherwise might be habitually behind schedule. Even more effective is to add unscheduled stops or small tour attractions for groups who are regularly on time and make it clear that their punctuality made these extras possible.

A Tour Manager Must Exceed the Client's Expectations

Adding "surprise stops" to a tour not only rewards a group for punctuality, but also serves as a "value-added" bonus. Such extras are a fine way to satisfy and even surpass a tour group's lofty expectations. Tour planners hold back a few minor tour components from their brochure prose and then encourage their compa-

ny's tour directors to add these surprises. In other instances, it's the tour conductor who finds ways to exceed what the client expects.

For example, one tour manager who conducted the "Canadian Classic" itinerary described in Chapter 3 regularly surprised passengers with:

▼ a stop at a Quebec farmhouse to sample fresh-baked bread and maple butter;

▼ a visit to the Welland Canal Locks to watch a ship pass through;

▼ Montreal postcards provided free by that city's Convention and Visitors Bureau;

▼ thank-you notes from the escort, which he slid under clients' hotel room doors on the tour's last night.

His most impressive "miracle working" feat was to have Niagara Falls light up at 9:30 P.M. with the precise colors that the clients had chosen earlier in the day. He was able to do this because he knew the worker who operated the lights on the Falls!

A Tour Manager Must Be Firm When Facing Disruptive Behavior

Chronic Complainers. Experience once prompted a veteran tour conductor to propose a one-out-of-three theory: out of every three tours conducted, at least one will have a passenger whose purpose seems to be to make life difficult for the tour leader. Chronic complainers do exist. They travel around the world in a bad mood, seemingly bent on finding everything that's wrong with a vacation rather than concentrating on all that's right. What makes them that way? Perhaps a recent problem has created their ill feelings, and the tour manager must suffer the consequences. Even more vexing are the complaints that stem from a deep-rooted, misguided need for attention. The complainer has discovered that the squeaky wheel gets the oil.

On a tour, the cause of complaining is often an individual's inability to submerge personal needs to those of the group. There *are* people who are ill-suited for the tour experience. Individualistic and strong willed, they become deeply irritated by tour regimentation and sometimes take it out on those around them.

As a tour manager, what should you do about a complainer? First, consider whether the criticism is justified. If it is, then solve the problem or at least explain that you are working on it. If the complaint isn't reasonable, then you may still have to respond—up to a point. What is that point? Lynette Hinings-Marshall, who has conducted tour management training programs, argues for a "rule-of-three" strategy: the first time a client complains, it may be justified; the second time may be a warning signal; the third time probably indicates the problem is in the person, not in the tour.

What should you do with a chronic complainer? You must draw the line, and quickly. You will have to be diplomatic but firm, explaining in a private and discreet moment that you have done all you can and that the person will just have to accept the way things are. Some people, after all, *want* to be told no.

You might choose to ignore the complaints, but this often leads to even worse predicaments. The hidden purpose of the complainer may be to get attention, not to have the problem solved. Ignoring the complaint may cause the complainer to escalate his or her efforts to get attention. Disgruntled feelings often spread through a group like an infection.

Above all, realize that unjustified complaints may come from recent misfortunes or deep-seated neuroses. A little compassion, rather than irritation or resentment, will provide a good defense against this very vexing dilemma. At the same time, don't let a chronic complainer monopolize your attention or color your perception of the group. Concentrate instead on the 99 percent of tour members who are easy to be with.

Chronic complainers, however, aren't the only clients who require a tour manager to be firm yet understanding.

The Chronically Late. Never cater to individuals who are repeatedly tardy. Otherwise the whole group will resent the fact that their tour's smooth structure is crumbling before them. Clients who are always tardy must be given an ultimatum: Be on time or we will leave you and you will have to find your own way to the next destination. This essential rule can often be expressed to the entire group in a humorous way: "Please return from your highway rest stop by noon. If you return at 12:30 and the motorcoach isn't here, don't worry. We have another tour going through here next week at the same time and they'll be glad to pick you up . . . ." Your point has been made.

But what if someone who is chronically late continues to be tardy? Then you may have to make good on your promise. After waiting twenty minutes or so (if you work for a tour operator, there may be an official time limit), have your on-time group members note the precise time (so the tardy clients cannot claim that your watch was fast) and leave.

Know-It-Alls. This *will* happen to you: You'll be giving a tour and suddenly a passenger will amend, add to, or outright contradict what you have said.

There are people who pride themselves on their knowledge and are genuinely informed. They offer you an opportunity to learn. Know-it-alls, on the other hand, *think* they are better informed than you, even though they probably aren't. Your instinct will be to get into a debate with them. Avoid the temptation. Pretend to be interested, be patient, and realize that the other clients on the tour will soon begin admiring your composure.

Bores. Some people are starved for attention. Their way of getting it is to talk incessantly to anyone too polite to escape their verbal grasp. This can be quite disruptive for a tour conductor. It's your job to listen to passengers, but you also need to spread your attention around. You often have more pressing things to attend to than listening to this one person. You'll have to give *some* attention to the person, but find excuses to eventually get away. (You may even tell them that you must spread your attention around, even though you "enjoy" talking to them. This usually works.)

Bores and know-it-alls are an annoyance. Chronic complainers can become extremely irritating. But those rare clients who drink too much alcohol, who seem to be on drugs, or who may be stealing things cause problems that may severely disrupt a tour. As a last resort, you must invoke the clause almost all tour companies print in their brochures: "The company reserves the right to terminate the tour of any person who is objectionable to other passengers or who disrupts the operation of a tour."

To drop someone from a tour is a serious matter, since it exposes you and the tour operator to a possible lawsuit, but it may be necessary. Document the client's actions carefully on paper, and get the names and addresses of witnesses to the client's behavior.

A Tour Manager Must Encourage Client "Adulthood"

Many of the behaviors we have reviewed—chronic tardiness, jealousy, a need for attention—have their roots in childhood and have solutions that parallel wise parenting. But tour directors mustn't fall into thinking of clients solely as children. They must use reasonable group-management strategies that encourage an adult client's right to make his or her own decisions within a tour's rules and regulations.

Several tactics work to encourage the "adulthood" of tour members. They also tend to counter-balance (but not subvert) the flock factor by reinforcing identity and independence.

▼ Use clients' names when speaking to them. Relate to them as individuals.

▼ "Interview" each client, if possible, on the tour's first day.

▼ Give them lists of your recommendations for places to eat and things to do during their spare time. This will encourage them to get out and explore. ·

▼ Find out from each client what interests them and then suggest ways they might pursue their interest during the tour's free time. You might tell an art lover, for instance, about a particularly good museum in the city where the tour is staying. Someone who likes Mexican food would be interested in knowing about the best Mexican restaurant in town.

A Tour Manager Must Exercise Leadership

Consider the terms used in the touring profession. *Tour escort* implies a sensitive, service-oriented job, one in which the escort becomes the helping companion to a group of travelers. The terms *tour manager*, *tour leader*, *tour conductor*, and *tour director* all imply control.

Escorts, though they're members of a service industry, shouldn't be reluctant to exercise their authority. Their groups expect them to. On the other hand, that authority must be restrained; over-control is not the answer. An escort is neither an overbearing dictator nor a meek servant but a leader who is ever-mindful of the needs of tour participants.

Tour conductors lead by example. They strive to make a strong first impression through good eye-contact, a warm smile, and perhaps a welcoming handshake. They're not just on time, but are early for everything. They explain a day's schedule and stick to it. They're cordial in all situations and calm when necessary. They dress professionally whenever on duty. In short, they're role models for their group's behavior.

Tour managers quickly figure out the responsibilities of their leadership role and what happens when they fail to accept these responsibilities. "I was on a tour of Germany. We were scheduled to see two castles, yet we were very behind time," remembers Dr. Sue Cooper, a practicing psychologist who has a special interest in tour escort behavior. "It was clear there was no time for both castles, only one. The tour leader took a vote as to which one to see. Bad idea. By that action, he gave up his power, upset those who wanted to see the castle that 'lost,' and forfeited the entire group's respect." What should he have done? "He could have made a professional decision himself and framed his decision in a positive light by explaining why he chose the castle he did and why that decision was in the best interest of the group. Sure, some people would still be disappointed. But if you're not ready to occasionally be the 'heavy' as an escort, then you shouldn't be out there escorting."

A Tour Manager Must Be Flexible

Flexibility is a key word when it comes to managing group behavior. Tour leaders who treat each group exactly the same way, ignore the subtleties of client feedback, and fail to adjust to each group and situation soon find that their strategies are strangely out of kilter.

Flexibility is especially important when a tour conductor is assigned to an untraditional touring group. For example, tour directors for charter, affinity, student, or incentive tours need to do very little to mold their group into a cohesive, cooperative unit. Tour participants already know one another or at least have common interests. Many tour directors report that such groups are among the easiest to manage. Clients on these tours show enthusiasm for their trip much earlier than clients on a public, "per capita" tour. They're also much less likely to squabble over seats or demand constant attention.

On the other hand, a tour manager will find exerting leadership over such groups a delicate business. For one thing, the group may already have a leader. A student tour, for instance, will have a teacher; an adventure tour of scuba divers, its diving instructor; an incentive group, its corporate officers; a group of Shriners, its potentate; a religious group, its minister, rabbi, or priest. In such groups, it's the tour manager who, at least initially, is the outsider.

A tour conductor must quickly establish a relationship with the group's leader in which responsibilities are

A tour conductor is an important authority figure.
Courtesy of the National Tour Association

clarified. (The group leader, being on vacation, will probably want minimal responsibility anyway.) The tour manager must then delicately establish his or her authority with the tour members while warmly acknowledging and praising the group's leader. Keep in mind that the group's leader may have helped organize the group in the first place and will expect some sort of acknowledgment.

Incentive tours present especially subtle challenges. First, the clients are all winners. The tour is their reward for personal and corporate achievement. As a result, they expect their tour director to be more of a host or service person than a leader, and they expect that service to be professional and even-handed. Incentive travelers, the elite of their company, expect a first-class performance from every person they deal with on their trip.

Furthermore, incentive travelers aren't always in the best frame of mind when their vacation begins. "They may be irritated by certain rules of the incentive," explains Kathleen Kearney, former manager of Crimson Incentive Services. "For instance, they may not have reached a sales level that permitted them to bring their spouse free of charge, whereas the person sitting next to them did. Incentive clients can be somewhat cranky at the beginning, and the trip director should expect and understand this."

Finally, trip directors must understand that they represent *two* companies: the corporation sponsoring the tour and the incentive house operating it. On the one hand, they must identify themselves with the client's company, frequently underscoring the team spirit they share. At the same time, they must submit to the leadership of the incentive company. Trip directors must be prepared to attend frequent planning meetings, take on many humble tasks, and surrender their authority to that of the incentive supervisors. The traditional tour manager, used to on-the-road autonomy, may initially find this position disorienting.

Cultural Sensitivity

"The only distinguishing characteristic of the American character I've been able to discover is a fondness for ice water," said Mark Twain in a typical bit of wry satire. In reality, to a visiting foreigner, Americans seem to possess a multitude of unexpected cultural traits that often amuse, confuse, or fluster the visitor. In turn, Americans who travel abroad find certain foreign behavior patterns to be equally unusual or unsettling.

Television has hardly helped the situation. Though it has turned the world into a global village, with each citizen seemingly better informed than ever before, it has also terribly distorted the image we have of one another. People from other countries know a lot about America, but their preconceptions have been oddly shaped by the media. For example, many tours include the South Fork Ranch in Texas as a place for foreign visitors to see. It's where some of the old TV series *Dallas* was shot. Europeans really get excited about seeing it. It's strange to think that their expectations of America are probably very influenced by TV shows, like *Dallas* and *Baywatch*. Add to this the typical American's poor knowledge of geography and culture and the problem becomes clear—26 percent of the college students polled in a recent study stated that a principal language of Latin America is Latin.

Tour conductors need to develop an informed sensitivity to foreign cultural differences. Such sensitivity is especially important for those who deal with inbound foreign groups or who escort tours outbound to other countries. Cultural knowledge smooths interactions with foreign nationals, helps adjust expectations, and provides a rich topic for tour narration. If you specialize in taking groups to other countries, you'll have the task of helping them navigate in a foreign culture. As the escort who "stars" in the fine documentary, *The Grand Tour*, puts it: "My job is to change people's perspective." This is also true if you escort groups inbound to North America from other countries. In fact, in that situation you become an ambassador of culture. You may be the only citizen of your country that the foreign visitor will ever get to know.

Ethnocentrism and Stereotyping

The term most relevant to any discussion of cultural interaction is ethnocentrism. **Ethnocentrism** is defined as the belief that one's own nationality or ethnic group is superior to all others. Examples of ethnocentrism are many: the Texan who views Parisians as culturally deprived because they "don't know how to cook a good steak"; the Parisian who believes the Texan is crude because of his boisterous, good-time manner; or the Japanese tourist who visits the United States and wonders why there aren't Indians on every corner or gangsters on every street.

A second relevant term is **stereotyping**, the tendency to believe that an unvarying pattern or manner marks all members of a group. The previous paragraph about Texans, Parisians, and Japanese contains several stereotypes: statements that may apply to some members of each ethnic group but do not apply to all of its members. Certain supposed cultural traits have no validity at all. In fact, they're dangerous.

Perspectives for Avoiding Cultural Insensitivity

Tour directors who deal frequently with foreign places or people should avoid ethnocentrism and stereotyping. They should always keep the following points in mind.

The "Rightness" or "Wrongness" of Certain Practices Varies from Culture to Culture. Many American travelers find Spanish bullfighting to be a brutal tradition. They certainly have the right to that belief, but they must also understand that culture has a major impact on that judgment. Spaniards view bullfighting as a sport of bravery. Furthermore, Hindus consider the American practice of slaughtering cattle for meat just as barbaric as bullfighting. Tour managers mustn't impose their values on others. They must realize that cultural values are often neither right nor wrong, only different.

Cultural customs sometimes affect a tour manager quite directly. For instance, escorts often consider groups from Japan cheap, since they rarely tip the escort or driver. But the lack of gratuities has nothing to do with miserliness. Just as an American would not think of tipping a dentist, salesperson, or electrician, a Japanese tourist is simply not in the habit of tipping a guide or a tour conductor, who in Japan is viewed as a service professional.

Cultural Values Are in Constant Flux and Can Become Rapidly Outdated. An Asian traveler who visited the United States in the 1950s would certainly be surprised by current American values. The visitor who smokes would probably be annoyed by current U.S. smoking regulations. Most Asians don't perceive smoking to be a significant health hazard or a behavior that should be controlled through legislation. A tour conductor guiding a group of Asians might have to readjust smoking policy on the motorcoach (assuming it is legal) and ensure that restaurants seat the group in a smoking section. In turn, a tour leader will encounter real problems when taking a group of nonsmokers to Asia. Above all, tour managers should not impose their values on the group, except perhaps in the gentlest of ways.

Cultural Values Vary Within Regions of the Same Country. You wouldn't expect a New Yorker to behave like someone from Des Moines, so don't assume that all Belgians, for instance, will be the same. Someone from Brussels may have very different values than a person from the small town of Tielt. A Belgian of Flemish descent may think differently from a Belgian of Gallic ancestry. Individuals may not fit any predictable cultural pattern at all. A tour conductor should avoid any oversimplifications about culture, since it's always multi-layered.

On the other hand, certain generalizations about groups, when valid and useful, can be justified. Almost all tour managers comment that Australian vacationing groups, for example, expect a good-time, party atmosphere and don't especially appreciate receiving an array of facts and figures from their guide. On the other hand, German groups are said to expect much factual information, and they're usually sticklers for accuracy. In these matters, let honest experience, yours and your company's, be your guide.

Some Cultural Specifics

It is thoroughly impossible to prepare a tour manager for all aspects of worldwide cultures. A short discussion of a few aspects of general behavior, however, can help make one aware of the astonishing variety of cultural practices.

Again, remember that not every member of a culture will espouse each custom. For more specific information, you may wish to consult the fine Culturgram

series, published by Brigham Young University (see Appendix A), which culturally profiles over 100 countries.

Initial Contact

A tour conductor will greet a busload of clients at the start of each tour, and dozens of individuals during the course of the trip. In dealing with foreigners, sensitivity to different styles of greeting can enable the tour manager to make that important first impression a good one.

Shaking hands is the norm in many countries, although the United States and Canadian "pumping" handshake can seem strange to people from other nations. In some countries, especially those that are Moslem, women rarely shake hands. In Asia, a bow often replaces the handshake. In Europe, a hug and kiss (in the air, next to but not *on* the cheek) is a standard greeting between even casual friends.

The use of names also presents problems. A tour director can feel secure in using first names with Canadians and Americans once he or she knows them well. This practice might make a European uncomfortable, however. Remember that among many Asians, the family name is given first.

Two small but important reminders: First, many people consider it rude to wear sunglasses while convers-

In a foreign land, dining can be a very different cultural experience.

ing. In the United States and Canada, it might only be considered standoffish. Second, never show the soles of your shoes to a Moslem—it's considered very crude behavior in Moslem countries.

Punctuality

As we've seen, schedules, deadlines, and reservation times are critical to a tour. Yet the perception of their importance will vary depending on the origin of the group and the destination to be visited.

In general, punctuality is important to travelers from Northern Europe, Japan, Canada, and the United States (again, many exceptions exist). The concept of time is much more elastic in Latin America, Africa, the Caribbean, on South Sea islands, and around the Mediterranean.

Since punctuality is critical to a tour's workings, what can a tour manager do with a group that doesn't consider punctuality a high priority? The tour director must repeatedly and patiently point out to the group the importance of staying on schedule. The tour director might describe the dire results of missing a certain deadline. If the group is traveling in the United States, they should be told how seriously Americans take promptness. (Be prepared for a lecture from the group on why this is obsessive, insensitive, and stress-provoking behavior!) Canadian and American tourists need to be similarly prepared for experiences abroad that move at a snail's pace.

Remember that not every culture puts a premium on waiting in orderly lines. In many countries, service people try to handle everyone at once. To push for attention is therefore viewed not as rude but as sensible. Prepare your group for this. Also be aware that cultural values often override your plan for motorcoach seating. For example, Pakistanis have their own idea of what assigned seating or rotation should be: the men sit in the front and the women sit in the back.

Dining

In the movies, it's a stock scene. A visitor sits down to dinner in a foreign land and is confronted by some unidentifiable or terribly unappetizing treat, such as eel, brain, or chocolate-covered ants. Rarely does a traveler encounter such bizarre delicacies. Yet it's true that we each have strongly ingrained eating habits (especially with respect to breakfast) that may conflict with what another culture considers appropriate fare. Tour con-

ductors must be aware of worldwide culinary customs and how they affect a traveling group.

Among outbound groups from the United States and Canada, certain reactions are predictable. They'll see foreign service as awfully slow. Other countries consider dining a major event to be savored; in the United States and Canada, it's often something to be done quickly. A tour conductor must explain this fact to the group as well as guide them through unfamiliar fare.

A tour manager must also prepare foreign restaurants for American idiosyncrasies, such as the desire for water with every meal and the habit of eating salad *before* the main entree. (In many countries, the salad serves as an after-meal aid to digestion.)

Many other small, local quirks must be explained. In Egypt, eating all the food on the plate usually indicates you want more. In Switzerland, asking for salt and pepper is an insult to the chef. In Austria, cutting fish with a regular knife is uncouth. In many countries, eating food while walking down the street is considered uncultured.

In turn, many eating customs in the United States disorient foreign visitors. They'll be amused by salad dressing, baked potatoes, and water with their meals. They'll be astounded by the size of meal portions. Since any traveling group brings along its peculiarities of taste and appetite, a group may be intrigued by distinctly American dishes yet seek out, whenever possible, familiar fare. Since menu phrases may be difficult for a foreign group to understand, they may prefer cafeterias, where they can see what they will eat and order by pointing to the item.

Finally, the tour leader must explain a country's tipping practices. In New Zealand and China, for example, tipping a waiter is considered unnecessary and even gauche. In much of Europe, a 15 percent gratuity is added directly to the bill. In Italy, a waiter expects an additional tip over and above the 15 percent included in the bill.

Miscellaneous Factors

Small cultural factors often become large for anyone visiting another country. For example, we rarely think about public restrooms. Yet you, as the tour conductor, must always think about them, if only because forty people attempting to use two public restrooms in an exotic land is a daunting experience.

First, familiarize groups with the name used: bathroom, restroom, WC (water closet), or lavette (a term

---

What Most Germans Find Surprising When They Visit North America

▼ Doggie bags
▼ Mobile homes
▼ Orderly lines
▼ Vast distances
▼ Overt patriotism
▼ "Bottomless" cups of coffee
▼ The quantity of food at meals
▼ Mail boxes on posts
▼ Four-way stop signs
▼ Wheelchair accessibility

▼ Stores that are open 24 hours a day, seven days a week
▼ The incredible variety of food in supermarkets
▼ The fact that U.S. citizens have the right to bear arms
▼ The fact that young people can drive and marry before they can legally drink

---

used only in parts of Rhode Island). You must point out that in Europe "bathroom" means just that—a place to take a bath. It's not a toilet. A private bathroom for each hotel room is not always a given. The variety of bathroom plugs, faucets, and handles that exist worldwide (as well as overall design configurations) is mindboggling. A common experience in Europe, for example, is to mistake a pull chain dangling from the wall for a tub-draining mechanism. You yank it, and very quickly a maid bursts into your bathroom—you've pulled the emergency call device.

Another common source of social blunders is body language and gestures. The hitchhiking sign used by Americans and Canadians, for example, is obscene in Australia. The United States "okay" sign means "zero" in France and "money" in Japan and is an obscenity in Russia. In most countries, two people stand close together when they talk; this proximity, however, disturbs Americans, Canadians, and the British. There's no way that you can fully prepare clients for these sorts of subtleties, but they do serve as endlessly entertaining and enlightening sources of commentary.

One final critical point for touring: In many countries, what is called the second floor in Canada and the United States is labeled the first, and the first floor is called the ground floor, main level, or *rez-de-chaussee*.

Dealing with Fellow Workers

Tour conductors are usually only one part of a much larger team that services a tour group. Tour managers must apply their people skills to everyone they deal with, not reserve them only for clients. If a tour director shows arrogance to a hotel desk clerk or disregard for a motorcoach driver's skills, the clients' tour experience will surely deteriorate. Three categories of co-workers merit special discussion.

Flight Attendants

Once one of the most glamorous jobs in the travel industry, flight attending has become an increasingly stressful and thankless occupation. Modest pay, increased passenger loads, labor unrest, and frequent litigation have all taken some of the sheen off the profession. Yet flight attendants are professionals. Their job is hardly as easy as it seems. When the cabin door closes, *they* are in charge.

The tour director must perform a delicate balancing act when escorting a group on a plane. You must learn to maintain control of your group while at the same time deferring to the flight crew's leadership. Seat belt laws, for example, apply to you, too.

The best approach is to introduce yourself to the head flight attendant or those attendants who are serving the cabin section where your group is seated. Offer to help out in any way possible. Then stay out of their way. For instance, it's important for tour managers to circulate among tour passengers from the start, to help cement the escort-client relationship that will hold the group together. This should not be done, however, while attendants are moving carts through the aisles. Socialize in those "off" moments when nothing much is going on in the aircraft.

Drivers

On some intermodal tours, a tour leader can expect to work with a different motorcoach operator each day. On other trips, however, and especially on a motorcoach tour, the driver and the tour director become a team. A smooth driver-escort rapport powerfully enhances the tour experience. A bumpy one jars it terribly.

In most cases the person behind the wheel has years of touring experience. Drivers sometimes know more about a trip than the tour manager does. Drivers are important resources. They have many duties beyond driving: they load and unload luggage, assist disembarking passengers, help keep the coach clean, help plan routing, and occasionally supplement the tour manager's narrations or entertainment activities. In turn, the tour director often assists the driver in some of the above tasks. Above all, neither must attempt to usurp the other's prime responsibilities.

A few suggestions can help you maximize the driver-escort relationship:

▼ If feasible and appropriate, driver and escort should eat meals together. Clients will admire the friendship that exists between the two of you. Eating meals together will also give both of you a little respite from client attention.

▼ Introduce the driver at the very beginning of the tour. Refer to him or her frequently. Praise a fine driving performance at the day's end.

▼ Each evening or over breakfast, the two of you should discuss upcoming activities, routes, and responsibilities. Don't throw in an unexpected tour event without informing the driver first.

▼ If the route is familiar to you but new to the driver, it's perfectly all right for you to give him or her directions. Do it subtly, though, and off the microphone.

▼ Be open to driver suggestions. Remember, though, that in most things you are in charge. Some drivers have strong personalities and engage in a subtle struggle for tour leadership. Tour groups will judge you poorly if a driver begins taking command of the microphone. Yet some drivers try to do this. You must be very firm in such a situation.

▼ From time to time personality conflicts arise between driver and tour manager. If at all possible,

A motorcoach driver is an important resource person.
Courtesy of the National Tour Association

don't allow passengers to become aware of this discord. As soon as you return to your tour company for debriefing, discuss the matter fully with your supervisor.

Step-On Guides

When a step-on guide takes over the microphone, the group members' attention shifts to the guide, yet their loyalty and trust remain with the tour manager. This "split allegiance" can be awkward.

To keep things running smoothly, the tour conductor should hand over authority by warmly introducing the step-on guide by name. Acknowledge the guide's expertise and then pay attention like everyone else. In most instances the tour manager should stay with the group, even though someone else is in charge. Otherwise, the tour members will feel abandoned.

Preventing Escort Burnout

The statistics are troubling. The typical part-time tour director stays in the job for only four years; a full-timer, only seven. As indicated in Chapter 1, there are many causes. There's no doubt that the stresses of tour management can cause rapid burnout.

Much of this anxiety can be avoided. Certain tactics can sharply reduce the stress a tour conductor feels.

Sensitivity to One's Own Needs

When visiting a particular city, film director Alfred Hitchcock always stayed in the same hotel and requested the same room. For him, predictability was more soothing than variety.

Perhaps you're the kind of person who is unnerved by the unpredictable. Though unforeseeable events will always challenge you, you may prefer to do everything possible to reduce all stress-causing factors that can be anticipated. For example, many tour managers specialize in only one or two destinations. Then if a problem occurs, they know whom to talk to and are intimately familiar with the available options.

Other tour leaders treasure variety and are bored by predictability. If you're one of these persons, it's probably better to work for a company that sends you to a new destination each trip. For you, the stresses involved in dealing with the unfamiliar will be far outweighed by

the exhilaration provided by fresh, novel locations.

Whether you specialize in one trip or vary your assignments, your career will probably travel a predictable arc. For the first few months, the job will be quite stressful—there's so much new to learn. If you feel the same level of stress after six months or more, tour management may not be for you. Typically, however, you'll enter a period of satisfaction and balance. The job will still be demanding, but you'll know, deep in your heart, that you genuinely love tour management.

For some, this period of satisfaction lasts for years, even decades. Eventually, though, most tour managers reach a burnout stage. They become jaded or irritable, and the joy is replaced with cynicism or boredom. They must listen to their needs—the need to find a new career. They should either work at rekindling their energy and commitment or move on to something else, often in some other segment of the tour and travel industry. Here they can find job satisfaction again, where the challenges are better suited to their present stage in life.

Awareness of Body Rhythms

You may consider yourself a morning person or you may work better at night. Whatever the case, you must closely monitor how your body clock affects your job performance. For instance, if you normally sleep late, you'll have to do all you can to break that habit, since touring often begins at 9 A.M. or earlier. You may seek to escort those tours that operate primarily at night, such as New York theater and nightclub tours. Conversely, a "morning person" who is listless at night will have to find a way to become energized for an evening tour activity. You might want to take a short nap in the late afternoon when your group has returned to the hotel after a day's touring.

No factor affects one's body clock more dramatically than jet lag. Once thought to be primarily a psychological reaction to lengthy air travel, **jet lag** is now known to be a physiological phenomenon. Crossing time zones wreaks havoc on hormone levels, blood components, digestion, and overall mental alertness. For example, a trip from Houston to Helsinki can throw your body totally out of synchronization, since Finland's day is Houston's night. At 3 A.M. you wake up, your body ready for dinner. At lunch time, you may nod off into that soup in front of you—your body is telling you it is 4 A.M. (Remember, too, that your whole group will be having the same reaction.)

What do most medical authorities recommend to combat jet lag? Several medications are now being offered that help the body readjust quickly. More traditional strategies are listed below.

▼ Try to avoid hectic activities the day before your trip.

▼ Eat lightly and drink plenty of water while in flight. Avoid alcohol or sleep medication.

▼ Get as much rest as possible on the plane, especially when your group is sleeping or watching a movie.

▼ Shortly after departure, reset your watch to your destination's time.

▼ After traveling west to east (the toughest for most), get outside early the first morning, but avoid late afternoon exposure to light. East-to-west travel requires staying outdoors in the late afternoon and for at least a few hours in the morning. This helps to reset those rhythms cued by sunlight.

▼ Keep active on your arrival day, but try to get to bed early.

Tour directors are often tempted to overdo both play and work. Pace your work carefully during the day and don't stay out late at night.

Home-Duplicating Patterns

The movie *The Accidental Tourist* (and the book it was based on) describes a travel writer who invents every conceivable way to cushion himself and his readers from the rigors of travel. Although the story's central character is obsessive about the stress of travel, there's no doubt that being on the road cuts us off from the comfortable patterns we treasure when at home. Tour directors should do everything possible to preserve some of the important links to their more everyday lifestyle.

▼ Eat the same quantity and types of food, when possible, as you do at home. Traveling (and free food) should not be an excuse to overindulge.

▼ Try to work some sort of exercise program into your daily routine. Use the hotel's health club facility.

▼ Make friends among those with whom you work. A network of out-of-town "allies" does much to cushion the potential loneliness of escorting. Telephone your friends and family back home on a regular basis, for they miss you, too.

▼ Don't obsessively overwork. You may, for example, want to turn down a tour to remain home for a sensible amount of time between assignments.

▼ Make your hotel room an extension of your home. Bring a few personal mementos with you that have no purpose except to comfort you. Call room service occasionally so you can dine in a relaxed setting free of interruptions.

Guarding Your Privacy

Some movie celebrities are truly gracious to their fans, but others can be rude. Why? One reason is that they may resent the constant assaults on their privacy.

It's not enough that you're the "mother" and "father" to tour members. You play another role as well. To the group, you're an instant celebrity, a "personality," a *star*. They want to talk to you, to find out everything about you, to have their picture taken with you. They may even ask you to autograph their itineraries.

You should deal with this loss of anonymity with tact, warmth, and a sense of humor. This kind of attention comes with the job. But you should also protect yourself from the stress that this little dose of fame brings.

▼ Carve out blocks of off-duty time, if possible, to enjoy attractions that *you* want to see.

▼ During free time, eat your meals in restaurants other than the ones in your hotel, or use room service.

▼ Set aside moments to simply enjoy being alone in your room.

▼ For companionship, rely on friends you make in each city your tour visits (this will be easier if you specialize in one itinerary) or on your driver.

▼ Unless you don't mind a constant stream of conversation, avoid sitting among clients on a motorcoach, in a restaurant, or on a plane, even when you're on duty. Stay close and visible, though. They do need to feel that you are there for them.

▼ When off-duty, dress casually. The group so associates you with a uniform or professional attire that you'll be able to walk right through a client-filled lobby without being recognized at all—one of the more amusing phenomena of the tour business.

Whether tour conductors should or should not announce their room number to clients is a much debated question among tour companies. Giving out such information emphasizes that a tour manager is accessible and ready to serve. On the other hand, tour

A tour director must often deal with a diverse group of people.

participants have a bad habit of disturbing their tour director's privacy with a barrage of trivial requests, such as a need of towels or soap, when they could just as easily have dialed housekeeping.

No matter which approach you take, you definitely should be available to satisfy a client's reasonable or pressing needs. Therefore, tell the front desk or operator to put through all necessary calls from tour members, and let the front desk know where you will be when you go out, in case an emergency occurs.

Above all, you should feel that you are with your group by choice, not that you're chained to them. A good tour manager feels honest affection for tour members. Once they sense it, group travelers will return this affection willingly and with respect.

Summary

Tour conductors face powerful psychological forces when managing a group. Its members have high expectations, wish to be a part of the group, and may revert to childlike behavior. To manage a group effectively, a tour director must be fair, praising, firm, flexible, encouraging of adult behavior, and willing to exceed expectations and to lead. To be culturally sensitive, tour managers must avoid ethnocentrism and stereotyping. They need to be aware of the variety and ever-changing nature of cultural values. They must also remain alert to the needs of their fellow workers as well as to their own physiological and psychological reactions to the tour-leading profession.

■ ■ ■

QUESTIONS FOR DISCUSSION

1. Describe three psychological forces that mold group behavior.

2. List seven general strategies that a tour director should employ when managing a group.

3. Explain ethnocentrism and stereotyping.

4. What four points about foreign cultural values should a tour manager keep in mind?

5. You are escorting a group to Venice. What cultural factors might you discuss with your group regarding the way Italians greet one another, dine, and treat time?

6. Describe the working relationship that should exist between a tour manager and a flight attendant crew.

7. Give six ways an escort can maximize the driver-escort relationship.

8. Identify four ways a tour conductor can avoid job burnout.

9. What is jet lag, and how can it be minimized?

10. List at least four ways a tour manager can maintain some sense of a normal home life while on the road.

■ ■ ■

ACTIVITY 1

▼ Psychological insight is required to meet many of the challenges that a tour manager faces. Six situations are described below. In a paragraph, describe how you would deal with each:

CASE 1: You are taking a group of twenty in an outdoor elevator to the top of a tower that rises above a major city. Two-thirds of the way up, the elevator stops. The elevator operator presses the intercom button; it doesn't work. He presses "emergency descent"; that doesn't work either. Your group is getting nervous, as the elevator hangs 600 feet in the air in the full heat of the sun.

CASE 2: A client arrives for your motorcoach tour and claims that, because she gets motion sickness, someone in your office has promised her the front-row seat for the entire trip. This is clearly contrary to your company's seat rotation policy. There is no memo in your briefing materials about this client's special request.

CASE 3: You are the tour manager on a twelve-day European motorcoach tour. Your company's policy is to inform clients through the tour brochure that "gratuities to escort and driver, if deserved, should be given individually—no group tip collection, please." Your driver, however, who works for a European bus company (not the tour operator), informs you that he expects you to organize a group collection for him or to at least manipulate a client into doing it. You get the feeling that if you do not agree, he and his driving will soon become a problem.

CASE 4: It's the end of a motorcoach tour. You have two official drop-off points for your Floridian clients: the bus terminals in Pompano Beach and Miami. However, between these two cities, a client says that you will be going right by her house in Hallandale—could you just drop her off? It would only take a minute.

CASE 5: You are escorting an inbound group of forty from China. Despite your company's no-smoking policy, several in the group insist that their travel agent told them your company permits on-coach smoking. You say that this is not the case, yet as soon as the motorcoach begins to roll, many in the group start smoking.

CASE 6: A passenger tells you that this tour is turning out to be very different than she expected. She shows you a copy of the itinerary in her brochure. It turns out to be an old, out-of-date one. The tour has changed since her version was printed. One hotel is different, a minor attraction has been dropped, and the "scenic drive" along a certain road has been replaced by a faster, less interesting one.

■ ■ ■

ACTIVITY 2

PRETEST: Respond to each of the following statements with either A (agree) or D (disagree).

1. Bullfighting is a barbaric custom. _____

2. Smoking should be banned in most public places. _____

3. Americans are generally polite. _____

4. At seventy, a person often knows and remembers fewer things than he or she did at thirty. _____

5. Dying for one's country is usually not worthwhile. _____

6. Time is money. _____

7. If someone gives you a gift, the first thing you should do is say "thank-you." _____

8. You should memorize the first names of individuals on your tour as soon as possible. _____

9. To be polite, you should finish as much of the food on your plate as possible. _____

10. The practice of paying little bribes to get your way in some countries is disgusting. _____

11. Foreigners often smell funny, but Americans rarely do. _____

12. Women who don't shave their legs are usually unattractive. _____

▼ Upon completion of the above, go back and read the chapter. When you've finished the chapter, complete the remainder of this activity.

Now that you've read the chapter, you should realize that a tour manager must have a global perspective on cultural practices. Go back over the above statements and see whether you have changed your mind about any of the responses you gave. Below each statement, explain your new perspective in one or two sentences. If your point of view hasn't changed, state this, but acknowledge another point of view that may exist. (Note that several customs referred to above weren't directly discussed in the text.)

EXAMPLE: I still dislike bullfighting, but I know that Spaniards perceive it as a sport that demonstrates the courage of both the matador and the bull.
    or
Bullfighting is probably as repugnant, from an animal rights or religious perspective, as our own slaughtering of animals for meat.

■ ■ ■

ACTIVITY 3

▼ Foreign language skills are important if your tour operator deals with non-English-speaking people. Even if you work with English-speaking foreigners, however, you may sometimes find yourself mystified. The comments below contain terms commonly used in Australia. Try to fathom their meaning and complete them appropriately.

1. "Everything is apples" means _____.
   (A) the information is in the computer
   (B) things are under control
   (C) it's spring
   (D) everything is going wrong

2. If an Australian says, "Break it down!", he _____.
   (A) wants you to stop
   (B) is getting angry
   (C) wants you to share a drink with him
   (D) is expressing disbelief

3. "Enjoy the bush, but beware of the Marchies. They might _____ you."
   (A) enlist
   (B) eat
   (C) confuse
   (D) bite

4. If a salesclerk asks you, "Are you right?", she wants to know if you _____.
   (A) wish to purchase the item you are looking at
   (B) need assistance
   (C) are not feeling well
   (D) have shoplifted

5. "I'll be back this avro. I'll see you _____."
   (A) this afternoon
   (B) tomorrow
   (C) next week
   (D) next year

6. "These opals are fair dinkum, they're _____."
   (A) genuine
   (B) well priced
   (C) so-so-quality
   (D) huge

Working with Hotels

Chapter Objectives

After reading this chapter, you should be able to:

▼ Explain the impact hotels have on tour conductors, clients, and companies.

▼ Enumerate the six characteristics that mark a successful tour hotel.

▼ Explain how best to negotiate with a hotel.

▼ Identify information that must be given to tour members about a hotel.

▼ Compare the advantages and disadvantages of three methods of group check-in.

▼ Specify seven typical problems that arise for hotel-lodged groups and suggest solutions.

▼ Chronicle the specific steps a tour manager must take while staying in a hotel.

▼ Describe the pitfalls to be avoided during hotel checkout.

"YOU SHOULD WARN YOUR GROUP THAT THEY MAY HAVE JUST A LITTLE TROUBLE FINDING THEIR ROOMS."

Next to the destination, perhaps the most important element of any tour is the hotel," maintains Edward Camara, president of Camara Tours. As you begin escorting groups, you may soon decide that Camara has understated the situation. At times, tour members will seem more preoccupied with their lodging than with the destination itself, even though they'll spend only a few waking hours in their hotel rooms.

The reasons for this are subtle. In the most basic sense, a hotel or motel becomes a second home. Your tour members see it as a calming refuge from the trip's stimulating but stressful pace. Indeed, modern marketing strategy plays directly to this yearning for homelike environments. Bed-and-breakfast inns, condo resorts, all-suite hotels, living room-like lobbies, and extra-amenity floors have succeeded grandly for this very reason.

You'll also discover that tour members view a hotel not just as a second home but as an idealized, perfect one. Air-conditioning, maid service, a swimming pool, a phone in the bathroom—if any of these hotel luxuries aren't in proper working order, your tour members will surely let you know about it. Be tolerant of such seemingly overcritical behavior. Part of your job is to assure clients that their home-away-from-home dreams will be fulfilled.

A hotel (often called a **property** in travel industry terminology) is equally important from the more down-to-earth perspective of a tour operator. Lodging usually accounts for the single greatest outlay in a tour's budget. Therefore, hotel value and service take on considerable fiscal importance for tour planners.

Hotel personnel—at least those in upper-echelon management—understand that tours inject enormous profits into their hotel's operation. (Unfortunately, others sometimes view tours as cut-rate and troublesome.)

An intriguing study by Southeastern Advertising (SEA) underscores the dramatic impact a tour can have on a hotel's balance sheets. SEA analyzed one single tour, Tauck's six-day motorcoach trip to New England. They estimated that forty-five passengers would travel on each tour and that all forty-three scheduled departure dates would operate. (This may have been an overly optimistic projection. On the other hand, SEA did not factor in the probability that on many peak-season departure dates, one or more motorcoach groups might be added.)

The study's results are striking. This single tour, over only one tourist season, would be worth $238,165 in accommodations alone. It would also probably generate another $100,000 for the hotels, as the groups would take many of their meals in the hotels' dining facilities. To get an idea of how significant the packaged tour is to the lodging industry, consider that the New England tour was but one of the over eighty tours that Tauck advertised in its brochures, and Tauck is only one of hundreds of tour companies that operate worldwide.

At peak times tour members, whose rooms are substantially discounted, displace regular, full-paying customers and therefore cut into hotel profits. However, this imbalance is more than offset by tour arrivals at times of low occupancy. From a hotel's perspective, therefore, the tour operator, tour director, and clients should be in the foreground, not the background, of attention and service.

Researching a Hotel in Advance

A tour company's staff can't possibly visit all the lodging choices available. To narrow the options, the tour planner consults several industry reference books. Most of these research tools publish the hotel's official rates (**rack rates**), location, facilities descriptions, address, phone and fax numbers, and the name of the hotel manager. Some feature photographs of the property, **locator maps** (which show where the property is located and what is nearby), and rating evaluations.

Below are listed the most commonly used reference industry sources.

The Star Service. The most opinionated of all lodging research sources, this book gives detailed analyses and ratings of thousands of hotels worldwide (no photos, maps, or ads).

The Hotel & Travel Index. This reference work doesn't rate hotels, but it does cover a multitude of hotels (especially in North America). It gives all the basics on each and features both maps and ads with photos (often in color).

The Official Hotel Guide. A multi-volumed work, the *Official Hotel Guide* has a worldwide perspective. It has ads, maps, photos, and ratings—all presented in an easy-to-read graphics style.

The OAG Business Travel Planner. This reference tool, updated quarterly, covers over 29,000 North

American hotels. It also includes amenities, prices, ratings, destination information, maps, airport diagrams, climate charts, ground transportation, and an events calendar.

Computer Programs. Electronic versions of the above guides are growing in popularity as reference tools.

The Internet. The Internet is a powerful tool for researching hotels. Virtually every major hotel chain has a Web site where you can look up its individual properties. Remember, though, that these sites are promotional and sales-oriented: the information and photos are biased to make each hotel look as splendid as possible. Several "objective" lodging information sites also exist; these portray all hotels, not just those of one brand. Hotel information is also sometimes available through tour operator and travel agency sites.

Note that many consumer books—like those in the *Fodor, Frommer,* and *Fielding* series—also provide extensive and usually reliable reviews of hotels.

Having narrowed the lodging choices, a tour planner will visit the properties that seem most interesting. The tour planner may also be so confident in the above research tools that he or she will simply contact the hotel and try to work out a deal, sight unseen. If the company is thinking about changing hotels on an existing tour, the tour manager may instead conduct the inspection and perhaps negotiate as well.

The Ideal Tour Hotel

It would be wonderful if every hotel used by a tour operator were an ideal one, assuming that such a property existed. In reality, each overnight stop is a compromise. It's often a tour conductor's job to play up the hotel's strengths and discover ways to offset or minimize its weaknesses. Even if the ideal hotel did exist, the perception of its strengths could easily shift according to the nature of the group. A great resort hotel such as the Acapulco Princess impresses young groups with its pool waterfalls, indoor tennis courts, and broad beaches. But would all these amenities contribute to an older adults group's enjoyment of Acapulco? Such tour members might instead complain about the hotel's isolated location (a factor that's often seen as an asset by others). If these clients were on a budget tour, would they admire the remarkable value they were getting by staying at one of the world's great resort hotels, or

would the relatively high cost of its restaurants, room service, and laundry inconvenience them?

Tour planners must seriously analyze lodging choices when planning a tour. So, too, must tour managers, for three reasons:

▼ Tour operators often ask tour conductors to evaluate hotels for them. It's far cheaper and more direct than sending someone from the office (see Figure 5–1).

▼ Upon arrival, a tour leader must identify (or, ideally, find out through a pre-tour company briefing) those factors that may make his or her clients' stay pleasant or difficult. To be forewarned, at least when it comes to hotels, is to be forearmed.

▼ Some tour companies will ask a trusted tour manager to evaluate competing properties and even negotiate with them, with an eye to improving overnights for the next tour season.

Characteristics of a Successful Tour Hotel

If you've been assigned to evaluate a hotel, what should you look for? Below are a few guidelines.

The Ideal Tour Hotel Is Well Managed and Well Staffed. Mark Twain once said, "All saints can do miracles, but few of them can keep a hotel." Innkeeping, as the Holiday Inn chain quaintly calls hotel management, is a difficult and demanding profession. As a tour director, you'll interact with all levels of management and staff: front-desk clerks, bellhops, restaurant personnel, maitre d's, concierges, and doormen. An efficient bell captain and helpful front-desk manager, as you'll soon discover, are critical to a tour's success.

You'll also quickly discover that behind the controlled, stolid surface of a hotel sometimes lurks inefficiency, understaffing, or indifference. Communication lines occasionally break down between the sales office and the **front desk** (the hotel check-in area), between housekeeping and the front-desk manager, or between accounting and the cashier. The ideal hotel ensures efficient communication among its various departments, staffs each department fully, pays close attention to the security of its guests, and hires personnel who are genuinely concerned about the welfare of the guests. After only a few stays at a property, a perceptive tour director will sense how well a hotel fulfills these criteria and

HOTEL INSPECTION FORM

NAME OF HOTEL: _____ NUMBER OF ROOMS: _____
NAME/TITLE OF PERSON SHOWING THE HOTEL: _____
DATE: _____ TIME: _____
Please place an X under the category that best describes this particular hotel:

	Excellent	Good	Average	Fair	Poor	Comment
a. First impression of hotel	___	___	___	___	___	___
b. Accessibility of front entrance to motorcoaches	___	___	___	___	___	___
c. Lobby appearance and size	___	___	___	___	___	___
d. Number of elevators	___	___	___	___	___	___
e. Number of available bellhops	___	___	___	___	___	___
f. Number of staff at front desk	___	___	___	___	___	___
g. Appearance and diversity of dining areas	___	___	___	___	___	___
h. Appearance and diversity of entertainment and bar areas	___	___	___	___	___	___
i. Closeness to restaurants, shops, etc.	___	___	___	___	___	___
j. Closeness to public transportation or availability of hotel shuttle bus	___	___	___	___	___	___
k. Appearance/apparent safety of neighborhood	___	___	___	___	___	___
l. Size of guestrooms	___	___	___	___	___	___
m. Appearance of guestrooms	___	___	___	___	___	___
n. Appearance and supplies in bathroom	___	___	___	___	___	___
o. View from hotel room shown	___	___	___	___	___	___
p. Enthusiasm of person showing hotel	___	___	___	___	___	___
q. *Overall rating of hotel*	___	___	___	___	___	___

Use reverse side for additional comments.

Figure 5–1   **Sample hotel evaluation sheet**

in what manner its strengths and weaknesses should be played.

The Ideal Tour Hotel Values Group Business.
Hotel management that directs its sales staff to court tour business should also communicate the importance of that business throughout all its departments. If the front desk hasn't prepared your clients' keys for arrival, if your passengers tend to get rooms with poor views or locations, or especially if *you* get an inferior room, you can conclude that somewhere along the chain of command a decision has been made, consciously or not, to treat group business as secondhand business. This situation must be dealt with immediately. You or your company must communicate your displeasure to the front-desk manager, sales manager, or perhaps the general manager. Prompt action should result.

Don't assume when scouting new hotels that they'll automatically want your business. Even if you could meet its price, the Ritz in Paris is not likely to want buses pulling up to its front door. Conversely, there are hotels that seem to support themselves entirely through group business. Though they'll be quite accustomed to dealing with your needs, their overall quality level will probably be lower than average. The ideal tour hotel mixes group business with regular business and applies equally high standards to both. It reminds staffers that group check-in will be relatively simple, that problems will be funneled through tour managers, and that there's little chance that tour members will hold wild,

The front desk is a focus point in tour/hotel communications
Courtesy of Marriott International

guest-disturbing parties all night long. It may even build a separate check-in entrance for tour groups, as several hotels in Las Vegas have done.

The Ideal Tour Hotel Is Strategically Located.

People on tours tend to be less adventuresome in their free time than those who travel independently. To tell them that they're two miles from the nearest shopping, restaurant, or tourist centers but right next to a convenient subway station will do no good at all. Many will end up shopping only in the hotel's souvenir shop, dining in its coffee shop, and sitting idly in the lobby—all the while cursing their predicament.

The Tokyo Hilton discovered this not too long ago. Located a fairly short walk from the Shinjuku shopping area, it found out that its guests (many of them tour members) didn't wish to brave the exotically named streets that led there. For this reason, the hotel set up a regular shuttle bus service to and from Shinjuku.

Ideally, your group will be lodged in a safe, strategic location. You should carefully stress to the group how easy it is to get around, identify nearby places they may wish to visit, and discuss whether it's safe to walk around at night. If your hotel isn't well situated, it may be necessary to use your motorcoach to take them almost everywhere or to organize group expeditions on the hotel shuttle bus or on public transportation. Be aware, however, that such makeshift alternatives can become logistical nightmares with a large group. Guides in Russia regularly take visitors down into

Moscow's splendid subways and because of the crowds, regularly lose them there.

In some cases, tour planners have no choice. A destination may have no strategically located hotels. This is often true of overnight, isolated motorcoach stops between distant destinations, where lodging next to highway exits may be the best you can do. It can also apply to large cities. Los Angeles is a case in point. Once described as seventy suburbs in search of a city, Los Angeles was designed around freeways, not pedestrians. It's somewhat difficult to find a hotel within walking distance of shopping centers, restaurants, and attractions. Tour operators, therefore, tend to situate their groups in lodgings that are close to the freeway. A tour leader may have difficulty explaining this subtlety to hotel-bound clients and will almost certainly have to sugarcoat the situation in some way.

In two other situations, centrally located hotels aren't necessary to a tour: when staying at airport hotels (especially if the group arrives on a late flight and will be moving on the next day); and at resort properties, which are designed to be "away from it all" and usually offer all the amenities the client wants.

The Ideal Tour Hotel Is Relatively New or Extremely Well Maintained.

New hotels are a favorite with tour operators. They often represent extraordinary value. Still relatively unknown to the public, such hotels are usually quite willing to bargain with tour companies. Furthermore, everything is

The ideal tour hotel is well situated. *Courtesy of Marriott International*

sparkling new: the paint is fresh, the beds firm, the staff unjaded, the rooms spacious and of equal size. (There's nothing worse than having some tour members get large rooms and others get tiny ones, as often happens in older hotels. Those clients with the roomy accommodations are sure to invite the others over to envy their good fortune.)

Tour managers soon learn, however, that there's a downside to recently opened properties. Inexperienced staff, untested routines, and architectural surprises can blunt a hotel's mint-condition charm. A tour director should tactfully forewarn his or her group members that they may have to put up with some minor inconveniences in order to stay at what will surely become a popular vacation favorite.

On the other hand, tour conductors may find that well-maintained older hotels please their clients the most. A 1,400-room giant like Toronto's Royal York Hotel, which courts group business, has managed to remain competitive against dozens of gleaming new challengers. Its twelve fine restaurants and lounges, a uniquely dramatic lobby, an unbeatable location, and meticulous upkeep make it an enjoyable place to stay. (Most hotels are fully renovated every five to seven years; resort hotels need renovation every three to five years.) The Royal York's one drawback, common to many older North American properties and most European ones, is its small rooms, many with single beds. (Newer hotels almost always have rooms spa-

cious enough to accommodate two double beds.) Hotels like the Royal York also cater to convention groups, which can lead to some noisy nights.

However, the quality of a hotel can slide downhill in a matter of months. Tour leaders should be vigilant and report any such trend to their company when it becomes obvious.

The Ideal Tour Hotel Has Great Ambience and Interesting Views.
Some hotels are like boxes stacked next to other boxes. The rooms may be pretty, but what kind of feeling do they evoke?

A good tour hotel often has a pleasing, unique "personality." Maybe it's cultured in an Old World sort of way, like New York City's Tudor Hotel. Perhaps it's playful, like many of Disney's Orlando properties. Or it may seem straight out of the future, like Los Angeles's Bonaventure Hotel.

Another plus is a room with a view. Which would you prefer, a room that opens onto Waikiki Beach or one that looks out on a parking lot? This is why tour operators are willing to pay a little extra to ensure that clients get a hotel's "view" rooms or why they seek out properties where all the rooms face something lovely.

The Ideal Tour Hotel Is of at Least Medium Size.
It would be wonderful if tour managers could bring groups to that thirty-room Victorian bed-and-breakfast in San Francisco or reconverted castle in Limerick—such ambience! As picturesque as they may be, though,

such lodgings pose distinct problems for tour operators. What if a few regular guests stay over and there are not enough rooms for the group? Can the dining facilities handle forty or fifty people at once? Can the motorcoach access the facility easily? In truth, small hotels, motels, and inns rarely consider groups. From their point of view, one canceled tour (for which rooms have been set aside for months) could spell economic disaster.

Generally, hotels and motels with about 300 rooms or more welcome tours. (Surprisingly, less than 6 percent of all United States hotels have over 300 rooms, and a similar pattern prevails worldwide.) The choice, then, can be limited, especially at less-populated destinations. Yet staying at a large hotel has many advantages for tour groups. It's likely that the hotel will feature restaurants at several different price levels, that a client dissatisfied with a room will be able to get a better one, that there will be enough clerks at the front desk to attend to the tour manager's needs, that several bellhops will be available when the motorcoach arrives to take luggage promptly up to the rooms, and that there will be in-house entertainment lounges. Larger hotels also tend to have spacious lobbies, a real advantage when your group gathers for a departure.

Negotiating with Hotels

Negotiating with a hotel is a little like playing cards. You want to know as much as you can about the sales manager's hand, but you don't want to reveal *your* cards until you are well into the game. To do this, consider the following tactics:

▼ **Do plenty of advance research.** Find out before your meeting at your preferred hotel what the rack rate is, if there is an "official" **tour** or **group rate** (a discounted rate offered to tours), when the "slow slots" occur, either weekly or yearly, and what the usual deposit requirements are, etc. Sometimes it's as easy as asking. Just call in advance when you make your preliminary inquiry. You might also try to find out from your research sources if the property has certain weaknesses, such as a mediocre location, considerable competition (some areas are overbuilt) or, in the case of newer hotels, unfamiliarity.

▼ **Begin negotiations as far in advance as possible.** Most hotels have a "group ceiling," a maximum number of rooms that can be allocated to

groups. To get best rates and availability, you may have to negotiate as much as a year in advance. Hotels usually will grant bigger concessions six months or more out, since it reduces unpredictability. It also helps the tour operator, since rooms at the preferred hotel may not be available later. Be prepared, though, to have a deposit payable sixty days before departure.

▼ **Negotiate in person.** It's much too easy for a sales manager to say no on the phone.

▼ **Make a list of everything you really want** and a separate list of what you could live without. These lists will become your game plan as the negotiation unfolds. They'll ensure that you don't leave out anything.

▼ **Always have a backup hotel in case you can't get what you want from your preferred one.** Indeed, having several choices to negotiate with is wise. Alternatives make you feel more confident as you negotiate. It's even acceptable to mention what a competing (but second-choice) property has offered you. Be careful, though. The person you're negotiating with knows what the competition is likely to offer, so don't try to bluff.

▼ **Ask more questions than you answer.** By taking control of the conversation with your questions, you'll find out more about the sales manager's "cards" sooner than he or she will find out about yours.

▼ **Assume almost everything is negotiable.** Sales managers often counter your requests by saying that certain things are non-negotiable because of hotel "policy." All this means is that this particular item, which is often merely a hotel *guideline*, may be more difficult for him or her to negotiate. *Be firm or strick*

▼ **Be assertive, not aggressive.** An assertive person makes his or her needs known clearly, emphatically, but diplomatically; the negotiation becomes a cooperative activity where both sides are working toward a common goal. An aggressive person views a negotiation as a battle and the opponent as an enemy to be defeated. Such an approach creates ill-will and rarely brings positive results.

▼ **Personalize your requirements.** As you negotiate, say, "Here's what we need," or "Can you

Hotel brands come at virtually every quality and price level imaginable. Here's a quick review of the primary North American hotel chains:

Luxury	High End	Mid-Range	Budget
Four Seasons	Crowne Plaza	Clarion	Baymont
Peninsula	Fairmont	Crown Sterling Suites	Best Western
Regent	Hilton International	Doubletree	Comfort Inns
Ritz-Carlton	Hyatt Regency	Embassy Suites	Days Inn
	Inter-Continental	Hilton	Econo Lodge
	Marriott	Holiday Inn	Hampton Inns
	Meridien	Hyatt	Howard Johnson
	Omni	Radisson	La Quinta
	Renaissance	Ramada	Quality Inn
	Sheraton Resorts	Sheraton	Red Roof
	Sofitel		Rodeway Inn
	Westin		Travelodge

help me with this?" This draws the sales manager away from being the extension of an impersonal hotel and toward a team-like cooperation.

▼ **Reveal your principal need, for a discounted room rate, first.** What kind of tour discount can you expect? Fifty percent off rack rate is common, especially for mid-priced chains like Sheraton or Hilton. Top-rated luxury hotels, like those of Ritz-Carlton, rarely give better than 10 to 20 percent, since they rarely court tour business. Budget properties like Days Inn or Hampton Inn also rarely give better than 20 percent, since their rates are so low in the first place. Here, too, is the time to ascertain room taxes and if the rate is **commissionable** (usually 10 percent back after the trip) or **net** (no commission).

▼ **Try to have the hotel representative quote you a rate first,** rather than ask you what rate you're seeking. There's an old saying in hotel negotiations: Whoever gives a price first loses.

▼ **Never assume that the first rate quoted is the best rate.** Sales managers will often quote you a rate that's 10 to 20 percent higher than what their real final offer would be, just to see what will happen.

▼ **Next, play your other cards.** Now is the time to offer other things that will motivate the hotel to bargain further: taking meals in the hotel, holding special catered functions (e.g., a welcome party), guaranteeing a very large number of tours, or perhaps accepting less desirable rooms. (Expect the sales manager to try to find this out *before* quoting a rate.) The sales manager will also favor requests for dates when the hotel is less full, such as weekends (for airport hotel properties, but not for resorts) or seasonal slumps. As another saying in the lodging industry goes: "Put them in the valleys, not on the mountains."

▼ **As negotiations draw to a close, ask for a few small concessions.** Here's when you should ask for a complimentary room for the tour leader and for the driver, if there is one. If meals are included, these too should be provided free of charge to the tour leader and driver.

▼ **Request a written confirmation of the agreed-upon conditions and prices.** Be sure that the letter, when received, spells out exactly what was agreed upon. Also check to see when the hotel expects to receive a rooming list (usually seven to thirty days out). Any minor adjustments to the rooming list can be phoned or faxed in by the tour company within a few days of arrival. Such last-minute changes, however, sometimes never make it from the sales office to the front desk. The tour conductor, therefore, should carefully review the list upon arrival at the hotel.

The Algonquin Hotel in New Brunswick, Canada, has clearly defined high, low, and shoulder seasons. *Courtesy of the National Tour Association*

Preparing for the Hotel

Group voyagers arrive at a hotel with a peculiar mix of anticipation and exhaustion. They've probably traveled for some time by plane, motorcoach, train, or ship. Gritty and cranky, they can't wait to freshen up, unpack, or take a nap. At the same time, they want to get out and see the sights. A tour conductor must be sensitive to these conflicting needs, as well as to his or her own condition, for one of the most potentially taxing parts of the tour-managing job is about to begin.

As a tour manager, you would do well to prepare your passengers in advance for the arrival. You should first look over your notes to see whether any clients have made special requests, such as a room on a lower floor, adjoining rooms, non-smoking rooms, or a queen-size bed. (Unless told otherwise, hotels almost always try to assign two-bedded rooms to tour guests.) Before getting on the transfer bus at the airport or station (or at an earlier rest stop on a motorcoach tour), call ahead to the hotel's front-desk staff and alert them to the probable arrival time. Very often this call will serve to nudge a busy or procrastinating staff.

On the motorcoach, you should brief tour members on the hotel's location and amenities. Suggest that they pick up a hotel-embossed matchbook in case they get lost and can't remember the hotel's name and address. This is especially critical in foreign countries. Remind them to write their room number on that matchbook:

card keys don't list the room number. With the multiple hotel stays of a tour, it's easy to forget one's room number. Briefly review with them the itinerary for the remainder of the day and, if appropriate, for the following morning. Be clear and precise, and repeat vital information several times.

Also discuss hotel tipping practices with the group. Usually a tour company pays baggage charges—the client doesn't have to tip the bellhop when he or she arrives with the luggage. Some countries officially forbid tipping, but clients should be warned that a small gift of cigarettes, candy, or gum to the bellhop, floor concierge, and housekeepers is expected.

Indeed, culture-specific information must always be underscored. Your clients need to know that German corridor lights may be on timer switches, that Tahitian hotel rooms sometimes have no locks, what French bidets are used for (this could be a tricky one), that in-the-room tea service is often standard upon arrival in Hong Kong, and that in some foreign hotels, you're supposed to check your room key with the front desk or concierge whenever you leave. (Most larger hotels have replaced real keys with card keys, which you don't drop off.) This would also be a good time to discuss whether the hotel has an in-room pay movie system (and how it works); where to buy stamps; whether money exchange rates are most favorable at the hotel, bank, or exchange bureau; and that phone calls made from their hotel room and charged to the room bill are far more expensive than those made via a charge or calling card from the room or from a lobby phone booth.

You might also put your group at ease about some of their anxieties. Is the area around the hotel safe? Does the hotel have good fire procedures? (These subjects should be mentioned with great tact so you won't aggravate clients' fears.) You should certainly emphasize the need to lock rooms and to place valuables in the hotel safe or in-room safe, if one is available. If you know the hotel will have in-room mini-bars or refrigerators, do warn clients that anything consumed will be billed to them and probably at a high price. If you're not sure about any of these considerations before you get to the hotel, ask when you arrive and tell the group then.

Arriving at the Hotel

The arrival itself presents a dilemma. Should passengers remain on the motorcoach while the tour leader obtains the keys, or should they disembark, gather in the lobby, and receive their room assignments there? There's no perfect answer. Each choice has certain advantages and drawbacks. If the group stays on the motorcoach, the tour manager can work out potential problems with the front desk calmly and without distractions. You won't need to herd the group together in the lobby to call out names and pass out keys—an undignified practice often associated with everything that's wrong with touring. The controlled environment of the motorcoach is certainly a more suitable place to announce room assignments.

The disadvantages, though, are several. The motorcoach may be monopolizing important parking space, its engine spewing exhaust in order to keep the passengers air-conditioned. Clients may become anxious watching their luggage being unloaded, no matter what precautions are taken. Most of all, they'll be immensely restless and want to *move*.

The alternative, to disembark immediately upon arrival, must be handled just right. The tour manager gets off first (presumably the driver will assist exiting passengers) and leads the clients directly into the hotel lobby. He or she must then gather them together in one area before going alone to the front desk. That area must be well away from the front desk so passengers won't be able to look over the tour conductor's shoulder. Then the tour manager must carefully review the

hotel copy of the rooming list and correct all oversights. Have all special requests been honored (for example, for adjoining rooms)? Were any last-minute changes made to the rooming list that weren't reflected on the hotel's copy? Has the hotel prepared a photocopy of the rooming list for the tour manager? (The front desk usually does this as a matter of course and distributes additional copies to all its divisions.)

The tour director is now ready to distribute the keys or room access cards, which hotel staff usually place in envelopes marked with the clients' names. If it's a card key, explain to the group how it functions. Make sure to hand the keys out randomly, so the persons listed on the top of the rooming list don't get called first at each hotel. Before handing out the keys, you should point out the locations of in-house restaurants, elevators, and the tour bulletin board, if any. Then explain that you'll be in the lobby for a half hour in case problems arise. You may also choose to announce your own room number. (As indicated in Chapter 4, there is great controversy about this last point.)

Collect passports if the hotel and host country require it. Hand out any mail that may be waiting for passengers. In the meantime, the bellhops will already be offloading and checking off luggage. Their fee (usually about $2 per bag) will automatically be billed to your account.

A clever way around the on-coach off-coach dilemma is possible if you arrive at your destination in the late afternoon or early evening. If practical, you and the driver can take the group to dinner before going to the hotel. After ordering your meals, you and the driver leave the group, drop off luggage at the hotel, pick up keys, sort out problems, then return to the restaurant. Have your own dinner, then circulate among your clients and distribute their keys. When you return to the hotel, all luggage will have been delivered, tour members won't have to wait, and most problems will have been solved already by the hotel staff. You'll have to explain the advantages of this procedure to the group, though, for they'll be anxious to get to their night's lodging.

Morning arrivals at a distant destination, often after a long overnight flight, present an even greater problem. In such a situation you must drop off luggage and take the group sightseeing, shopping, or whatever, since the hotel, unless it's in the midst of a low-occupancy period, will not have the rooms ready. This situation, while unavoidable, is certainly vexing. The tour members will be in no mood to buzz around sightseeing after hours of traveling. You'll have to tactfully explain to your group why this inconvenience is necessary.

Potential Arrival Problems

The thirty minutes of "lobby duty" that follow hotel check-in are critical. You should be ready for anything. When possible you should solve problems by delegating to front-desk and bell personnel, so you can remain in the lobby area. Other clients may come down looking for you. What are the most common problems?

An Occupied Room. "My room is occupied." This happens more often than you would think. A guest may note a 1 P.M. check-out time, settle his account through video check-out or at the cashier, indicate that he is leaving, and then stay in his room. The hotel believes the room is unoccupied. Presumably housekeeping will find out, but sometimes the cross-check system doesn't work. Your tour member walks in on the guest, walks out very quickly, and comes to you. Ask the front desk to assign a new room to your client.

An Inoperative Television. "My television doesn't work." TVs have become our home companions. When the hotel television doesn't work, it's distressing. If the set is broken, the hotel will fix it or bring up another one. More often the maid has accidently pulled the TV plug from the outlet while vacuuming. It

often happens. Have the client check and phone down to you if that is not the problem.

Too Few Beds in the Room. "There are three of us in the room but only two beds." In some parts of the world, a "triple" will be assigned a room with three single beds. In North America they'll be given one with two double beds (called a **double double**). Almost no hotels in the United States or Canada have rooms with three beds. (Sometimes the third bed is a convertible sofa.) The tour manager must phone housekeeping and have a rollaway bed delivered or the sofa opened up.

No Towels. "There are no towels in the bathroom." Laundry service often lags behind the rest of the hotel's operations. Stolen towels strain the system even further. All you can do is make a list of the rooms involved, phone housekeeping, and assure tour members that the towels are on their way. This problem is more likely to occur if you arrive early. Many itinerary planners think that a tour ideally should arrive between 4 and 7 P.M. During this time period, all hotel services have finished their work, but a strain has not yet been put on the number of hotel rooms available. You and the hotel will have flexibility in the event of an emergency.

Unsatisfactory Room. "I don't like my room." A few clients are unreasonable, but there *are* valid and typical complaints. They generally result from the front desk's passing off an "ah-ha" room to a client. (Arthur Hailey,

A standard "double double" hotel room. *Courtesy of the National Tour Association*

in his novel *Hotel*, calls an "ah-ha" room any room that elicits an "ah-ha..." when you walk in and look around.) There are distinct subcategories of "ah-ha" rooms: ones that the architect shoved into a weird angle of the building; ones near a noisy ice machine or laundry chute; ones that have poor views (if the brochure promised "a panoramic view of Waikiki's surf" and the client has a panoramic view of a parking structure, you're in trouble); and ones that are in fact suite sitting-rooms, with only a convertible sofa for a bed.

Whichever of these problems confronts you, be firm with the front desk. If they can assign a new room, they should. If they absolutely can't, you'll have to exercise all the diplomacy you can muster to persuade the client to accept the "ah-ha" room. You might offer to ask the front desk at your next hotel stop to assign a special room to your unhappy customer. (In a pinch, you might have to sacrifice your own room for the client.) Remember that older hotels and foreign hotels tend not to have full-sized double-double rooms; their rooms are relatively small by current U.S. standards.

Undelivered Luggage. "My luggage wasn't delivered to the room." No complaint strikes greater fear in the heart of a tour conductor than this one. If you've carefully followed the luggage-tracking procedures outlined in Chapter 3, you should be relatively certain that the baggage was offloaded from the motorcoach into the hotel. You might check with the bell captain. He or she often keeps a list of the number of pieces delivered to each room. It may be necessary to back-track to the airport, the airline, or even the tour departure point.

In all probability, however, the luggage was delivered to the wrong room in the hotel. Hopefully, the persons occupying that room will report the presence of this unexplained luggage when they return. But what if the room is unoccupied? The bellhops may have to institute a comprehensive hotel search. If the building is large, the task could be formidable.

There's a shortcut, however, that many veteran tour managers use. In almost all cases the mistake occurs because the bellhop who writes the room numbers on the luggage tag transposes numbers. Thus, you should first look at rooms with numbers that resemble the intended room number. If the actual room number is 2332, try 2323, 3232, and 3223. Also, check to see what the client's room number was at the last hotel visited. The bellhop may have failed to cross that figure out. If the bellhop left luggage in the corridor in front of the room's door, do a corridor search to see if stray luggage remains. In the meantime, you must remain confident and composed, if only to reassure a client depressed by the thought of wearing the same clothes for days.

Wrong Kind of Room. "We were supposed to have connecting rooms." Couples or families traveling together often wish to have rooms next to each other. When two rooms are next to each other, they're called **adjoining rooms**. When a door connects them, they are called **connecting rooms**.

An anxious client makes sure that her luggage is on the coach.
Courtesy of the National Tour Association

Unfortunately, for logistical reasons, hotels can't always arrange for connecting rooms. They can, however, ensure that the rooms are relatively close to each other. If they've forgotten to do so, ask them to reassign the rooms.

At least half the time, absolutely no complaints or problems at all will filter down during your lobby duty. In that case, use your thirty minutes in the lobby to catch up on all the little things that need to be done. Set up the next day's wake-up call, through either the front desk or the hotel operator. (As a precaution, you should bring your own travel alarm clock in case the hotel operator forgets to call you.) Remind the bell captain of your luggage pickup and departure times. Contact each attraction you'll be visiting and each restaurant where you'll be eating to remind them of the time your group will arrive. If a welcome or farewell reception is planned, check the arrangements. Post a daily itinerary, with precise times, on the tour bulletin board. Reconfirm your group's departure flight. If there's time and they're not too busy, chat with the front-desk and bell staff. They're important allies who will appreciate a friendly, sociable tour manager.

The Hotel Stay

Once lobby duty is over, a tour director's dealings with the hotel are minimal until checkout. You yourself will certainly want to freshen up. If you and your company are on good terms with the hotel, you might even find yourself assigned to a suite (which may serve double duty as the host area for any planned group receptions).

After relaxing, reconfirm everything that you didn't have time for during lobby duty. Make sure throughout the stay to arrive a little early in the lobby, outside for departures, or at in-house restaurants. The example you set will be important to the group. If you have to leave the hotel for an extended amount of time and leave your clients on their own, let the front desk know where you will be. While on the road, a tour director may have time off but is never really free from responsibility.

Hotel Checkout

Checking out is perhaps more frantic than checking in, since a departure deadline is involved. Meticulous time management is a must.

The day before departure, the tour conductor should carefully go over departure-morning procedures

with tour members. Review with them what time the group wake-up call will take place (do not trust clients to use in-room alarm clocks); at what hour luggage must be ready for pickup; how breakfast will be handled; where and when the motorcoach will pick them up; and what documents (such as passports) will be needed. Also remind them to pay all incidentals that night; in the morning the cashier will be too frantic to take care of such things efficiently. (**Incidentals** are the small extra charges, such as those for telephone calls and movies, that are added to a client's bill.)

That evening before retiring, the tour manager should reconfirm everything necessary with the bell staff, front desk, and hotel operator. At this time, it might be wise to remember that hotel personnel generally work, with some overlap, on a 7-A.M.-to-3 P.M., 3 P.M.-to-11 P.M., 11 P.M.-to-7 A.M. schedule. It's best to discuss the next morning's details with those individuals who will handle your departure. Set up a separate, earlier wake-up call for yourself and finish packing.

The next morning, have breakfast a few minutes before the group, if possible. During breakfast, check out the dining area. Are any clients noticeably absent? You may have to call their rooms. Then you must go to the lobby to carry out several critical tasks.

Examine the Group's Financial Record

Examination of the group's financial record is essential. Hotels use two systems to track tour expenditures. The first puts all expenses on one bill. The second has one **folio** for group charges (room, tax, and group functions) and another for incidentals incurred by individuals on the tour, including the escort. In either case, the tour conductor must review the charges carefully. Uncontested billings will travel on to the home office, where they'll become a nightmare to unravel.

Was the tour billed for the proper number of rooms? Sometimes accounting uses the original rooming list as a working document; last-minute additions or deletions are not reflected in the room count. If part of the company-hotel deal was to have free rooms for the tour manager and the driver, was this arrangement honored by accounting, or did they mistakenly bill the company for those rooms? Your copy of company-hotel correspondence should indicate all agreements. Are all dining charges accurate? Again, food and beverage services may have been working from an obsolete rooming list; if dining prices were fixed, there could be an error. Have all incidentals been paid? If not, talk to the clients in question as soon as possible. Are there some peculiar incidentals outstanding? Erroneous phone, bar, and movie charges are common.

Any billing questions should be discussed with the front-desk manager, who is usually quite amenable to clearing up the matter quickly. If not, alert the home office; you can't stand around arguing when your motorcoach is leaving. Do set aside about a half-hour for the cashier checkout procedure. Some tour companies prefer that the tour manager not examine the master billing, since they want the hotel-tour operator agreement to remain confidential. In this case, incidental billings are all the tour conductor sees.

Luggage Pickup

Luggage pickup should be scheduled for about forty-five minutes to an hour before departure. Two bellhops will usually handle the job. They can deal with the baggage of a single group in about twenty to thirty minutes. The bell captain or concierge will oversee the job. The bell captain may even handle the pickup: a group departure is generally a quick, lucrative enterprise for bellhops.

Bellhops almost always insist that tour guests place their luggage in the corridor outside their room doors. It's more efficient for the bell staff (no need to use passkeys) and also protects bellhops against accusations that they've stolen things from unoccupied rooms. On the other hand, tour managers and group members may feel uneasy about this procedure. A thief could simply walk down a hotel corridor at 7 A.M., grab unattended luggage, and walk right out the front door with it. A real danger exists here, and it's usually completely impractical for a tour director, busy with so many other departure activities, to watch over several corridors. A tour manager should try to talk bell captains into an in-room, luggage-by-the-door system. They may reluctantly agree, though pushing too hard could be counterproductive. One minor consolation: the incidence of thieves carrying off group luggage from hotel corridors is quite low.

As soon as the bell staff has delivered the luggage to the motorcoach, the bell captain informs the tour direc-

tor of the number of pieces picked up. He or she will generally assume that if the count matches that of the first day, if forty-five pieces came in and forty-five are going out, then all is well. Yet, an efficient tour manager knows this is not enough. As outlined in Chapter 3, you must cross-check names, rooms, and baggage. One person may have added a piece and another forgotten to put his or her own out, rendering the total count meaningless. Once you're sure that all baggage is accounted for, the individual pieces can be loaded onto the coach.

On the Motorcoach

About fifteen minutes before departure, you may open the motorcoach for passenger seating. About five minutes before leaving, check to see if anyone is missing. If so, look around in the lobby or coffee shop. If the clients aren't there, call their room immediately. If there's no answer, don't panic; they're probably on their way down.

When everyone arrives, do a last-minute check over the microphone. Have your clients dropped off their hotel keys? Has anything been forgotten in the hotel safe or security boxes? If needed, do they have their passports with them? Assure them that their luggage has been carefully checked onto the motorcoach. You can be pleased that one more chapter of your tour conductor career has been handled gracefully and well. (Figure 5–2 is a checklist of items to remember at each stage of your hotel stay.)

Summary

Lodging is a critical component of any tour. The ideal tour hotel is well managed and staffed, values group business, is strategically located, is new or well maintained, has interesting features, and is sizable. When negotiating with the hotel, several tactics may be used to create the best possible deal. Tour directors must carefully plot out their responsibilities at each stage of the hotel experience: pre-arrival, arrival, the stay itself, and departure.

ESCORT'S HOTEL REMINDER LIST

Before arriving, have you:
- ☐ Checked to see whether any clients made special lodging requests?
- ☐ Called to tell the hotel that you're on the way and ask necessary questions?
- ☐ Briefed tour members on the hotel?
- ☐ Discussed tipping at the hotel?
- ☐ Discussed where to exchange money and buy stamps?
- ☐ Explained that calls made from a hotel room are expensive?
- ☐ Warned clients to place valuables in a safe?
- ☐ Discussed in-room mini-bars and pay-per-view TV?
- ☐ Mentioned any miscellaneous cultural details?
- ☐ Sketched out immediate schedule plans?

Upon arrival, have you:
- ☐ Checked the room list for the accuracy of clients' names and special requests?
- ☐ Pointed out the hotel bulletin board?
- ☐ Explained that you'll be in the lobby for a half hour?
- ☐ Announced your room number?
- ☐ Set up tomorrow's wake-up call?
- ☐ Arranged your luggage pickup and departure times with the bell captain?
- ☐ Reconfirmed reservations at restaurants to be used in the next 24 hours?
- ☐ Cross-checked welcome or farewell reception reservations?
- ☐ Posted a daily itinerary on the bulletin board?
- ☐ Reconfirmed your group's departure flight?

Each day, have you:
- ☐ Set up tomorrow's wake-up call?
- ☐ Reconfirmed reservations at restaurants and attractions to be visited in the next 24 hours?
- ☐ Left word at the front desk as to where you'll be, in case of emergencies?

On the day before check-out, have you:
- ☐ Reminded clients to pay all incidentals before leaving?
- ☐ Told clients to carry their passports with them the next day?
- ☐ Reviewed departure times and procedures with your clients?
- ☐ Set up your own wake-up call and that of the group?
- ☐ Reconfirmed luggage pickup times with the bell captain?
- ☐ Reconfirmed breakfast arrangements at the hotel?

On the departure day, have you:
- ☐ Checked whether any clients are noticeably absent from breakfast?
- ☐ Examined carefully the group financial record?
- ☐ Cross-checked to make sure luggage is being picked up as arranged?
- ☐ Checked off luggage carefully?
- ☐ Opened the motorcoach for seating?
- ☐ Asked clients on the coach if they've handed in their keys?
- ☐ Asked clients whether they've forgotten any valuables in the hotel safe?
- ☐ Asked clients if they have their passports with them?

Figure 5–2   **Sample escort's hotel reminder list**

QUESTIONS FOR DISCUSSION

1. Why do tour members place such importance on their hotel? Why is a hotel important to the tour operator? Why is tour business important to a hotel?

2. Describe the six characteristics that mark a successful tour hotel.

3. Discuss at least ten steps to maximize negotiations with a hotel.

4. What tips should be given to a group just before arrival at a hotel?

5. What are three general ways to handle a group at hotel check-in?

6. Identify seven typical problems that may confront a tour manager during his or her arrival lobby duty. How can each be solved?

7. What cross-checks and short activities should be carried out during lobby duty or shortly afterwards?

8. What checkout items should be discussed with a group the day before departure? What checkout procedures should the tour conductor carry out the evening before leaving?

9. List four mistakes to watch for on a hotel group financial record.

10. Describe each step of luggage pickup and how pitfalls may be avoided.

11. What safeguards must be taken and reminders issued just before the group departs from the hotel?

■ ■ ■

ACTIVITY 1

▼ Study the following rooming list and then fill in the information requested below.

ACME TOURS: Eight-Day Florida Circle Tour (Series #1000)
ESCORT: Ed Norton
DRIVER: Ralph Kramden DATE IN: 3/5 DATE OUT: 3/9 # NTS: 4

Room No.	Tag No.	Name	Special Instructions
	1001	Mr. Ernest Rollo	VIP clients
	1002	Mrs. Anna Rollo	
	1003	German Ruiz	room close to 1005, 6
	1004	Leah Ruiz	
	1005	Mark Aston	room close to 1003, 4
	1006	Nancy Aston	
	1007	Nancy Herr	
	1008	Judi Salmond	
	1009	Mary Kaun	
	1010	Thomas Brazie	
	1011	Jeannie Brazie	
	1012	Ramon Iacovelli	request firm bed
	1013	Carol Iacovelli	
	1014	Thomas Girvin	
	1015	Trace Gelgood	
	1016	Monica McLaughlin	
	1017	Geri Harding	request low floor
	1018	Chris Harding	
	1019	Cathy Harding	
	1020	L. Minkoff	request smoking room
	1021	V. Minkoff	
	1022	Gerald St. Amand	room close to 1024, 5
	1023	Frances St. Amand	
	1024	Roland Masse	room close to 1022, 3
	1025	Mrs. Roland Masse	
	1026	Robyn Keith	
	1027	Mr. Gordon Hayford	
	1028	Mrs. Gordon Hayford	
	1029	Larry Olson	
	1030	Adrienne Olson	
	1031	Robert Perry	
	1032	Frank Serafine	
	1033	Sharon Sterling	
	1034	Robyn Sterling	

Room No.	Tag No.	Name	Special Instructions
	1035	Mr. Jeff Wootan	
	1036	Mrs. Michele Wootan	
	1037	Michael Kelly	
	1038	Jan Wetrick Kelly	

1. Number of singles: 2

2. Number of doubles: 15

3. Number of triples: 2

4. Rooms close together   4

5. Special requests: 4

ACTIVITY 2

▼ You are checking out from a hotel. Your group, which required twenty-one rooms (tour manager and driver were comp), stayed for four nights. Examine the bill below.

THE GRAND HOTEL
35 Picturesque Lane
East Overshoe, Florida

Date	Reference	Description	Amount
3/5	00912	Room serv—Keith	18.75
3/5	00678	Luggage handling	90.00
3/5	00715	Tel—Kaun	8.50
3/5	00850	Room bar—Girvin	.75
3/5	00264	Reception meal	978.00
3/5	00265	Reception A/V charges	165.00
3/5	00654	Tel—Hayford	14.85
3/5	00915	Rollaway cot—Harding	16.00
3/6	00913	Room serv—Ladner	10.50
3/6	00944	Tennis courts—Olson	20.00
3/6	00962	Group breakfast	684.00
3/7	00963	Group breakfast	684.00
3/7	00974	Health club—Bonomo	10.00
3/7	00971	Movie—Minkoff	8.00
3/8	01100	Group breakfast	684.00
3/8	00990	Tel—Wootan	2.00
3/8	01423	Group dinner	1,525.00
3/8	01260	Mini-bar—Masse	4.00
3/9	01120	Rooms 16 D; 3 S; 4 T x 5 nights + tax	17,250.00

TOTAL:

1. Circle the room charges (billing for singles, doubles, and triples) with a red pen. If they are correct, place a checkmark next to them. If not, correct the mistakes in red. (Consult the rooming list from Activity 1.)

2. Circle all group dining charges in green.

3. Circle the luggage charges in blue.

4. Draw a blue rectangle around all client incidentals.

5. Indicate any omissions or mistakes at the bottom. (Again, consult the Activity 1 rooming list.)

■ ■ ■

ACTIVITY 3

▼ Using the form below, evaluate a local hotel that would be appropriate for tours. You should do your evaluation, preferably, as part of a class "field trip" group. If this isn't feasible, you might be able to inspect public areas of a hotel on your own and address at least a few of the items below. Do *not* go into guestrooms on your own.

HOTEL INSPECTION FORM

NAME OF HOTEL:_____ NUMBER OF ROOMS:_____

NAME/TITLE OF PERSON SHOWING THE HOTEL: _____

DATE:_____ TIME: _____

Place an X under the category that best describes this particular hotel.

	Excellent	Good	Average	Fair	Poor	Comment
a. First impression of hotel	___	___	___	___	___	___
b. Accessibility of front entrance to motorcoaches	___	___	___	___	___	___
c. Lobby appearance and size	___	___	___	___	___	___
d. Number of elevators	___	___	___	___	___	___
e. Number of available bellhops	___	___	___	___	___	___
f. Number of staff at front desk	___	___	___	___	___	___
g. Appearance and diversity of dining areas	___	___	___	___	___	___
h. Appearance and diversity of entertainment and bar areas	___	___	___	___	___	___
i. Closeness to restaurants, shops, etc.	___	___	___	___	___	___
j. Closeness to public transportation or availability of hotel shuttle bus	___	___	___	___	___	___
k. Appearance/apparent safety of neighborhood	___	___	___	___	___	___
l. Size of guestrooms	___	___	___	___	___	___
m. Appearance of guestrooms	___	___	___	___	___	___
n. Appearance and supplies in bathroom	___	___	___	___	___	___
o. View from hotel room shown	___	___	___	___	___	___
p. Enthusiasm of person showing hotel	___	___	___	___	___	___
q. Overall rating of hotel	___	___	___	___	___	___

Additional comments:

■ ■ ■

PROFILE

The first thing that strikes people about Craig Loughrin, a sightseeing driver-guide for Scenic Tours of Auckland, is his encyclopedic knowledge. "Though New Zealand's countryside is incredibly beautiful," says Craig, "there doesn't seem to be all that much to say about it. That's why I make a point of having a story about just about every tree, bush, bird, cow, and town I drive by."

Like any fine tour guide, Craig enlivens his commentary with humorous or interesting anecdotes. "I like to say that New Zealand's population is 73 million: 3 million people and 70 million sheep."

An accounting major in college, Craig later spent ten years as a policeman in Hong Kong. "Law enforcement gave me many skills that have proved valuable to me as a courier-guide. Police work taught me how to deal with people, solve unusual problems, stay outwardly calm, and be infinitely patient. Furthermore, Hong Kong is a real crossroads of languages and cultures. Working there really sensitized me to the variety of ways of thinking that people can have."

Craig feels that three skills are essential to successful guiding. "First, you have to be orderly. Some driver-guides don't put a high premium on organization or paperwork. They're also among the first to resign from the industry. There's an old saying that especially applies to guiding: 'Fail to prepare, prepare to fail.'"

The second strategy that Craig recommends is to constantly seek out fresh, useful information. "Maybe this comes from my police detective work, but I find it really enjoyable to do research, to observe, to know things, and to then tell others what I've learned. I read everything I can get my hands on and am lucky enough to absorb information very easily. And what I don't know, I look up."

Finally, Craig places a high premium on people skills. "When you're a driver-guide, it's easy to spend too much time thinking about things like coaches or routes rather than about people. That's why I set little goals for myself: to know each passenger's name by lunch, to try to find out about their prior travels, their hobbies, things like that. That's why I like to conduct smaller groups in small motorcoaches. Twenty people are easier to get to know than forty or fifty."

"The bottom line," concludes Craig Loughrin, "is that as a driver-guide, you're your own boss. You're not at a desk. Nobody is looking over your shoulder, except, of course, the people you're there to please: your passengers."

6

Air Travel and Tours

Chapter Objectives

After reading this chapter, you should be able to:

▼ Explain how tour operators negotiate with airlines.

▼ Discuss what a tour manager must do before a group arrives at an airline terminal.

▼ Explain a tour member's preboarding activities.

▼ List a tour conductor's in-flight responsibilities.

▼ Describe the procedures that face a group and a tour director upon arrival at a destination.

"SO, DOES YOUR GROUP HAVE ANY SPECIAL SEATING REQUESTS?"

Air travel has vastly expanded the range and scope of touring. It permits tour groups to access virtually any corner of the globe within a day. It reduces the necessity of long bus rides; only a few decades ago it was common for travelers from, say, New England, to take a ten-day Florida tour in which six days were spent on the road getting to and from Florida, leaving only four for the destination itself. Air travel has also altered how tour planners and tour directors do their jobs.

Negotiating with Airlines

As you've seen, tour managers are sometimes asked to negotiate with hotels. This is not the case with airlines. Since contracts for air space are so complex and the sums of money involved so large, it's almost always the planning and/or operations department of a tour company that handles airline choice and negotiations.

Some airlines (also called **carriers**) are quite supportive of the tour operator-airline alliance. Others, unfortunately, seem to perceive group bookings as an annoyance. Airlines that have their own tour operations are reluctant to cooperate with tour companies who, in effect, are their competitors. Furthermore, the bureaucracy at many mega-carriers makes smooth, swift agreements a near impossibility: they may be supremely slow in quoting or confirming anything to the tour planner, yet they will then set strict deposit and final payment deadlines (typically thirty to sixty days in advance of the flight).

If you're a tour planner, you'll do well to remember the following:

▼ A few airlines (often those that are new or that are having financial problems) cooperate more enthusiastically with tour operators than others do. Their service level, however, may leave something to be desired.

▼ The rates airlines quote may be **noncommissionable** or net (no percentage of the ticket price will come back to you), or they may be **commissionable** (a percentage of the ticket cost, not including taxes, will be paid back to you. Most airlines have severely "capped" the amount of commission they pay per ticket.)

▼ Airlines may offer **overrides** (commissions over and above the typical cap) if your business is especially desired or if you have a sales track record.

▼ Airlines usually offer one free ticket per fifteen passengers. The first one would be used for the tour leader. A second or third free ticket might be used for a client or for a later trip. (A price may still show on the ticket.) This one-per-fifteen standard, however, is no longer predictable. Some airlines will offset very low rates or overrides by giving no free tickets.

▼ Assume that some airlines' sales reps will be slow in getting back to you. Keep calling them. Make sure you get a confirmation *in writing* of all that has been agreed upon. Be aware that once the agreement has been reached, your account will be handed over to a **group desk**, which is a part of the reservations operation at the airline.

▼ Never call just one airline for a bid, wait for its response, and then, if unsatisfied, contact a second carrier. Always contact at least three or four airlines on the same day so you can compare several bids at once. You don't want to waste time.

▼ There's nothing wrong with playing one airline's bid against another's in order to get more favorable treatment, although certain airline reps hate this. The best strategy is to decide which carrier you really want. If that carrier gives you a good bid, go with it. If it doesn't, use the other bids as leverage with the preferred airline.

▼ If you're setting up air travel to and from a cruise, you may not need to negotiate with the airlines at all. Cruise lines book large blocks of air space with the airlines, often at a discount. They may then resell this air space to your tour company at a price lower than (or pay a commission higher than) what you could negotiate yourself.

Tour Managers and Air Travel

Perhaps the most challenging aspect of any tour manager's trip is its air portion. First, the tour conductor is at the mercy of each airline's procedures. At no point on a tour does a tour conductor feel more powerless than on a plane or at an airport. Second, airport departures and arrivals are often frantic. A tour manager feels as if a staff of ten wouldn't be enough to handle the avalanche of boarding rituals, baggage counts, and passport checks that must take place in an hour or

Wide-body jets are common on international flights.
Courtesy of the National Tour Association

two. Third, the overburdened nature of the air travel system itself often keeps both clients and airline employees tense and cranky. Good planning and efficient strategies, therefore, go far to minimize the stress on a tour director during a tour's air-related activities.

Airline Industry Terminology

It might be useful to review some of the general terms used in the airline industry. Flights may be nonstop, direct, or connecting. A **nonstop flight** is exactly that: the plane flies to the passenger's final destination with no stops. A **direct flight** would stop at one or more intermediate airports, but the passenger usually doesn't change planes at the intermediate airport. A **connecting flight** always requires the passenger to change planes.

The **terminal** is the building where travelers report for their flights. Larger airports may have many terminals, each serving one or more carriers. The **check-in counter** is that part of the terminal (usually near where passengers arrive) where individual travelers and groups check luggage, reconfirm seating, have their tickets checked, and receive a **boarding pass** (a card indicating that a passenger has completed check-in and has a seat assignment).

Most airlines have gone to a "ticketless" electronic (e-ticket) system: no actual hard-copy ticket is issued.

Instead, the passenger's flight is tracked by a reservation number and perhaps a confirmation document. The passenger (or tour conductor) presents the number at check-in and the airline representative issues a boarding pass. It's not unlike checking into a hotel. Sometimes a tour company can issue boarding cards in advance. This doesn't mean that the passenger can just walk onto the plane, however. Usually the airline still wants the holder of these pre-issued boarding passes to check in somewhere, either at the check-in counter or gate. A few carriers (usually the low-cost ones) don't even issue boarding passes. They conduct first come, first served seating.

The **security gate** is that area where carry-on luggage is x-rayed and passengers must pass through metal detectors (a precautionary measure to screen for weapons). The **gate area** is that portion of the terminal from which all flights depart. Each gate has a **podium** where airline representatives reconfirm tickets or reservation numbers and handle latecomers and standby passengers. Seat assignments and boarding passes may be given out here, too, to those who by-pass the check-in counter. The up-to-date departure time for a particular flight is posted at its gate; departure and arrival times for all flights are posted throughout the terminal.

Skycaps, also known as **porters** or **baggage handlers**, are available to take care of luggage at curbside and again when a client arrives from a flight. Check-in attendants staff the check-in desk and are coordinated by a supervisor. Gate attendants work at the podium at each gate. **Flight attendants** (once called **stewards** and **stewardesses**) are those responsible for looking after passengers once aboard the plane. The pilots, flight engineer, and flight attendants, as a group, are called the **flight crew**.

In some cases, you may deal with tour flight situations that are extremely simple in nature. For example, a tour may include a one-day trip, via a small aircraft, from Los Angeles to the Grand Canyon and back. Tauck World Discovery offers its Western Canada Tour participants the option of visiting mountaintops via helicopter. In each case, the terminology you'll need to know and the procedures you'll need to follow will be very uncomplicated.

Before Your Clients Arrive

On the first day of a conventional tour, a tour manager must arrive at the airport terminal at least a half hour before the time clients have been asked to report for check-in. For a **domestic flight** (a flight completely within one country), a tour conductor should be at the airline check-in desk about 2 hours before scheduled departure. For the more complex demands of international itineraries, more time is needed: 2 1/2 to 3 hours in advance is ideal. In some cases, your tour company may assign a helper to assist you in the pre-boarding activities.

You should first ask for the airline's check-in desk supervisor. Among the questions you should ask are:

Does the Supervisor's Copy of the Airline Manifest Identify Members of Your Group? The

manifest is the official list of all passengers on a flight. Sometimes an airline prepares a separate manifest of group clients; more often the general manifest flags the names of group participants through a coding procedure. You may wish to check the manifest against your own passenger list or at least determine that the number of seats reserved for your group matches the number of persons (including you) on the tour. If the supervisor has no special group information on the manifest, it might be wise to hand over a copy of your own list of tour members for airline reference purposes.

How Are Your Clients to Be Seated? Airlines follow one of two procedures: they preassign a seat to each of your clients, or they block off seats for the entire group. The latter approach—though rare today—

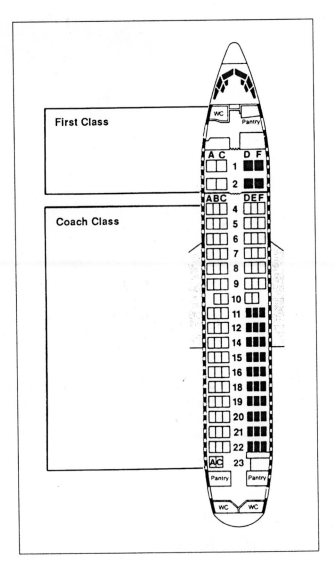

Figure 6–1   Seating chart for a Boeing 737 jet

will require you to assign seats to your tour members via boarding passes, which the supervisor or agent in charge will give you.

To make your job easier, ask the supervisor if a blank seating chart specific to the aircraft is available so you can write in the clients' seat assignments in advance. (See Figures 6–1 and 6–2.) If none is handy, draw one of your own, based on the seating configuration of that particular aircraft. (Either verbally or through an up-to-date seating assignment chart, the supervisor can tell you which seats are assigned to the group.) Make sure that your clients' smoking/nonsmoking (only an issue on some international flights) and special meal requests have been noted. (If you have to work out the seating yourself, deal with these special requests first.)

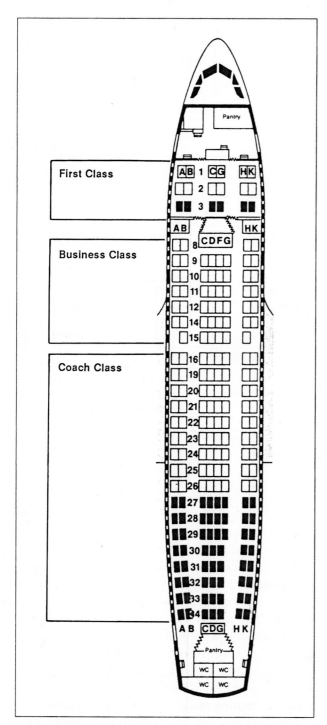

Figure 6–2 **Seating chart for a wide-body Airbus A310**

Which Seat Has Been Assigned to You, the Tour Manager?

A tour conductor should request an aisle seat to permit easy movement to and from clients. If you've been assigned block seating, simply give yourself an aisle seat. Some tour directors, in order to remain visible to the group, prefer a seat toward the front of the cabin. You'll have much paperwork to do, however, so it might be advisable to avoid sitting next to a tour member. Clients often feel obliged to converse with the tour conductor throughout the flight.

Some tour managers ask supervisors if it might be possible for them to be seated apart from the group, in the business or first-class section. The reasoning here is that since tour conductors must be in tip-top shape upon arrival at the tour's destination, a little peace, quiet, and pampering couldn't hurt. It does make sense. On the other hand, tour members may become annoyed when they find out that their tour leader has abandoned them for the luxuries of first class. The problem, though, may be academic. Increasingly, airlines resist upgrading tour conductors to better seats and assign them to coach class with regular tour passengers.

From Which Gate Will the Flight Leave, and Is the Departure Time Unchanged?

Your clients are sure to want this information. Other details you should ask about include: Where is the airport dining area located? How far is it to the gate? Where are the **duty-free shops** (the stores in international terminals where travelers can buy goods on which import taxes have not been levied)? Are there transport services to the gate for elderly or physically challenged clients? Where are the restrooms? If you have time, you should reconnoiter the airport area well in advance or study an airport layout map, usually found in an industry reference work called the *OAG Business Travel Planner.* (See Figures 6–3 and 6–4.)

What System Will Be Used to Check In Passengers?

Airlines usually deal with groups in one of three ways. The first is to check in each tour client separately in the regular lines open to the general public. (The tour manager may choose to greet clients when they check in or later, aboard the aircraft.) The second is to have a special, separate group counter or check-in position that handles each tour member separately, usually with the tour conductor's assistance. Both of these systems require that each client present his or her reservation number or ticket, passport, visa, and luggage to the agent, who then returns the documents, with a baggage-claim stub and boarding pass, to each individual. These first two systems are almost always required for international flights, since the agent must verify a client-passport-ticket match. They may be used for domestic check-ins, as well.

The third way (on some domestic flights) is for you, the tour director, to gather the group and its luggage

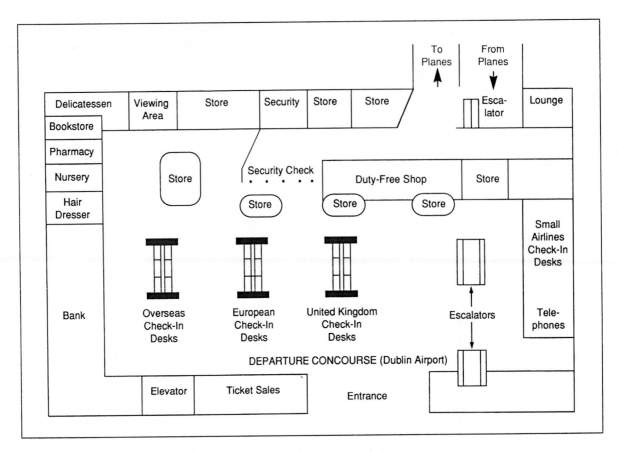

Figure 6–3 **Floor plan of Dublin Airport (departures)**

together in one spot and inform the agent or supervisor when everybody has arrived. You collect the clients' tickets or reservation documents as the clients show up (assuming you didn't have the tickets or e-ticket reservation numbers in the first place, which is sometimes the case). You then present all of this material together, loading the pieces of luggage one after another onto the reception counter scale. As you do this, the agent will tag the baggage and give you all the stubs together. The agent will then give all the group's tickets, boarding passes, and other documents to you. You'll then redistribute them to your clients so they can board the aircraft.

Depending on the time, you may then wish to tell your clients that they can visit the coffee shop, bar, or stores, as long as they don't forget to arrive at the gate with time to spare. This is especially critical on an international flight, when various checks may delay the walk from terminal to gate.

Among the three check-in systems described above, the second, in which each individual checks in with the

agent at a special group counter, is the best. It provides personalized group service yet doesn't require you to assemble a complete group before you can begin. The first system, putting tour members in the regular check-in line, requires much waiting time. The disadvantage of the third system is that it forces the tour manager to deal with the documents en masse, including baggage stubs that haven't been cross-referenced to individual passengers. If luggage is lost later, you must go through a lengthy process of elimination to find the claim check for the missing piece. To avoid this dilemma, ask the agent to come out from behind the counter and help you ticket the suitcases. On the back of each claim stub, write the corresponding client name or number for future reference. On an international flight, you may want to *insist* that they check in each of your tour members one at a time.

One other hint: when a ticket has actually been issued, each individual flight in the client's tour itinerary is represented by a separate piece of paper or card called a **coupon** (see Figure 6–5). These coupons are

***Figure 6–4* Floor plan of Ankara, Turkey Airport (arrivals)**

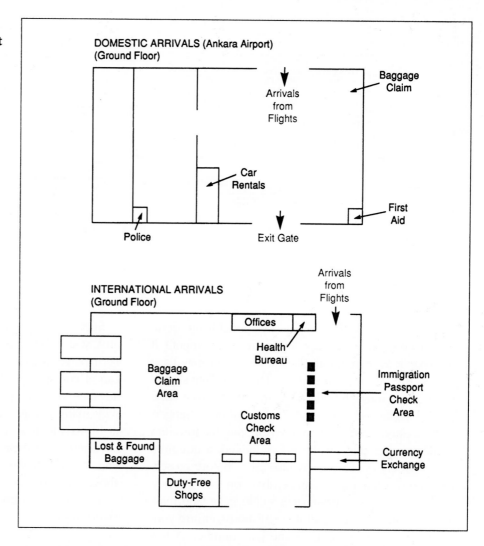

DOMESTIC ARRIVALS (Ankara Airport)
(Ground Floor)

Arrivals from Flights

Baggage Claim

Car Rentals

Police

Exit Gate

First Aid

INTERNATIONAL ARRIVALS
(Ground Floor)

Arrivals from Flights

Offices

Health Bureau

Baggage Claim Area

Immigration Passport Check Area

Customs Check Area

Lost & Found Baggage

Duty-Free Shops

Currency Exchange

gathered in one ticket folder or packet, which in turn is placed in an envelope-like jacket. When the passenger checks in, the agent pulls from the packet the coupon that matches the upcoming flight. However, coupons sometimes stick together, and an agent may pull several coupons at once, leaving the passenger with no coupon for the next flight. The tour leader or client should check each ticket before leaving the check-in counter to ensure that this costly mistake has not occurred. This potential problem may soon be eliminated, as airlines move toward ticketless bookings.

A few final comments are in order. Though three general check-in systems exist, all sorts of hybrids and variations are possible. You can occasionally talk a supervisor into following your favorite procedure. More often, though, the airline will tell you what it wants. What it usually wants is to handle the group in one check-in, with all documents handed over together by the tour manager, since this system makes most efficient use of airline counter personnel.

As Your Clients Arrive

You'll be able to identify your tour members by your company's luggage tags or name tags. (Now you know why these items are often so brightly colored.) Your clients will also be looking for you. (Now you know why a majority of tour operators insist on uniforms, or at least name tags, for their tour leaders.)

Be sure to greet your clients warmly—remember, the first impression is critical. Then you must immediately find out if your clients have their tickets (if your company mailed them out in advance, rather than giving them all to you for distribution) and if they have their passports, visas (for international trips), or other necessary identification. If any client has forgotten to bring the necessary items, you'll have to decide quickly whether there's time for the client to rush home, telephone home and ask someone to bring the documents, or find a notary public at the airport to validate the client's place of birth. (Before you look for a notary

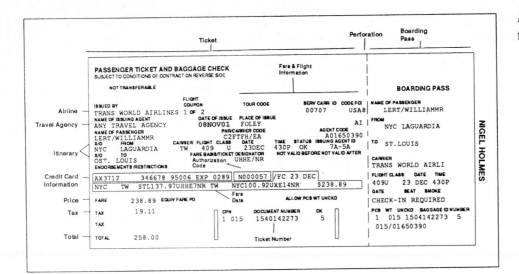

NIGEL HOLMES

Figure 6–5 **Sample flight coupon**

public, however, ask the airline personnel if the destination country will accept a notarized statement.) If these options aren't available, the passenger may have to miss the trip or catch up later. The later flight should be arranged through both the airline and the tour company. Heightened airport security requires passengers to have photo identification to ensure that the traveler's name matches that on the ticket. Indeed, a question-laden screening process will take place before passengers can check in luggage and embark on their journey.

After checking in passengers and luggage (and making sure carry-on pieces satisfy regulations), inform your clients of the boarding time and gate number. A few airlines have a separate group lounge where your clients can wait. If not, they'll probably be on their own until boarding, so show them the direction to the gate. Pass out whatever materials should be distributed—for instance, flight bags, updated itineraries, tickets, or boarding passes needed to get on the plane. Answer questions about airport facilities. Reiterate the importance of starting out for the gate *early*. Warn them to keep a careful eye on their carry-on bags and tickets. Although you'll probably be at the gate, tell them to board at the gate when ready, not to wait for you.

Now rest. You'll need to gather your energies after so much hectic activity. If you have the time, spend a few moments in the coffee shop or get an okay from the supervisor to wait in the airline's executive lounge. Then head out to the gate, ask the gate attendant if he or she can preboard your group (usually they won't, but it doesn't hurt to ask), make small talk with your passengers in the waiting area, and board the aircraft at the "last call."

Suppose after checking off luggage in the terminal area, you find that someone on the tour is still missing. Perhaps your clients checked their luggage with a sky-cap at curbside, contrary to the instructions mailed in advance to them, then went straight to the gate. This is why many companies give all the tickets for the first flight to the tour manager—it prevents clients from checking in on their own. Ask the gate agent to see if your missing clients checked in. If they're genuine no-shows, call your company to advise them of that fact. (For a visual summary of preboarding activities, see Figure 6–6.)

Aboard the Aircraft

As mentioned in Chapter 4, once you step aboard an aircraft, the flight crew is in charge. It's useful to introduce yourself to the head flight attendant and those attendants serving your cabin. You might even ask the lead attendant to announce a special welcome to your group over the P.A. system—write it out in advance on an index card. No matter how many times you've heard it, pay attention to the attendant's safety explanation. You'll set an example for the group, and the information will prove useful in the unlikely event of an emergency. Circulate among your clients only if the aisles are free. This is a good time to discuss what procedures await them when they arrive at their first destination. Otherwise, sit back and take care of whatever paperwork needs to be done.

***Figure 6–6* Visual sum-mary of how airlines check in groups**

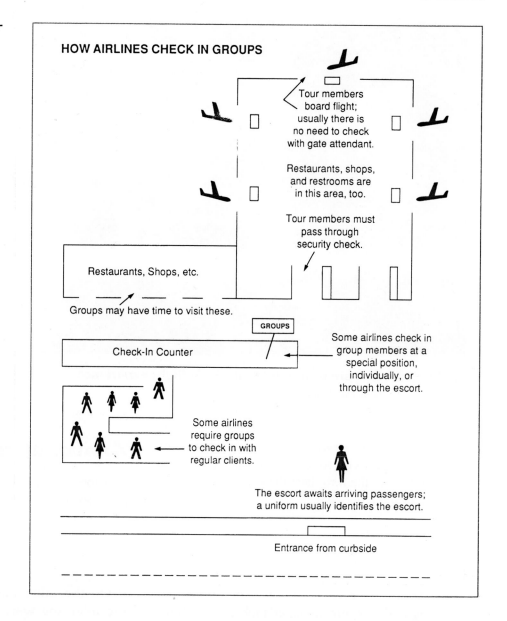

Your on-board tasks may include collecting airline tickets from your clients. Since travelers occasionally lose their tickets, some tour companies require tour directors to hold all group passenger tickets between *all* flights, not just for the first one. This is an enormous responsibility. You should scrupulously guard the tickets and place them in the hotel safe immediately upon arrival.

An efficient way to handle this process is to circulate in the plane with an envelope for tickets (take them out of their ticket jackets). Cross-check the tickets against a passenger list to make sure all are accounted for. The tour director returns the tickets to the clients just before the next air portion of their journey. Be sure to get a receipt for bundled tickets handed over to airline per-

sonnel for checking purposes. The receipt should indicate the number of tickets.

What if a client loses a ticket? Sometimes the airline will issue a duplicate ticket at no cost (perhaps taking a credit card imprint) and make a financial issue of it only if the original ticket is used at a later date. More typically, the airline will charge the client for a replacement ticket and give him or her a Lost Ticket Refund application to complete. If the original ticket is never used, the airline will refund the cost of the lost ticket several months later.

A client may inform you or the tour company that he or she has special dietary requirements—kosher, Hindu, Moslem, vegetarian, diabetic, low sodium, or low cholesterol. The company should have told the air-

Flight attendants are critical to a satisfying flight experience.
Courtesy of the National Tour Association

line of this at least twenty-four hours in advance of flight. If it failed to do so, contact the airline for your client so that on the next flight the client can have the meal he or she requested.

Arrival at Your Destination

Before arriving, you should have a sense of the airport's layout. An *OAG Business Travel Planner* map will

Some airports are models of efficiency; they make a tour manager's job easy. Others are quite the opposite. *Conde Nast Traveler* magazine rates the following airports as the best worldwide:

1. Singapore
2. Amsterdam
3. Pittsburgh
4. Zurich
5. Orlando
6. Hong Kong
7. Tampa
8. Reykjavik
9. Vancouver
10. Sydney

On the other hand, in an Excedrin poll, the following were once rated as the most "headache-provoking" airports in North America:

1. Chicago O'Hare
2. Atlanta Hartsfield
3. New York Kennedy
4. Los Angeles International
5. New York LaGuardia
6. Dallas/Fort Worth
7. Denver Stapleton (now closed)
8. San Francisco International
9. Washington National
10. Miami International

be helpful, as well as the maps sometimes found in the back pages of the airline's in-flight magazine.

If you're on an international flight, you and your group will have to deal with immigration and customs. Travelers often confuse the two. Basically, immigration deals with people, and customs with things. More specifically, **immigration** is the process by which a government official verifies a person's passport, visa, or birth certificate. Since the airline check-in person examined these documents before departure, there shouldn't be a problem for your tour participants. Most countries move travelers through this process quite quickly.

Once through immigration, it's time to deal with the luggage. This can be an awkward process. If you're arriving in a country that permits a representative of the ground operator to enter the baggage claim area, that person, perhaps with the help of porters, will help you and your clients locate the tour's luggage and will place it on large carts. Once again, you should check off luggage or at least take a count.

The carts will then be moved through customs. **Customs** is the procedure by which government agents inspect goods and baggage entering a country to check for illegal items and to assess whether a duty, or tax, is due on anything. If a ground operator is allowed in the claims area, a group will probably clear customs en masse, with only a spot inspection.

If reception personnel aren't allowed into the baggage area, you, as the tour manager, will have to choreograph the whole thing. Try to find small carts for each client or traveling couple. Passengers will then claim their luggage from the **carousel** (the circular baggage claim device) in the same way they would if they were individual travelers. Then they'll pass through customs one at a time. Tell them to wait for you on the other side. You should be the last person through, in case a suitcase has been lost.

If a suitcase is missing, you'll need to help the client fill out the lost-baggage form at a luggage claims counter in the baggage claim area. Make sure to ask the airline representative if your client is eligible for a cash allowance and/or overnight supplies kit. Before you get to the other side of customs yourself, the ground operator probably will have already identified your tour members. The immigration/customs procedure may be easier than you think—some countries operate on an "honor" system where people with nothing to declare can pass through customs unchecked.

Things will now start calming down. A driver and a representative from the ground operator (sometimes the same person) will help you shepherd the group to the waiting transfer bus and load luggage onto the coach. Discrepancies sometimes exist between what your tour company expects and what the reception tour operator has planned; therefore, you should briefly review the itinerary for the next few days with the ground operator. Before leaving for the hotel, take a head count to make sure everyone is on board. Once under way, use the motorcoach P.A. system to explain upcoming activities to your group participants. (For a visual summary of deplaning activities, see Figure 6–7.)

Midtour Flights

Often a tour has multiple destinations, each with a different flight. For example, a tour could leave from Washington, D.C., for London, stay three days in London, then fly from London to Paris, stay four days there, and then fly back to Washington, D.C. The group would have to make three airport departures: one from Washington, D.C., one from London, and one from Paris. Departure procedures at foreign airports will generally be the same as those previously described, with three significant exceptions. Upon leaving one country for the next, clients may have to pay a departure tax; they may be obliged to deal with a special security check or with customs; and, where applicable, they may be able to obtain refunds of taxes on goods bought.

In the Washington, D.C.-London-Paris tour described above, the formalities would be minimal. Tour members would probably declare what they had acquired in England and in France before reentering

Passing through immigration

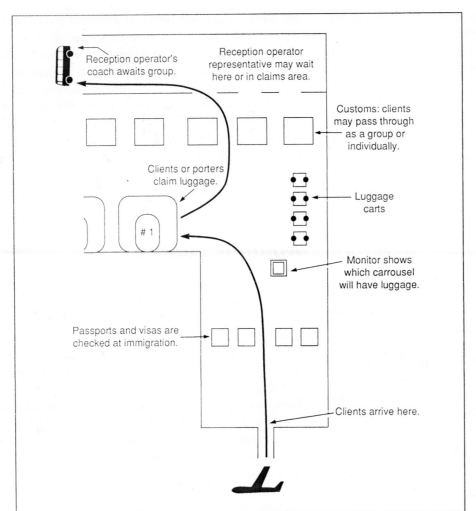

Figure 6–7 **Visual summary of deplaning activities (international flight)**

Reception operator's coach awaits group.

Reception operator representative may wait here or in claims area.

Customs: clients may pass through as a group or individually.

Clients or porters claim luggage.

Luggage carts

1

Monitor shows which carrousel will have luggage.

Passports and visas are checked at immigration.

Clients arrive here.

the United States; clients might also obtain refunds of taxes on items bought as they left each country. Unlike England or France, some host countries (for example, China) take extra steps to determine whether you're taking out something you shouldn't or (in Israel, for instance) whether you're a threat to the plane you're boarding.

What happens when your group lands in a country solely to continue on to a final destination? Let's say your group is going from Vancouver to Bangkok, Thailand, but your plane lands in Tokyo along the way. If the same plane continues on to Bangkok, you probably won't have to deal with Japanese immigration and customs. You'll be kept on the jet or in a secured waiting lounge. If you change to another plane on the same airline, you'll probably still avoid the hassles of immigration and customs, since the entire international terminal gate area of an airline is a sort of "free" secured zone (sometimes called the "sterile zone") where international passengers can transit from one gate to anoth-

er. If you must change to an airline in a different terminal, though, you may have to go through immigration, baggage pickup, and customs inspection before boarding the next flight.

Another example of a mid-tour flight is a "**flight-see**." Passengers board a small aircraft or helicopter for a short trip to a scenic wonder. Two examples are an air journey over the Grand Canyon or a helicopter excursion over an erupting volcano in Hawaii.

Returning Home

Travel is a wonderful yet arduous experience. Returning from a successful tour is both a sad and a comforting experience. On international journeys, though, it's made complicated by customs. (Immigration will also enter the picture.) Be sure to inform your clients before the tour's end about requirements for reentering the country. Warn them, too, not

A "flightseeing" group visits the Grand Canyon.
Courtesy of the National Tour Association

to joke with customs officers. The customs formalities upon return can be the most serious that your tour members will face over the course of their trip.

One final point: although group flight-related activities sound terribly complex, they tend to sort themselves out, no matter how many small things go wrong or are forgotten. If you've ever been on an international trip, you've probably moved through the complexities described above without giving them a second thought. Air and government personnel are used to dealing with unimaginably complex transit problems. View them as an important source of support in carrying out your escort duties and ensuring your tour's success. (For the tour manager's air-related checklist, see Figure 6–8.)

Summary

Negotiations and bookings with airlines are a complex process, usually carried out by a tour planner. The air travel portion of a tour is the most challenging. Airport activity is usually hectic, the air transportation system is overburdened, and the tour director has little control over what goes on in an airport or on an airplane. Reconnoitering an airport's facilities well before the clients arrive is a good way for a tour manager to prepare. An escort should be thoroughly familiar with preboarding procedures. Aboard the aircraft, the tour conductor's responsibilities are minimal. On arrival, the tour director should facilitate the passage of a group through immigration, baggage claim, customs, and the airport-hotel transfer.

AIR TOUR CHECKLIST

Before your clients arrive, have you:
- ☐ Checked with the supervisor about check-in procedures?
- ☐ Checked with the supervisor about client seat assignments?
- ☐ Confirmed all special seating and meal requests?
- ☐ Made sure you, the escort, have a seat?
- ☐ Determined from which gate your flight will leave?
- ☐ Figured out where restaurants, restrooms, and shops are?

As your clients arrive, have you:
- ☐ Asked clients if they brought passports, visas, etc.?
- ☐ Asked clients if they have airline tickets (or distributed them)?
- ☐ Checked off their luggage for future tracking purposes?
- ☐ Passed out necessary documents?
- ☐ Informed them of the departure time and gate?
- ☐ Warned them to protect their valuables?
- ☐ Made sure everyone has arrived?

Aboard the aircraft, have you:
- ☐ Introduced yourself to the flight crew?
- ☐ Collected airline tickets from clients (if company policy)?
- ☐ Organized baggage-claim stubs?

Upon arrival at your destination, have you:
- ☐ Sought out the ground operator?
- ☐ Helped organize clients' luggage claims?
- ☐ Found a porter to help you?
- ☐ Made sure all luggage has arrived?
- ☐ Taken a baggage count before loading the transfer coach?
- ☐ Taken a head count before leaving on the transfer coach?

Figure 6–8   **Sample air tour checklist**

■ ■ ■

QUESTIONS FOR DISCUSSION

1. List at least five things you must keep in mind when negotiating for group air space.

2. Give three reasons why dealing with air travel can be a challenging experience for a tour conductor.

3. What are the two approaches airline personnel take toward group seating in an aircraft cabin?

4. Explain the three ways airline personnel might check in groups.

5. Discuss the advantages and disadvantages of a tour manager's sitting in business or first class, apart from the group.

6. Which two questions must a tour director ask of each arriving passenger?

7. Describe an efficient way of handling a tour group's airline tickets and baggage-claim stubs once you and the group are on the plane.

8. What happens if a client forgets or loses an airline ticket?

9. What is the difference between immigration and customs?

10. In what three ways do midtour flight check-ins at foreign airports differ from the first check-in at the beginning of the tour?

■ ■ ■

ACTIVITY 1

▼ On the following drawing of the departure area of a small domestic airline terminal, label the following: check-in counter, security check, restrooms, dining facility, and gate departure area.

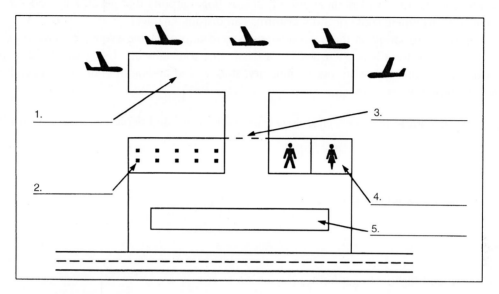

1. _____
2. _____
3. _____
4. _____
5. _____

▼ On the following drawing of a typical arrival area of an international airport, label the following: arrival gate, immigration, customs, baggage claim, and reception area.

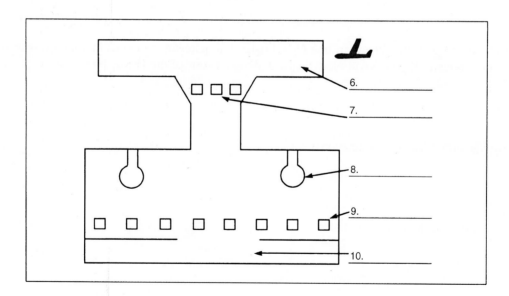

6. _____
7. _____
8. _____
9. _____
10. _____

ACTIVITY 2

Creating an efficient and cost-effective air itinerary is a subtle skill. The ideal itinerary (1) uses only one airline for the entire trip; (2) uses only nonstop flights or direct ones (in which the aircraft stops at an intermediary city, but continues on to your group's final destination); (3) avoids huge airports that get heavily congested; (4) avoids airports at certain seasons where snow or thunderstorms can disrupt air travel.

It's often impossible to satisfy all these considerations, and unpredictable events can always occur. This activity, however, challenges you to at least *try* to fashion a hassle-free tour itinerary. Using any research resources at your disposal (including the Internet), work out an itinerary, starting and ending in your home city, that is efficient and based on actual current airline routings.

1. A "Mayan Adventure" tour for archaeology buffs, with arrival and departure from Cancun, Mexico.

    a. Airline(s) and flight(s) to get there:

    b. Airline(s) and flight(s) to get home:

2. A "Fall Foliage" tour that begins in one New England air gateway and ends in another, with motorcoach travel in between. (If you live in New England, design a tour of the Pacific Northwest.)

    a. Arrival airport/city for destination:

    b. Airline(s) and flight(s) to get there:

    c. Departure airport/city to get home:

    d. Airline(s) and flight(s) to get home:

3. A "Classic Europe" tour in which the group visits three capital cities, flying between each:

   a. Arrival airport/city and flight(s) to get there:

   b. Second airport/city and flight(s) to get there:

   c. Third airport/city and flight(s) to get there:

   d. Departure flight(s) to get home:

■ ■ ■

ACTIVITY 3

▼ You've arrived at the airport ahead of your group. The airline desk supervisor tells you that the airline has blocked off group seating for your group, but hasn't assigned specific seats to your individual clients. You'll have to do that yourself. The supervisor has neither a manifest nor a blank aircraft seating chart at her disposal. She does give you an up-to-date seat assignment chart for your flight, which will go from Lima, Peru, to Miami.

Examine the following two documents. The first is your passenger list (18 PAX). The second is the aircraft seat assignment chart that the supervisor has given to you (seats reserved for your tour are labeled T). Work out the seating solutions on a separate piece of paper. Then indicate on the next page which clients you have assigned to which seats. Note that you can request open seats (O) to offset any logistical problems you may encounter or to correct any oversights or mistakes the airline may have made. Good luck!

Tour Passenger List

101.   Mr. Ted Striker and Mrs. Elaine Striker
102.   Harve and Irma Blakely
103.   J. Kerouac (requests smoking and aisle seat)
104.   Dr. and Mrs. Pangloss (Mrs. Pangloss requests window seat)
105.   M. Polo
106.   Rose Sayer and Charles Allnut (request smoking)
107.   Mr. L. Gulliver (requests aisle seat)
108.   Mr. and Mrs. D. O. Guerrero
109.   Clark and Ellen Griswold

       Audrey Griswold

       Rusty Griswold

110.   S. Bertrille (requests seat next to exit)

Airline Seat Assignment Chart

TransAmerica Flight #209
Code: T = tour; R = reserved; S = smoking; O = open

Row	Seats							
	A	**B**	**C**	**D**	**E**	**F**	**G**	**H**
22	R	O	R	R	R	R	T	T
23	R	R	R	R	T	T	T	T (exit)
24	O	O	T	T	T	T	R	R
25	R	R	R	R	T	T	T	T
26	R	R	R	R	R	O	R	R
27	O	O	O	O	O	O	O	O
28	SR	SR	SR	ST	ST	ST	SR	SR

Assignments you have made (to be transferred to boarding passes):

22 G	24 F
22 H	25 E
23 E	25 F
23 F	25 G
23 G	25 H
23 H	28 D
24 C	28 E
24 D	28 F
24 E	Other:

Do you have any changes to request of the supervisor?

PROFILE

Except to promote their services and attractions, destination-based organizations rarely get involved in the day-to-day activities of groups. However, Ontario's Niagara Parks Commission is very much an exception. Founded in 1885, the organization seeks to preserve, restore, commemorate, and keep beautiful the Canadian lands at and near the famous Falls. Assisting and managing groups is a big part of the NPC's mandate: a quarter of those people who visit the Falls come as part of a tour. And very much a part of those efforts has been George Bailey, the NPC's now-retired Director of Communications.

Raised in the city of Niagara Falls, Ontario (his father was captain of the famous *Maid of the Mist*, which sails to the very base of the Falls), George began as a newscaster for a local radio station. He left the Falls area only briefly, to oversee an attraction at the Thousand Islands. He returned to manage the Foxhead Hotel, still one of the prime lodging facilities at the Falls. "I was a people person, so I loved dealing with the visitors who came from every spot on the globe to see our attraction. I also learned plenty about groups, since a substantial number of people who stayed at the Foxhead came as part of tours."

Upon joining the NPC, one of the first things George did was to help establish a Group Tour Department. This enabled the NPC to better provide easy access motorcoach parking, special menu group meal opportunities (the NPC operates several restaurants), a sightseeing newsletter, and other value-added benefits to tour operators. "Consistency is the key," George explains. "We want visitors to the Falls at any time of the year to experience great service."

A key part of the NPC mandate—as far as touring is concerned—is its licensing of guides. "We strongly feel that those who deliver information on the Falls should know their stuff," argues George. Each guide candidate must pass an 80-question test that assesses their knowledge of everything about the Falls: its history, geology, ecology, attractions and—yes—the many daredevils who have challenged the Falls. "Even though we require guides to take the test every three years," explains George, "many take it each year. They want to keep themselves sharp." Currently, about 1,000 people hold an NPC guide license and many serve as step-on guides for visiting motorcoach tours.

And their skills are even more in demand today. Twenty years ago, the Niagara tourist season extended only from June through early September. Outside of that stretch—and especially in winter—the Falls area was largely devoid of tourists. Indeed, most of its hotels closed their doors for the winter season and restaurants had to depend almost exclusively on locals.

That changed with another idea that George contributed to: The Winter Festival of Lights. For two months before and after Christmas, the Falls area is now ablaze with decorations, lights and special, seasonal activities. As a result, hotels are open year-round, restaurants have much more business, tour guides can find many more job opportunities, and 400,000 people visit during a time when only a few thousand once did.

Now that he's retired, George is pursuing a new career: setting up shows to help promote other destinations. But Niagara Falls will always be close to his heart. "I think people have a much better idea now about what the Falls and Canada are about," states George. "There was a time many years ago when I actually saw some tourists arrive at the Falls with their skis—in the summer. My job is to ensure that people now come with more accurate expectations and when they leave, that they take with them a fascination with the Falls that will remain with them forever."

7

Suppliers and Attractions

Chapter Objectives

After reading this chapter, you should be able to:

▼ Discuss how a tour manager can enhance a group's cruise experiences.

▼ Explain the distinct nature of group rail travel.

▼ Identify the kinds of dining services that work best for tour groups.

▼ Enumerate the considerations a tour leader must have in mind when a group visits an attraction.

"YES, I DID TELL YOU WE WERE GETTING INTO INTERMODAL TOURS, BUT THIS IS ABSURD!!"

Hotels and airlines are certainly the most obvious companies that a tour manager will deal with. Many other providers of tour services, though, bear discussion. Restaurants, cruise lines, and railroads, among others, may influence a tour's shape and efficiency. The travel industry calls such tour-supporting services **suppliers**. Theme parks, historical buildings, museums, and the like, a special subdivision of suppliers, are called **attractions**. This chapter takes an in-depth look at suppliers and how a tour director can best deal with their procedures and personnel.

Cruises

Once a dull and dowdy segment of the travel industry, the cruise has been reincarnated as a glamorous mode of transportation. Perhaps the original 1970s television series "The Love Boat" did it. Maybe a nostalgia for the grand cruise ships of the early twentieth century is the cause. A more probable reason is the shift from the transatlantic trips of yesteryear to cruises in concentrated destination areas, such as the Caribbean. The most important reason is the modern cruise's comprehensive yet efficient nature. A cruise is the ultimate all-inclusive packaged tour, since the vehicle—the ship—doubles as a hotel, restaurant, and entertainment facility. Through a cruise one can visit a half dozen Greek islands, take in the great beach cities of the Mexican Riviera, voyage up the Mississippi, or explore the majestic Inside Passage of Alaska—and not once have to repack one's luggage.

Not surprisingly, tour manager positions that include cruises are much in demand. In many cases, the cruise *is* the tour; other forms of organized transportation aren't included. (In other words, the clients have to fly to the originating port on their own.) In other instances, the cruise comprises only one portion of a more extended intermodal tour. For example, a motorcoach tour of the western Canadian Rockies may end with a round-trip Alaskan cruise. Certain companies, such as Holland America Line-Westours, specialize in just such intermodal packages. For companies like Princess Cruises, cruise-motorcoach tours are only a sideline to cruise operations. Affinity groups such as the American Association of Retired People and the American Automobile Association also organize frequent cruise-motorcoach excursions.

In virtually every case, a tour manager on a cruise works for a tour company and not directly for the cruise line. We'll bypass the responsibilities of a shore excursion guide here, since the job requirements are almost identical to those of a regular tour guide (see Chapter 2). In the next few pages, we'll concentrate on what a tour conductor on a cruise tour must know and why people take a cruise as part of a group.

Terminology

Before hosting a cruise tour, a tour manager must become acquainted with the ship's layout, its onboard activities, the inclusiveness of the tour package (for example, does the price of the package include tips?), and the special terminology of cruising.

▼ A **stateroom** or **cabin** is the sleeping room on a ship. It's usually quite small. An **outside stateroom** has a porthole, a picture window, or even a full sliding-glass door that opens onto a verandah. An **inside stateroom** usually has no view and, to some, can be somewhat claustrophobic. A larger, more luxurious room is called a **suite**. Usually all tour members have the same class of stateroom; occasionally, clients on a cruise tour will each have their own category of stateroom—some inside, some outside, some more spacious than others—depending on what they paid.

▼ A **deck** is one of the floors of a ship. Usually the higher the deck, the more expensive the rooms.

▼ The front of the ship is the **bow**; the back is the **aft** or **stern**. When one is facing the bow, the left side is called **port**; the right side, **starboard**.

▼ The **chief steward** oversees meals and housekeeping. The **maitre d'** heads the dining room, while a **table captain** may oversee a group of tables within a dining room, along with its waiters and busboys. There are other stewards as well: the **room steward** cares for the passengers' rooms. The **deck steward** manages deck facilities, including the serving of drinks.

▼ The **passenger service rep**, or **PSR**, is the ship's troubleshooter; he or she also often handles logistics for pre- and post-cruise flights.

▼ The **chief purser** is the equivalent of a hotel manager and is, in general, in charge of all financial functions and passenger services, including shore excursions. **Shore excursions** (tours at each port) are often coordinated by the shore excursion manager.

▼ The **cruise director** (also known as the **social director** or **activities director**) is, in essence, the head escort for the entire ship. The cruise director makes sure passengers are kept entertained, active, and informed. The cruise director will most certainly tailor activities to the type of client who frequents the ship. For instance, Carnival Cruise Lines tends to attract a younger clientele; World Explorer appeals to those who wish to learn; and Seabourn ships attract the older, well-heeled traveler. The cruise director also controls function rooms; if you want to have any special events on the ship, this is usually the person to talk to.

As "mega-ships" have become more commonplace (a mega-ship is one that accommodates 2,000 passengers or more), cruise lines have assigned **groups managers** to each vessel. A groups manager can be a boon to tour conductors; he or she becomes a "one-stop" service person who facilitates all logistic matters, including those other personnel normally handle: special events, function rooms, group shore excursions, stateroom problems, and the like.

Groups on Cruises

Why do some people want to take their cruises as part of a group tour experience? The obvious reason is that the tour operator has added something (e.g., a multi-day land portion before and/or after the cruise) that brings extra value to the experience. But many other reasons account for the popularity of the tour-cruise combination:

▼ Because they buy cruise space "in bulk," tour operators can often offer a cruise at a price lower than what appears in the cruise line's brochure.

▼ The tour manager is onboard, providing added, more personal attention to the tour member.

▼ The tour company may provide other value-added features, such as a welcome reception onboard, a shore excursion included in the price, and the like.

▼ The purchaser, especially if he or she has already taken and been pleased with trips from the tour operator, trusts that company. The cruise line, however, may be unknown to the client.

▼ Travelers who enjoy group tours are comfortable with other group experiences, such as cruises. According to an NTA survey, 64 percent of tour-takers have cruised at least once.

In some cases, the cruise-tour is custom-designed for a special affinity group. This brings additional benefits:

▼ Group members will be with people they may already know or at least have something in common with. He or she will feel far more comfortable with the cruise experience (especially if he or she is a first-timer).

▼ This will be most obvious when dining. On cruises, passengers are often seated with people they don't know. With a preformed group, however, you may be seated with someone you do know, or at least with whom you have something in common.

▼ There may be someone onboard who brings to the group experience a special sense of authority, comfort, leadership, or expertise. Some examples: a church group's minister, a club's president, or a famous chef on a culinary tour. These are called pied pipers. (More about this in Chapter 9.)

On today's mega-liners, the ship's environment can be vast.
Courtesy of Cruise Lines International Association

▼ If the group is onboard for business or as part of an incentive experience, the ship provides a controlled and supportive environment that supports the company's goals.

A Tour Manager's Cruise Activities

If you're already at the port from where the cruise will depart and the clients have yet to arrive, your tour company will probably have arranged an early-boarding pass for you. Try to get on the ship about three hours early and do the following:

▼ Go to your stateroom and read the ship's daily activities sheet or newsletter; the cabin stewards place them in all rooms. It will list all the ship's activities for the first and second days and give you vital information with which to answer clients' questions. Also review the ship's deck plan (the tour company should have given you a copy or get one on the ship), and explore the ship if you need to.

▼ Go to the purser's office and check your passenger list, stateroom assignments, and shore excursion arrangements with those of the purser.

▼ Go to the cruise director or groups manager and reconfirm or arrange the reception party, the special briefing meeting, the farewell party, and your "office hours." Many tour directors make a point of being in a particular place—a function room, a lobby table, or a lounge—at the same time each day so clients can find them if they need to. Other tour managers rely on the evening dinner to update clients about upcoming events.

▼ See the maitre d' to verify meal seatings (times) and table assignments. (These probably have been set up in advance, in which case you need to make sure that your information matches the maitre d's.)

▼ If you have informational handouts, welcome cards, or anything else for your passengers, use your passenger stateroom list to find their rooms (usually near one another), and slip the necessary documents under their doors. (The staterooms may even be open, so you can leave things on the bed or dresser.)

You may then exit the ship and begin meeting clients as they arrive at the dockside check-in area. However, if you arrive with them—from a pre-cruise tour, for instance, or on their flight—you'll have to do all the above immediately after everyone gets on board. That's no easy task, since the ship's personnel will be quite busy.

You'll handle passengers as in an airport arrival: identify clients by tags, greet them, facilitate their check-in, and take care of luggage. If you're coming off a motorcoach portion of the tour, this process will be easier.

The cruise experience is well-suited to group travel.
Courtesy of the National Tour Association

Baggage personnel often track luggage through a color-coded, letter-labeling sticker or baggage tag system: they assign a letter according to the person's last name and/or a color according to stateroom class and deck. Ask the baggage staff to give a single letter (perhaps the first letter in your company's name) to all your group participants. If they're all on one deck, a single color code will do. (Increasingly, cruise lines provide passengers with special coded luggage tags in advance.) Once luggage is taken care of, send your clients to the check-in desk (often on the dock). There they'll be given informational material, their stateroom key (unless it's in the unlocked stateroom), and perhaps a credit card-like item that lists their stateroom number, booking number, dinner seating, table assignment, and the like.

The Briefing Meeting.

The briefing is of vital importance. The ship will hold its own briefing meeting for all passengers, usually the first night out or the next day. You may also wish to schedule your own meeting (perhaps during a welcome party) to explain those things of special interest and to strengthen the bond between you and your clients. If the cruise is at the end of a motorcoach trip, you could conduct this briefing the evening *before* the cruise, as long as you have all the information needed. A briefing meeting usually covers the following points.

The Ship's Environment. How is the ship laid out? What activities are available? Which shore excursions will be offered, and is their price included in the tour cost? What shopping bargains can passengers expect? What will the lifeboat safety drill be like? (It's often one of the first things that happens on a ship.) How can one avoid lines and waiting? How does one check valuables? Handing out a deck plan to clients and reviewing the activities sheet is very helpful.

Tipping. Whom must you tip? (Usually the cabin steward, the waiter, the busboy and, sometimes, the table captain and/or maitre d' expect to receive gratuities.) How much should you tip each? Are tips included in the tour package—that is, has the tour company taken care of them? (Upscale cruise lines may have a no tipping policy.)

Dining. How is dining handled? Smaller ships usually have only one principal dining facility and possibly another facility for very informal, snack-like food. Larger ships have more options.

For example, on the mega-liner *Majesty of the Seas,* tour members could have breakfast and lunch in one of two formal dining rooms (at tables assigned to the group), in a more informal, open-seating area on the pool deck, or in their rooms. The choice is up to each individual client. Dinner would probably be in the for-

Just about everything is included in a cruise—including meals.
Courtesy of Cruise Lines International Association

mal dining room (this is the time for the group to "bond"), although room service is an option. Snacks are served poolside in the late afternoon, and a spectacular buffet is presented each night at midnight.

On such a large ship, the passengers dine in the formal dining room in two shifts: a first (early) seating and a second (later) seating. Your group will be assigned to one of the two seatings well in advance. You'll also have to explain the dress code for each meal. (Much of this will also be outlined to them on the activities sheet.)

Problem-solving. How can passengers find you when they need help solving problems? Usually tour members can leave messages for the tour leader at the purser's office, through the ship's telephone operator, or even under the tour conductor's door (assuming that you give out your stateroom number)—or they may wait until the tour manager's office hours.

During the Cruise. Once the briefing meeting and the "welcome party" are over, a tour director's job becomes seemingly easy. The biggest challenge on a cruise is for the escort to make clear to the clients that he or she is still doing a job for them. That's not easy when you're competing with social directors, maitre d's, and the Broadway revue dancers.

A tour manager should above all strive to be visible. Walk around the ship, make small talk with the passengers you encounter, tend to their problems, be present at entertainment and dining activities, and generally be a *host* rather than a manager. You might consider scheduling brief daily receptions for your group or arrange special tours of the bridge and galley. A group walking tour of the vessel early in the cruise is a good idea. You might even serve as a mini-cruise director, organizing little tournaments or games for your group and encouraging them to participate in the ship's "Talent Night." (If such events occur, slide invitations under your clients' stateroom doors the night before.) Remember, too, that your company may expect you to fill out a ship evaluation form in your spare time. (See Figure 7-1.)

You'll also be expected to accompany your group on any shore excursions included in their tour. Get off ahead of your group and block off a bus for them. Then stand with a sign so your tour members can find you.

The End of the Cruise. If the cruise marks the end of the tour, an onboard farewell get-together may be planned for the last evening. Remind clients to pay any incidentals that they may have charged to their rooms. Review your own master account as you would in a hotel. You may also wish to slide a card or letter under your clients' doors, thanking them for the opportunity of being their tour manager. Note also that many cruise lines require passengers to pack their luggage and leave it outside their stateroom door on the last evening (keeping their overnight items in a carry-on bag).

On the final morning of the cruise, clients will disembark according to decks and/or luggage tag colors. Checking out will be a simple process, not unlike checking out of a hotel. At dockside, the baggage handlers will once again separate luggage by letter and/or color codes. If your tour is continuing, get a baggage handler to help you transport luggage to your airport transfer vehicle or motorcoach. If this is the end of your tour, it's the time to say a final farewell to the group.

The pages you've just read about cruises only skim the surface of this increasingly important topic. For more information, consult *Cruising* by this book's author, and Brooke Bravos' book, *Cruise Hosting*.

Negotiating with a Cruise Line

Do tour managers also negotiate next season's rates and space with cruise lines, as they sometimes do with hotels? In most cases, the answer is no. Someone in tour planning will do this (though their negotiations may be based on the tour leaders' and clients' evaluations).

However, in most ways negotiating with a cruise line is like dealing with a hotel: cruise companies, who appreciate the business tour companies can bring them, are willing to discount their fares by 20 to as much as 50 percent. Most of the strategies you read about in Chapter 5 apply: booking staterooms for the off-season, guaranteeing a large number of tours, accepting less desirable staterooms, and booking way ahead all can optimize the rate you'll receive. You can also negotiate for a free tour director stateroom, a free reception party, extra room amenities (such as a little gift on the first day), and ship credits (a set dollar amount that each client gets for beverages and the like).

Three components leave little room for negotiation: air space that the cruise line may offer from the city of origin to the port city; hotel space that they reserve at a hotel near the port; and shore excursion prices. Large tour operators can better negotiate their own air and hotel space directly with the airline or hotel, rather than tap the cruise line's inventory. (This eliminates the "middle man.") For smaller tour companies, the cruise line may indeed be able to provide the best hotel and air rates.

```
SHIP INSPECTION REPORT

SHIP'S NAME: _____     PREPARED BY:
SHIP'S CRUISE LINE: _____     _____
DEPARTURE PORT: _____
PORTS OF CALL: _____
NATIONALITY OF CREW: _____
PASSENGER CAPACITY: _____
NUMBER OF CABINS: OUTSIDE_____ INSIDE _____
NUMBER OF POOLS: _____
NUMBER OF DINING ROOMS: _____
```

Facilities/Services	Excellent	Very Good	Good	Poor	Not Applicable
Cabaret Show	☐	☐	☐	☐	☐
Cabins - Outside	☐	☐	☐	☐	☐
Cabins - Inside	☐	☐	☐	☐	☐
Casino(s)	☐	☐	☐	☐	☐
Child Care	☐	☐	☐	☐	☐
Children's Programs	☐	☐	☐	☐	☐
Cocktail Lounges	☐	☐	☐	☐	☐
Deck Area	☐	☐	☐	☐	☐
Dining Room	☐	☐	☐	☐	☐
Disco(s)	☐	☐	☐	☐	☐
Hair Stylist	☐	☐	☐	☐	☐
Health Club	☐	☐	☐	☐	☐
Library	☐	☐	☐	☐	☐
Movie Theater	☐	☐	☐	☐	☐
Pool(s)	☐	☐	☐	☐	☐
Quality of Food	☐	☐	☐	☐	☐
Shopping Area	☐	☐	☐	☐	☐
Singles' Programs	☐	☐	☐	☐	☐
Teenage Programs	☐	☐	☐	☐	☐
Overall Assessment	☐	☐	☐	☐	

```
Comments:



```

Copyright © Delmar Publishers

Figure 7–1   **Sample ship inspection report**

Rail Travel

Like cruising, rail travel is enjoying a renaissance. Its success has been somewhat mixed, however, since the governments that usually control rail service are slow to respond to new markets and demand. Still, train trips have become an integral feature of many tours. Short rides on old-time steam trains are a popular tour activity. Full-day train rides are common on intermodal tours of the Canadian Rockies. A multi-day train trip carries many groups through Mexico's majestic Copper Canyon. "Murder Mystery" train excursions, where actors aboard the train stage a performance and the passengers must "solve the crime," are a unique feature on a few tours. A ride on the high-speed bullet train highlights most tours of Japan. A voyage on a luxury train such as the magnificent Orient Express enriches several upscale tours of Europe.

The Features of a Modern Train

The layout of today's trains may be different from what you expect. Consider the sleeping facilities. Many people remember old movies in which the Marx Brothers terrorized passengers asleep in stacks of curtain-partitioned cubicles. This configuration has virtually disappeared.

Rail travel is an efficient way to visit Alaska.
Courtesy of the National Tour Association

Here are the most common options that may be available to passengers on overnight trains. The most basic: passengers sleep in their seats, as they would on a long plane ride. Occasionally, the seat can recline almost to a horizontal position; such a seat is called a **sleeper seat**. Another option is an open bunk called a **couchette**. The train car is divided into compartments, each containing four or six seats, half facing forward and half facing backward. At bedtime a porter enters and drops down small bed surfaces in each compartment. However, passengers in couchettes sleep in their daytime clothes: the compartments offer little privacy and aren't necessarily same-sex.

On some trains passengers can pay for a private, compact sleeping room called a **sleeper, roomette,** or **wagon-lit.** Each room contains one or two berths

(though some have up to four berths) and usually also have a sink with hot and cold water. Rooms may even have toilets.

During the day your clients will travel in their compartments or in an open lounge car that resembles the interior of a motorcoach. The lounge cars are usually larger than buses and accommodate sixty or more people. In some areas these cars are even double-decked and domed, with seating on the top level and dining or lounge facilities on the bottom.

Getting to know the personnel is a simpler task on a train than on a cruise ship. The porters handle luggage, the conductors care for passenger logistics, and a maitre d' is in charge of dining services (assuming that the train has more than a snack bar). A few railroads even hire a "singing brakeman" to entertain passengers. Finally, a sort of step-on guide particular to railroading is the car manager. The **car manager,** sometimes employed by the tour company, sometimes by the rail company, comments on the passing sights.

Check-in and Onboard Activities

A tour manager's check-in procedures for a train are nearly identical to those required for air travel. You'll have to hand over the passenger tickets and check luggage with the porter or at the ticket counter. You'll need to explain sleeping accommodations and whether tour members will travel in small compartments or large cars. Note that since the largest motorcoaches accommodate no more than fifty-three passengers and a typical train car seats sixty or more, your group may share a car with regular travelers, especially if the train is quite full.

You'll also need to explain dining services and whether they're included in the tour price. Since dining coaches have limited seating, you may have to organize your group's meals in shifts. Make group reservations with the maitre d' early in the trip. In many cases, the tour operator will have made these arrangements in advance. In fact, some tour companies reserve a dining car exclusively for their group and determine the menu selection. One tour operator, unaccustomed to dealing with rail travel, specified that lunch was to include little melon balls. It was a nice touch—until the melon balls began to roll all over the swaying car.

The psychology of rail travel is unique. First of all, clients approach a train experience with a sense of adventure. (You'll find that many are already rail buffs.)

A group enjoys a formal meal on a restored vintage train.
Courtesy of the National Tour Association

For the first few hours at least, trains manage to beguile almost anyone. However, unless the passing panorama is genuinely breathtaking, monotony can set in. A tour director must therefore make much small talk. If the train is divided into small compartments, the process will be a bit awkward. If a car manager is present, his or her narration will certainly enhance the experience. At long stops, clients may be able to disembark for a while, and of course they'll have the wonderful freedom of walking around their vehicle as it clanks along.

When your group leaves the train, immediately find a porter to help with the luggage—assuming there *is* a porter. In many places only limited baggage services exist. It may be necessary to have your clients push their own luggage on carts, as individual travelers must. Occasionally, a multi-day train trip features overnight hotel stops along the way, rather than requiring passengers to sleep on the train. In this case, your baggage moves will be frequent indeed.

Dining and Tours

The saying is well-known: "An army travels on its stomach." So, too, does a tour. The quality of meals and the ambience of dining do much to color a traveler's perception of how well a tour is going. Choreographing meals in a careful and creative manner is one of a tour manager's most important responsibilities.

Selecting a Dining Facility

Tour managers usually have very little say as to which hotels, airlines, bus companies, cruise lines, or attractions a tour will use. Not so for restaurants. When a tour company sets up dining reservations, it is generally on the recommendation of tour managers, drivers, or ground personnel who are acquainted with the destination. In some cases, the selection of places for the group to eat is left totally to the tour director. (This is especially true when the meal isn't included in the price of the tour.)

Tour conductors who have been asked to choose a restaurant should ask themselves the following:

Does the Itinerary Dictate that the Meal Be Quick and Efficient or Lengthy and Worth Savoring? A lunch stop during a city tour or a motorcoach trip from one destination to another shouldn't take more than 90 minutes. The restaurant should be able to handle large groups with relative ease. Cafeterias or buffet restaurants are perfect in this situation, since there's no need to order and wait for one's meal. A conventional restaurant can serve a group faster if the tour arrives before the regular rush of patrons—say, by 11 A.M.

For dinner, however, there's no real need to rush things. A pleasant restaurant with a strong ambience, an interesting view, and, perhaps, entertainment is ideal for tour group dinners or leisurely lunches. Indeed, entertainment restaurants, which encourage clients to stay long and enjoy a show with their meals, have become magnets for tours. Two examples are Medieval Times (with knights battling it out) and Wild Bill's (a Western-themed show).

Does the Dining Facility Have an Interesting Ambience?
Entertainment restaurants certainly provide a fun context for a meal. So, too, do "theme" restaurants, such as the Hard Rock Cafe, the Rainforest Café, and Planet Hollywood. An outdoor restaurant might be a wonderful option on a warm summer night. And a historic inn might help the group sense the tradition behind the destination they're visiting.

Is the Dining Facility Large Enough to Accommodate Groups?
Many fine restaurants simply aren't big enough or don't have sufficient staff to handle forty people at a time. Don't take chances just because you like the food at a smallish restaurant that assures you it can "squeeze your group in." Also, take into consideration the ease with which your driver will be able to drop off and pick up the group.

Does the Restaurant Have a Wide Variety of Foods?
"There's no accounting for taste," goes an old Roman proverb. Because food preferences vary widely, the more choices your clients have in what they eat, the more satisfied they'll feel about the tour in general. Just because you adore seafood and Captain Ahab's has the best in town doesn't mean that even a majority of your tour members will be pleased to go there. This is one more reason why tour operators frequent cafeterias and buffets: the wide selection, ease of ordering, speed of service, and reasonable prices all contribute to the ideal tour meal experience. For the same reason, breakfast buffets have become commonplace in hotels.

Keep in mind, too, that some of your tour members may have special dietary needs: vegetarians, Orthodox Jews, Moslems, and those on specially restricted diets (e.g., seniors on low-cholesterol regimens). The restaurant should be prepared to handle their requests—and not just with salads.

What Do Meals at the Restaurant Generally Cost?
Tours come in three general dining configurations. In the first, all meals are included in the price of the trip. (This is a feature of the **all-inclusive tour**, also known as the **all-expense tour**, in which the price paid covers just about every cost associated with group traveling.) In the second, no meals are included in the tour price. The third option, the most common, includes some meals (usually breakfast each day and a few lunches and dinners) as part of the tour package price; for all other meals, clients must pay out of their own pockets.

If you, the tour manager, must choose a restaurant for a meal that the company pays for (actually, of course, the client has paid for it), you'll have little choice in terms of price. The tour operator will tell you how much is budgeted for that particular meal. It's usually a reasonable figure. Then you'll have to find someplace that fits (including tax and tip). If the meal isn't prepaid, it's almost imperative that you find a very reasonable restaurant. The clients are, after all, captives of your itinerary. Some will certainly balk at an overly expensive choice.

Will the Restaurant Even Consider Taking Groups?
Some dining facilities are so busy or exclusive that they reject tour groups. Others dread the number of orders that will flood into the kitchen. Don't waste your time trying to talk such restaurants into serving your group (unless, of course, you're in the wonderful situation in which your group's arrival at an off hour, such as 5 P.M., appeals to them). At the other extreme, some dining facilities seem to exist only to cater to group travelers. Be wary of such restaurants. Some do a fine job, but others take groups too much for granted and treat them in a bored, apathetic manner. A restaurant that caters to a mix of groups and regular customers is ideal.

Finding the Right Restaurant

Finding the right restaurant is no easy matter. Restaurant guidebooks rarely help—they're not geared to group considerations. Because tour companies find it difficult to plan dining in a distant destination, they must count on the recommendations of field representatives, such as tour managers, local guides, convention and tourist bureaus, or ground operators. If you, as escort, have been assigned the task of choosing a restaurant, don't fall into the easy trap of deciding to go where every other tour goes. Instead, ask locals where they would eat. Make sure, however, that they understand a tour's dining requirements. You may want to scout out area restaurants in your spare moments.

Negotiating the Meal

Negotiating with a restaurant is a process that must be handled carefully. If it's a sit-down restaurant, try to get full-menu choice for your clients, or a **tour menu** with at least three entree choices. There's nothing more irritating to tour participants than sitting down to a scrambled eggs-only breakfast or a chicken-only lunch. (Of course, it's a lot easier on the chef.) If the meal is included as part of the tour price, try to negotiate a set price that includes everything—all courses of the meal, beverage, tax, and tip. Remember that full-menu choice means different prices for each client and you'll have to estimate an average cost. Keep in mind that groups eat most heartily at a tour's beginning and less so at its end. (As their clothes get tighter, they begin to realize they may be eating too well. . .) Check to see whether the restaurant, in return for volume business, will give you a special price for meals or perhaps free desserts or beverages. Ask if escort and driver will receive free meals. (One complimentary meal per group is accepted practice.)

Breakfast calls for special conditions. In most cases clients will have their breakfast in the hotel. Hotel executives sometimes prefer that tour members arrive all at once, that the meal be served in a function room, and that one breakfast combination be served (for example, scrambled eggs, sausage, and rolls). This set-up is to be avoided if possible, unless it's for a first-day orientation breakfast. It's much better for the clients to be able to have breakfast in the regular coffee shop, at a time of their individual choosing (everyone wakes up at a different time), with full-menu choice or, preferably, from a buffet. They may charge the meal to their room number or identify themselves as tour members to the cashier, who will then transfer the costs to a master billing.

Note that breakfast rituals vary from culture to culture: Americans and the British like a hearty breakfast; many Europeans prefer a **continental breakfast** of coffee and rolls; the Chinese like porridge and dumplings. See if the hotel can adjust the menu to your group's tastes; if not, prepare the group for a new breakfast experience.

The Meal Itself

Before dining, clients need certain questions answered: What kind of food can they expect? Is the meal price incorporated in the tour package? Is the tip included? (When the company pays, clients need not leave a tip—it's already factored in.) How should clients dress? Is liquor included in the price? (It usually isn't.) What is the scheduled time for leaving the restaurant? Where are the restrooms? (Remind them to use the restrooms before leaving the restaurant.) All of these questions should be answered before you enter the restaurant. Make sure to reconfirm the meal and the number of clients with the dining facility; restaurants too frequently forget that a scheduled group is to arrive.

Once you arrive with your group, enter the restaurant first—keep your clients outside or on the motor-

Fine meals are an important ingredient in the tour experience.
Courtesy of the National Tour Association

coach while you go in and make sure that enough tables are ready. If they're not, you may have to keep your group occupied for a little while. When the tables are ready, go into the restaurant first. Your driver will assist in disembarking passengers. Help the hostess or maitre d' with seating.

Seating is a delicate matter. In some cases, tour operators or restaurants prefer that groups, for efficient service, be seated at large tables. This works well for the groups, too, since it helps them get to know one another. On the other hand, many clients look forward to dining as a time to be apart from the group.

If your group is to be seated at smaller tables, you must be sensitive to the restaurant's need to not give away all its tables. It must accommodate its regular customers as well. Given the choice, your group will want to be seated mostly by twos—especially in the early part of the tour when few members know one another. To do this, the maitre d' would have to give away all the smaller tables or seat one couple per table-for-four. The impact of the tour on the restaurant's seating capacity would be significant and unfair.

One solution is to suggest pairings of people likely to enjoy one another's company. You can do this as couples arrive at the restaurant's entrance. Do the same for singles and triples. You might even mention the problem at the very beginning of the tour so people can begin pairing up on their own. Within a few days, new friends will be made and the problem will solve itself. If you suggest a pairing that doesn't work, you'll hear about it quickly and avoid that particular seating combination in the future.

Once everyone is seated and you've ordered your meal, circulate among your passengers to make small talk. When you return to your seat, you'll experience an interesting phenomenon: all eyes will be on what you ordered ("Maybe I should have had what the escort is having . . ."), when you are served ("Why hasn't my order arrived yet?"), and, especially when you finish ("I'd better hurry; the escort's already done."). If the group is being served slowly, make a special effort to look unhurried. Otherwise, some of them will become anxious.

Do *not* ask clients how their meal was. Even the best restaurant dissatisfies a customer now and then. A single complaint, overheard, can convince otherwise satisfied clients that their meal wasn't all that great after all. When you finally get up to leave (which will set off a wave of clients who also decide it's time to get up), don't forget to give a healthy tip to the waiter or waitress even if your meal is complimentary.

Additional Dining Considerations

Below are a few miscellaneous remarks on dining.

Consider Jet Lag and Its Effect on Appetites. If your group has traveled over many time zones, you can expect, for the first few days, that they may feel hungry at odd hours. For example, clients who have gone from Portland, Oregon, to Miami, Florida, will probably feel like having their breakfast at 10 A.M., lunch at 3 P.M., and dinner at 9 P.M. You can actually profit from this, since scheduling meals at odd hours, at least until your passengers' biological clocks readjust, permits you to get into restaurants at times when they're the least busy.

Sometimes a Tour Itinerary Allows Free Time to Clients, During Which They Dine on Their Own. A printed list of convenient, recommended restaurants—prepared by you, by the tour operator, or by a tourist bureau—will be helpful and appreciated at such times. If a list isn't available, give the information orally.

Tour Groups Are Notorious in the Restaurant Industry for Their High Frequency of "No Shows." If the tour operator reserves a meal, it should inform the restaurant when a tour has been canceled. If you, the tour manager, are in charge, it's your responsibility to indicate in advance to a restaurant when an upcoming tour has been canceled.

Occasionally a Tour Will Stop at a Place with Many Small Dining Alternatives. A shopping mall is a good example. Be sure to remind clients to fan out to all the restaurants. The tendency will be for the entire group to follow the first person off the motorcoach to the same eating place. One warning: it's almost impossible for travelers to resist the temptation to shop in a mall after eating. If you must use a shopping center for meals, assign an official amount of time for shopping and be very firm about the exact time you want them back to the coach. Above all, don't expect your clients to return from a mall restaurant directly to the motorcoach.

Rest Stops Often Must Be Taken Along Your Tour Route, Usually in Midmorning or Midafternoon. Typical is a stop at a roadside rest area, fast-food restaurant, or donut shop. Such breaks should last no more than thirty minutes—enough time to grab a quick cup of coffee or to use the restrooms.

In Certain Unusual Situations, Picnics or Box Lunches Are Necessary for a Tour Group. Since this is rarely gourmet dining, the tour conductor should do everything possible to turn the situation into an informal, fun experience. Foreign visitors, especially, like to pick up snacks for free-time eating. Stopping in an American supermarket is often a novel, enjoyable adventure for them.

Be Alert For Special Occasions. If you find out it's a client's birthday or anniversary, be sure to have the restaurant acknowledge it with a special dessert (some tour managers bring a box of candles with them on all trips) or by having the waiters sing for the tour member.

Attractions

Attractions—the points of interest that help attract tourists to a destination in the first place—are the sites around which tour companies shape their itineraries. Some, like Vatican City, are extensive and inspiring, requiring a full day's visit. Others, such as Kauai's Wet and Dry Caves, take only a few minutes of a tour's time. Some attractions are manmade, like the pyramids of Egypt or the temples of Kyoto. Others are natural wonders, like Alberta's ice fields, Iceland's geysers, or South America's Iguazu Falls. Many take on importance for the layers of culture and custom we impose on them: the Blarney Stone is hardly a natural wonder, but it's certainly a must because of the kissing tradition that goes along with it. Others are strongly dictated by the group's interests. A shopping tour, for example, must have plenty of malls, markets, factory outlets, and/or duty-free stores to please the clients.

Tour managers need to ask themselves the following about each attraction:

How Much Time Will My Group Need to Visit This Attraction? It's terribly unfair to shortchange tour members when it comes to time spent at an attraction. Indeed, attractions are what originally made them choose the tour. Conversely, too much time spent at one place may crowd out other important events in the itinerary. Be reasonable in assessing the length of stay needed at each site, and make clear the precise time and place the motorcoach will pick up the group.

Is This the Best Time to See the Attraction? Though you mustn't ever leave out something the itinerary promises (unless some emergency occurs), you can certainly consider moving things around to adjust for weather or other similar factors. It's wise, for instance, to get your group to the Tower of London

early in the morning when the waiting lines are still reasonable, though your itinerary may list an afternoon visit. Even light and temperature can be factors: the beauty and mystery of Australia's Ayers Rock are most imposing in the red rays of an outback sunset, whereas the grand ruins of Mexico's Chichen Itza are best visited in early morning, before the jungle's heat becomes oppressive.

Of course, don't change your group's visit time if a prearranged appointment was required. Many sites will turn you away if your group arrives at an unexpected hour.

Will You Be Obliged to Orient the Group to the Attraction? In many cases an on-site guide will be assigned to your group and will explain everything to your group members. You should still give a short introduction to the attraction just before arriving. It will help build the group's anticipation. For a vast attraction, like

A tour manager helps his clients enjoy a "hands-on" experience at the Monterey Bay Aquarium.
Courtesy of the National Tour Association

What do people on tour shop for? When asked in a *Consumer Reports* poll, travelers responded this way:

Local handicrafts	61%
Souvenirs	37%
Clothing for self	35%
Clothing for others	29%
Art	24%
Books	23%

San Diego's Sea World or Beijing's Imperial Palace, it will be necessary to give a thorough introduction and "game plan," perhaps augmented by maps, in order to orient the group to the site and to ensure that their time will be used efficiently. Indeed, in some cases you or the on-site guide should take the group through the site, holding an umbrella or flag up so they can see you, ahead of the group, at all times. (Sounds corny, but it works well to keep the group together.) This would be very appropriate in the Imperial Palace, with its rich cultural history, but not at Universal Studios or Disneyland, which are planned around events and rides. When visiting these attractions, group members prefer freedom of choice.

Is There an Admission Fee Involved? In almost all cases, if the attraction charges an admission fee, that cost is included in the tour price. Unless you've been given the tickets in advance, you must get off the coach ahead of your group and go to a special customer relations or group sales window to obtain tickets. The admission tickets may have been prearranged (in which case you probably have a voucher for the tickets), or you may have to pay for them by company check or credit card. Make sure to get the group discount price and to give the exact number of clients. Don't include yourself in the count. If you want to go in, the attraction will probably give you complimentary admission.

In certain situations, an attraction is a tour option and admission is not included in the tour price. This is often the case when the attraction is physically demanding or adventuresome (for example, a raft ride). In this situation, you'll do best to collect money on the coach, before arriving, from those who are interested. This approach is more efficient, you'll pay for everyone at once, and will ensure a group discount for each participant.

"Factory" tours are popular attractions on some itineraries. Here are some of the most famous:

Celestial Seasonings, Boulder, CO

Ethel M. Chocolates, Las Vegas, NV

Federal Bureau of Engraving & Printing, Washington, D.C.

Louisville Slugger Museum & Factory, Louisville, KY

Hershey's Chocolate World, Hershey, PA

Mardi Gras World, New Orleans, LA

World of Coca Cola, Atlanta, GA

Ben & Jerry's, Waterbury, VT

Crayola, Easton, PA

Corning Glass Center, Corning, NY

Goodyear World of Rubber, Akron, OH

Levi Strauss Museum, San Francisco, CA

Miscellaneous Suppliers

Airlines, cruise lines, hotels, motorcoach companies, railroads, restaurants, and attractions account for perhaps 95 percent of all tour suppliers. Some of the most creative tours, however, include very unusual activities: ballooning, barging, white-water raft trips, and the like. Those who supply these activities are usually willing to spend a lot of time and effort to help you integrate their product into your itinerary. It's usually worth it: offbeat travel components can bring uniqueness and drama to your offerings.

Summary

A supplier is a provider of a tour service. Cruises are relatively simple for tour managers to handle, though tour managers must work at staying in contact with group members and maintaining group cohesiveness. Rail travel, too, is easily managed, though a tour director must deal with the unusual sleeping accommodations, the potential for boredom, and a layout that does not promote group cohesiveness. Meals are a key tour activity. Dining locations must be well chosen, appropriate, efficient, pleasant, varied, and cost-effective. Tour conductors must make sure that groups have enough time to visit attractions, that the visit is at an appropriate time of day, that the group is oriented to the attractions if necessary, and that the admission charge is handled smoothly. Unusual tour components can bring uniqueness and drama to a tour.

■ ■ ■

QUESTIONS FOR DISCUSSION

1. Define the terms "supplier" and "attraction." Give three specific examples of each.

   Supplier:

   Attraction:

2. Give three possible reasons for the renewed popularity of cruises.

3. How can a tour manager remain visible to tour members on a cruise?

4. Define the following: stateroom, bow, stern, port, starboard, room steward, purser, and shore excursion.

5. List at least ten subjects a tour conductor must discuss during a cruise briefing.

6. Describe three possible sleeping arrangements on a train tour.

7. Discuss three factors that affect the psychology of tour train travel.

8. What are four considerations in selecting a dining facility for a group?

9. Why are cafeterias and buffets well suited to tour groups?

10. What are four questions tour directors should ask themselves about an attraction?

ACTIVITY 1

▼ This is an exercise in evaluating restaurants and their suitability for hosting tour groups. Select six sit-down restaurants. The first three (A, B, C) should be within a half mile of your school or training classroom; they need not be ideally suited for tours. The second three (D, E, F) should be those restaurants within ten miles of your school that you feel would be most appropriate for tours. Use the chart below to rate each restaurant, with 3 being the highest rating in each category and 0 the lowest.

RESTAURANT EVALUATION FORM

Excellent = 3 pts.; Very Good = 2 pts.; Fair = 1 pt.; Poor = 0 pts.

	Restaurant/Dining Facility	Location	Variety of Food	Price	Amount of Space	View	Ambience	Total Score
A	Name: Address:							
B	Name: Address:							
C	Name: Address:							
D	Name: Address:							
E	Name: Address:							
F	Name: Address:							

ACTIVITY 2

▼ Few areas in the United States are richer in attractions than central Florida. Using whatever sources you can find (for example, guidebooks, tourist maps, and the Internet), list the seven major attractions within a two and one-half hour drive of Orlando that you would have your groups visit for at least a half day. In the right-hand column, indicate how long (half day or full day) you would give your group at the attraction. Assume that your group is made up mostly of families, with parents in their thirties and forties and children under sixteen.

Attraction   **Time for Visit**

1.

2.

3.

4.

5.

6.

7.

■ ■ ■

ACTIVITY 3

To succeed, a tour manager must be very outgoing. Assess how much of a "people person" you are by doing the following exercise.

"If I had to choose between the following two options (A and B), in most cases and most of the time I would rather:"

	A	**B**
_____	1. Attend a sporting event	Watch it on TV
_____	2. Go to a party	Read a good book
_____	3. Visit with friends	Work on a hobby
_____	4. Watch a team sport like football	Watch an individual sport like gymnastics
_____	5. Work with a committee of people	Work on a project myself
_____	6. Go shopping with family or friends	Shop on my own
_____	7. Take a cruise vacation	Get away from it all on a near-deserted island
_____	8. Play cards with friends	Work on a jigsaw puzzle
_____	9. Attend a "networking" business function	Read a useful newsletter
_____	10. Give a great office party	Master a new piece of office equipment
_____	11. Be a therapist	Be an author
_____	12. Take aerobics classes	Take long walks alone
_____	13. Play charades	Play computer games
_____	14. Be a talk-show host	Be a sculptor
_____	15. Talk on the phone	Do some gardening
_____	16. Attend a convention	Watch a series of motivational tapes
_____	17. Carpool	Drive to work alone
_____	18. Take my lunch break with fellow workers	Have lunch quietly alone
_____	19. Serve on a hiring committee	Reorganize my files
_____	20. Call a person and thank them directly for a favor	Send a written thank you note or e-mail to them

Total As _____ Total Bs _____

Your instructor or trainer will help you assess your "gregariousness quotient" from your answers to the above choices.

■ ■ ■

PROFILE

These days, the majority of tour conductors come from other endeavors. For many, tour management is a second or even third career. This was the case with Linda Cunningham, who for fifteen years had worked as a nurse. "I guess I was going through a mid-life crisis," she admits. "I felt I was getting burned out and needed to do something different with the second half of my life."

Nursing requires people skills and so does travel. "Dealing with people, helping solve their needs has always been a joy to me," explains Linda. "I wanted to find a new field where I could provide the same things I had provided in nursing: comfort and happiness. Travel seemed to be a promising and exciting option. I would be doing the very same thing for people, but in a different context."

Linda first signed up with a $495, "You too can be a travel agent" company, the kind that the industry calls a "card mill." "I soon found out that it was mostly a supplier of travel agent ID cards that supposedly provided travel perks. It wasn't about careers. I wanted a career. The perks could come later." She fortunately found out about a travel school near her home. "I took my first course," she explains, "and I knew this was the real thing."

At first Linda didn't know what sector of the travel business would best profit from her skills. After taking several courses, she narrowed her interests to two areas: cruises and groups. She quickly realized that the two could be merged. "My husband thought I was crazy to go into this, that there was no money in the travel business, but I was hooked."

Linda quickly proved to herself and to everyone else that there was indeed money in putting together cruise groups. She focused her efforts on people who had never been on a cruise. "One of the reasons people don't cruise," says Linda, "is that they're worried about committing to an entirely new experience. But they feel 'safer' as part of a group of other people who, like them, are taking a 'chance' on a new travel experience." Her first effort was an immediate success: sixty people signed up for a three-day Baja cruise. "That motivated me to learn even more about promoting cruises," states Linda. "I began to attend industry seminars and to read everything I could get my hands on."

Since then, Linda has refined her group-making skills. She convinced a church group of 170 to cruise and made their minister her "pied piper." She currently is working an even more novel concept: a cruise for twins. "A local radio announcer is a twin and she's helping me promote the sailing," explains Linda. "Those radio promos are a great way to spread the word on this unusual group departure."

Of course, Linda escorts every cruise group herself. "It's so easy to manage a group cruise departure," she says. "The staff onboard and the structure of a cruise departure make my task simple. The unexpected rarely happens and when it does, there are plenty of people to help me. Plus, it's so fantastic to see a first-time cruiser when they first set foot on a ship. They're awed by the ship's size and food. It helps me relive that first time I went on a cruise."

Expecting the Unexpected

Chapter Objectives

After reading this chapter, you should be able to:

▼ List six general strategies for dealing with unexpected challenges.

▼ Identify two types of client mishaps that can often be avoided.

▼ Explain the exact steps to take when a client loses money or valuables.

▼ Discuss the special needs of the physically challenged.

▼ Outline procedures for dealing with lost or damaged luggage, flight delays or cancellations, illness and accidents, client deaths, and hotel fires.

"NO MA'AM, GODZILLA WAS JUST A MYTH."

Sometimes a tour attracts people *because* of the unexpected. These are called **mystery tours**. Mystery tours are those in which the destination and itinerary are kept secret to the client until they join the tour. Indeed, they find out about the tour's features as the tour unfolds, often not knowing what's next from day to day.

Mystery tours often go to places that are hard to sell (e.g., ones that the public doesn't yet know well), but which have much to offer. Tour operators usually sell them during shoulder or low seasons, so that the prices can be low and the value high. (Purchasers of mystery tours are willing to "gamble" on an unknown itinerary only if the price is low.) Mystery tours especially appeal to the most loyal of a tour company's customers. They trust the company to provide an interesting travel experience, even in the absence of details about it. (Tour operators often do give at least a few hints in their promotion of a mystery tour to ensure that the appropriate type of client will be attracted to it.)

Tours are born, not made. No matter how much planning the company puts into a tour, things like weather, the group's personality, and, especially, an array of unexpected, unpredictable incidents will reshape the tour into its own unique form. No two tours are ever exactly alike. Both tour managers and passengers often remark that what they remember best about a tour are its unplanned occurrences.

Some of these unexpected events are thoroughly delightful, such as catching a once-a-year festival, crossing paths with a celebrity, or seeing some rarely visited but fascinating corner of a city that wasn't on the itinerary. However, not all surprises are wonderful. Every now and then something occurs that could potentially disrupt a tour's smooth flow. Tour conductors are at their very best when they, in effect, turn lemons into lemonade. This chapter will equip you with specific strategies that can help you cope with even the most formidable challenges.

Escorts should view other resource people, such as these theme park security guards, as allies.

Guiding Principles

There's a fine line between a tour de force and a tour de farce. A few general principles will help you stay on the safe side of that line by enabling you to deal with the unexpected in an effective and gracious manner.

Use Common Sense

Common sense is perhaps the most important thing an escort can have. Yet when it comes to common sense, some of us are more common than others. An escort really needs an *uncommon* sense of how to quickly assess a situation, to look at it from all sides, and to come up with a logical solution. Most importantly, a well-informed tour manager should be confident of his or her ability to clearly see the correct path in any challenging situation and take it with little or no hesitation.

Stay Calm

Panic is infectious and doubly so if it passes from a tour manager to the group. You must always seem to be in control, even if fear or confusion is simmering within you. No one deals with the unexpected with complete calm, but good leaders always *appear* to be doing so. Furthermore, outward composure has a way of moving within, reinforcing your own presence of mind and helping you make the right decisions.

Consult Your Company

If you have even a modest amount of time to deal with a problem, you should always contact your immediate superior at the home company. Tour operators have dealt many times with situations that you've never encountered before; they may have a premapped strategy for you to deploy. Furthermore, contacting the company helps absolve you of ultimate responsibility. No one, then, can accuse you of unilaterally going out on a limb that broke off.

Many tour operators provide escorts with what is called a **tour manual**. This book is a compendium of facts about the company, its rules and regulations, and, most importantly, official company procedures for dealing with accidents, sickness, receptive operator mistakes, and other unexpected occurrences. Keep the tour manual with you at all times, and always consult it when faced with an emergency.

Use Other Resource People As Allies

A common weakness of tour managers is to feel that they can rely on no one but themselves. You should remember that you're not alone. Motorcoach operators, airline personnel, hotel executives, restaurant managers, and local law enforcement officials are trained to assist you in specialized situations.

Tour passengers, too, can serve as resource persons. In an emergency you can often turn to clients on your tour who have medical training—perhaps a nurse or firefighter on vacation. In early tour conversations, casually determine who these people are, and turn to them if the need arises. Remember, too, that in a crisis, individuals in a group often band together for the common good. Be alert for this and tap into it.

If you're on an international tour, you may need the help of consular officials. What can your consulate (or your client's consulate) do for you? First, consuls will advise on legal aid. They won't pay your client's fees, but they will explain local laws, help find an attorney, and do what they can to smooth things out with local officials. Second, consuls will provide temporary replacements for lost or stolen passports. Third, they'll help unravel money problems. If a client runs out of funds or has a wallet stolen, the consul will explain how to have money transferred from the home country. Consular representatives also can facilitate the replacement of lost traveler's checks. Finally, consuls will find a client a local doctor, explain what the client's insurance (or a national health plan) covers, and report illness to family or friends back home. If a client dies,

they'll expedite arrangements for the transportation of the deceased's body.

Consuls will not deal with hotel disputes, lost luggage, lost airline tickets, or other such problems, which a tour manager should direct to specialized personnel.

Document Any Unusual Occurrence

In this age of persistent litigation, it's essential for you to document anything uncustomary that happens on a tour. Tour operators provide escorts with forms for this purpose. Fill out a form as soon after the event as possible. Get the names and addresses of witnesses. If relevant, find out if the client has travel insurance. Be sure to turn in the paperwork immediately at the tour's end.

Head Off Problems Before They Occur

The best way to deal with a messy predicament is to not let it happen in the first place. Of course, a tour manager must expect the unexpected. But many headaches can be avoided through a little preventive medicine and foresight. Firmness in the face of difficult clients, for instance, serves as an effective barricade against many potential nuisances. Making all information very clear to clients (and repeating it often) helps, too, in keeping a tour operating smoothly. For example, if you fail to mention where breakfast will be the next morning or if you forget to announce the next departure time, you're sure to create confusion and complications.

You must also be somewhat cynical about things happening as they should. Reconfirming every scheduled appointment is a wise strategy. So, too, is buying your own microphone and bringing it with you—you never know when the one on the motorcoach will be defective. And never be without maps. A closed freeway exit, for instance, can create a delay if you don't know which new route to take. So take Murphy's Law to heart, and remember that Murphy may have been an optimist.

How to Help Clients Avoid Problems

Two general types of mishaps can spoil your client's vacation experience: theft and sickness. Yet both can often be averted if a tour member takes certain precautions. As the tour manager, it's your duty to inform your group about how they may avoid both problems.

Money Matters

In many parts of the world, preying on vacationers has become a sinister art form. The most blatant example is pickpocketing. In some places, a thief can strip a man of his wallet with the skill and speed of a magician. In much of southern Europe, youngsters on mopeds can seize purses from strolling women without even slowing down. In Southeast Asia, luggage is pilfered all the time.

What can a person do? First, travelers should never carry money in a predictable place. A wallet is better kept in a vest pocket and cash in a money belt; a purse should contain only nonvaluable essentials. Some male tour managers even carry a "decoy" wallet in the obvious back pocket. If that escort becomes a target for pickpocketing, the thief gets an empty old wallet. The "real" one is elsewhere.

Second, valuables shouldn't be left in a hotel room. Instead, they ought to be placed in a hotel security box or safe. (Some hotels equip each room with a small safe.) Third, travelers must avoid dubious neighborhoods and should be alert to anyone who bumps into them or intentionally crowds them. Even little children can be well-trained pickpockets. Such precautions apply to tour leaders and clients alike. As a tour manager, you should not allow group luggage to leave your sight (or that of the driver or hotel personnel) for very long, if at all.

Tour directors also have an obligation to steer tour members away from scams. Overpriced souvenir shops, worthless attractions, black-market money changers, stores that sell phony brand-name items, land development promotions, and the like dot many a vacation destination. They're actually a subtle form of thievery. So, too, are many "bargains." Often clients end up paying more for articles in a Hong Kong shop or a Mexican mercado than they would have paid at home. True bargains do still exist, though. It's a tour conductor's job, with the help of step-on guides and other locals, to track them down and inform tour participants about the peculiar negotiating games that many cultures play on the way to a genuinely discounted price.

If you don't inform clients about the intricacies of **value added taxes (VAT)**, you'll in effect be helping others take money from their pockets. Started in Europe, the value added tax is a type of sales tax levied on merchandise and services. This tax can often be as high as 35 percent. Many travelers don't know that countries often permit travelers to get refunds of VAT paid on merchandise and even occasionally on lodging.

What's the procedure to receive a refund? In some countries you can have the VAT deducted immediately from the cost of a purchase if you have it shipped home from the store or delivered to the airport or railroad station for pickup at departure. In other countries, you must fill out a form at the store and have it processed at airport customs or at a special VAT refund desk. In some cases your refund will be issued on the spot at the airport. Usually, though, you'll have to mail the customs-stamped copy of the form back to the store while still in the country. The store will then send a refund check to your home. If the items were purchased with a credit card, the refund will be credited directly to your account (usually preferable, since it's simpler and less expensive—banks commonly charge high fees to cash foreign-denomination checks). In a few cases, you send the necessary form, with receipts attached, to a special government office, which then sends you a VAT refund check.

Remind your passengers of two things: First, many merchants will not tell your clients about VAT refund availability unless they ask. Second, some countries (or stores) won't refund the VAT unless purchases exceed a certain monetary amount.

Illness

Illness can't always be avoided. Certain precautions can be taken, however, to lessen the chance that you and your clients will suffer medical hardships during a journey. Chapter 4 discussed ways to ease the effects of jet lag. Below are other tips to help keep travelers in good health.

Food Poisoning Can Occur Anywhere. Food and water are generally safe in most of Europe, Australia, New Zealand, and Japan. In other countries, however, the situation isn't quite as good. Unfamiliar parasites and bacteria can contaminate water or food, causing diarrhea in visitors who haven't built up immunity to them. (Mexicans aptly call this condition "La Turista"; travelers label it "Montezuma's revenge.")

To ward off digestive distress, advise clients to drink only purified water. Counsel your clients to avoid brushing their teeth with tap water or eating uncooked vegetables. Eat only fresh fruits that are intact, with no breaks in the skin. Safe beverages include coffee and tea (if the water has been boiled), canned soft drinks, and bottled wine and beer. All meats and fish should be thoroughly cooked and, if possible, should be eaten hot. Be cautious about milk, custards, pastries, cold cuts, and salads. Freezing is no guarantee against bacteria, so try to avoid ice cubes in your drinks.

Many Cosmetics, Perfumes, and Medications Increase the Possibility of Serious Sunburn. Tour groups that visit sun resorts should try to avoid the mid-day sun, both to avoid burns and to reduce the chances of heatstroke.

Medication Should Never Be Removed from Its Original Container. Customs officials may confiscate anything that doesn't come in a labeled container. Of course, if tour members brought pills in pill boxes, it's too late to do anything about it. But you can at least prepare them to do some quick explaining or repack before reaching customs.

Insect Repellents Are Important in the Tropics. This is especially significant, since some mosquitoes carry diseases. Urge your clients to buy repellent if they didn't bring any along.

When Problems Do Occur

An ounce of prevention may be worth a pound of cure, but when a group has a problem, it's time for the tour manager to come up with a well-guided solution. The following is a general review of what you should probably do if a common tour dilemma arises. Remember that your tour company may have firm, precise steps that you *must* take in certain situations. And don't forget that by rising to a challenge, you prove your true professionalism as a tour leader.

Theft and Losses

No greater nightmare can be imagined: someone steals your wallet or purse and with it you lose your credit cards, driver's license, passport, cash, traveler's checks, and all the other things that are necessary when you're away from home. If this happens to one of your tour members, you must quickly show that your knowledge can turn such a calamity into a tolerable (though still major) inconvenience. Each item stolen or lost must be dealt with differently.

Cash. Money stolen is money gone. If the client still has credit cards and/or a checkbook, he or she may be able to get a cash advance from an automated teller machine, a bank, or the hotel. If cards and checks were also stolen, your client can have family or friends wire new funds, if needed. In this situation, their consulate, Western Union, or American Express can facilitate the transfer, which usually takes twenty-four hours. You may need to advance a little company or personal money to help out in the meantime—probably the only situation in which lending money to a passenger is justified.

Credit Cards. A person who loses a credit card usually is liable only up to $50 for fraudulent use. But you must have your client call the issuing institution as soon as possible. (Finding the number to call can present quite a problem, unfortunately.) If the passenger belongs to a credit card registry such as Credit Card Sentinel, one call will do for all cards. If not, the client must contact each individual issuing institution. Certain credit card companies have local offices that can issue a temporary card within a few hours. Most companies, though, will not be able to get your tour member a new card until he or she arrives home.

Traveler's Checks. Help your client contact the issuing company immediately. Many operate round-the-clock refund centers that can be reached by telephone. If the client has kept the purchase receipt with serial numbers separate from the checks (as the issuing company's directions advised), the company's nearest

In an emergency, tour members can have money wired to them from home.
Courtesy of Western Union Company

refund location may be able to replace some or all of the checks on the spot. If the serial numbers have been lost, it may take up to a few days to trace down the original purchase. These refund locations can also help in contacting credit card companies.

Passport. Loss or theft of passports occurs more often than you might think. According to the U.S. State Department, each year one in every two thousand United States tourists loses his or her passport. To replace a stolen passport, a client must report the theft to local police (a useful procedure for *all* stolen valuables) and then go to the issuing country's embassy or consulate. The consular officer will request a copy of the police report, ask for proof of citizenship or at least some form of identification, and require that new passport photos be taken. If it's a Saturday or Sunday, the consular office will probably be closed—the client will have to wait until Monday. You should, nonetheless, at least leave a message about the lost documents with the consulate's or embassy's answering service.

What if all identifying documents have been lost? Then the consular officials will contact the home country to verify the client's identity. They may trust the traveler and issue a passport before receiving an answer. But it's more likely that there will be a delay of hours or even a day or two. You may need to arrange separate lodging and traveling plans for your client, who at this point will be obliged to leave the tour.

Driver's License. On a domestic tour your client may need a driver's license to cash checks. Instruct the passenger to call the Department of Motor Vehicles in the issuing state or province. The DMV may then send a telegram verifying that the person holds a valid license or may express mail a temporary license. You can also have the local police contact the home DMV on your client's behalf. In either case, though, a temporary license usually won't go far in serving as identification. You may need to request that the hotel manager authorize limited check-cashing privileges for your client at the hotel.

Airline Tickets. Generally, airline tickets aren't lost or stolen but misplaced. They turn up later, deep in a purse, between shirts in a piece of luggage, or in some unexpected place. But that's no consolation if the client discovers the loss at the airport, just before departure. When a ticket is lost, the airline usually has the passenger fill out a Lost Ticket Refund application. It then usually requires the client to buy a new, *full-fare* ticket (often via credit card or check). If the ticket turns up

later or if it isn't used by someone else within a certain period of time, say, 60 days, the airline will refund the cost of the new ticket. If it has been used by someone else, then the passenger must report it to his or her insurance company (or credit card firm, if the original ticket or tour was charged) to receive reimbursement.

Miscellaneous Valuables. With your help, the client should report the loss of personal items to local police. Remind your tour member that homeowner's or renter's insurance often covers the theft of items away from home. If the items were stolen from a hotel room, the hotel may refuse to reimburse, since, in general, it's not legally liable. Press the issue for the client, though. To maintain good will, enhance its public image, and avoid litigation, a hotel is often willing to compromise and offer the client some compensation.

Company's Valuables. Since they're professionals, tour managers aren't expected to lose briefcases, company credit cards, vouchers, tickets, and similar items. No one is perfect, though. If such a catastrophe happens to you, follow the above procedures and contact your company immediately. To avoid such a problem in the first place, put all company valuables in a hotel safe when they're not in use. If you must carry certain essential items with you in a briefcase, consider buying a device that sounds an alarm when the briefcase is more than twenty feet from you. (This handy item, which can be purchased in certain electronics or travel supply stores, was discussed in Chapter 3.)

Luggage Problems

Previous chapters have explained how to avoid losing baggage and what to do if a piece of luggage disappears at a hotel or an airport. Be aware that if a tour operator concludes that a suitcase has been lost through escort negligence, it will often deduct the cost of retrieving the baggage from the escort's pay.

What if a suitcase is damaged? On behalf of the client, the tour manager must report the damage to the hotel, airline, ship, or train authorities responsible for dealing with any negligent handling that may have occurred. Then you must fill out a damaged property form, which your tour company has probably supplied. (See Figure 8–1 for an example.) Check to see if the client has luggage insurance. Above all, make absolutely no promises to the tour participant. It's completely up to the supplier and tour operator to determine whether compensation or repair is in order and who will pay for it.

```
┌─────────────────────────────────────────────────────────────┐
│  DAMAGED PROPERTY REPORT                                      │
│                                                               │
│  ESCORT FILLING OUT THIS FORM: _____  │
│  CLIENT'S NAME: _____  │
│  CLIENT'S ADDRESS _____   │
│         _____  │
│  CLIENT'S PHONE NUMBER: ( _____ ) _____   │
│  TOUR AND DEPARTURE DATE: _____   │
│                                                               │
│  Describe item damaged:                                       │
│  _____ │
│  _____ │
│  Describe nature of damage:                                   │
│  _____ │
│  _____ │
│  Describe circumstances that caused damage:                   │
│  _____ │
│  _____ │
│  Describe how and when you first discovered the damage:       │
│  _____ │
│  _____ │
│                                                               │
│  Answer the following:                                        │
│  Did you, on the first day of the tour, notice that the item was │
│  NOT worn or damaged?                          ☐Yes    ☐No    │
│  Did you, on the first day of the tour, notice that the item  │
│  WAS worn or damaged?                          ☐Yes    ☐No    │
│  If so, did you notify the client?             ☐Yes    ☐No    │
│  Did you ask the client if he or she had insurance that might │
│  cover the damage?                             ☐Yes    ☐No    │
│                                                               │
│  Nature of insurance: ☐ Homeowner's ☐ Traveler's ☐ Credit Card ☐ Other │
│  Name of insuring company: _____   │
│  Other comments: _____   │
│  _____ │
│                                                               │
│              Copyright © Delmar Publishers                    │
└─────────────────────────────────────────────────────────────┘
```

Figure 8–1   **Sample damaged property report**

On the tour's first day, tour managers should note any luggage that is damaged or could easily be damaged during the course of the trip. This will help determine liability if damage is reported at a later time.

Transportation Delays and Cancellations

Humorist Shelley Berman expressed it quite well: "The sooner you're there, the sooner you'll find out how long you'll be delayed." Delayed or canceled flights have become an all-too-common feature of the world's air traffic system. Weather, aircraft seat overbooking, late-arriving flight crews, mechanical problems, overburdened traffic controllers—all can change your group's flight plan. Calmness with your clients, patience in the face of factors that can't be controlled, and knowledge of your passengers' rights are your best weapons against the traumas of delays and cancellations.

What should you do if your flight is delayed? Consider the following:

If the Posted Departure Time for Your Flight Hasn't Changed, Keep Your Clients at the Gate.
In such a situation, air traffic control, connecting flights, or minor mechanical problems are probably holding up your flight. Once everything is ready, boarding will occur rapidly. Don't take literally any announcement

that "we probably won't be leaving for an hour at least." The delay could be called off at any moment.

If the Posted Departure Time Has Been Changed, Determine What the Gate Attendants Are Willing to Do for Your Group.

Each air carrier has its own protocol in such a situation. Remember that a barrage of questions and complaints has probably plunged the airline personnel you're dealing with into a bad mood. Be sympathetic, but act with the expectation that your large passenger group deserves special attention. For example, the airline may provide a private group reception room in which your clients can relax. It may also offer meal vouchers. Carry on these negotiations away from the group. If no special arrangements are forthcoming, it's probably not worth pressing the issue; increasingly, airlines are instructing personnel that delays warrant no special services for anyone.

Explain the Nature of the Delay to Your Passengers and Warn Them Not to Wander Too Far.

It's important that your clients know that you and the airline are doing everything possible for them. Show your concern, but remain composed and positive. (This will help defuse passenger frustration.) Assure them that you'll phone ahead to alert tour suppliers "downstream." Ask them to limit themselves to, say, the cafeteria, the duty-free stores, and the gate waiting area. This will enable you to easily round up stragglers who don't return to the gate for the new departure time. Never depend on the airport public address system to alert them about departure changes—airport P.A.s are notoriously easy to ignore.

What if the delay turns into an outright flight cancellation? The air carrier must try to find space for your group on an alternative flight (including those of other airlines). If a next-day flight is the only option, it may offer rooms, meals, transfer costs, and little toiletry kits. However, an airline may also offer nothing. Usually, it is company, not government, policy that determines what can be offered. In this case you must be very assertive: ask for a supervisor and make it clear that you expect the airline to absorb all delay costs. If it refuses, call your company immediately to find out what it can do to pressure the airline or whether it's willing to pick up the costs.

Physically Challenged Passengers

The Americans with Disabilities Act requires businesses to make reasonable efforts to accommodate both disabled customers and employees. It may take years to completely sort out its legal implications for the

Most hotels in the United States are sensitive to the needs of the physically challenged guest. *Courtesy of Marriott International*

tour industry. At the very least, it ensures that the physically (and mentally) challenged can have access to the same travel experiences and career paths as do others. For example, motorcoaches (or at least the newer ones) have special entrances that can lift a wheelchair-bound client or tour manager directly into the vehicle.

Two situations are likely to occur in the course of conducting tours. You may have a client who needs special assistance and care. Your company will almost always know of the situation in advance and will have taken the steps necessary to prepare everything. The physically challenged person will also probably be accompanied by someone who understands, and may assist you with, their companion's special needs: building accessibility, seating requirements, and the like. Fortunately, the United States, Canada, and many other nations are highly sensitive to the needs of the physically challenged. Certain other countries will not be; it will be your duty to think ahead at each hotel, restaurant, attraction, and mode of transportation.

The second possible situation is that you may have a tour made up entirely of physically challenged persons. In fact, this is becoming one of the tour industry's most interesting niche markets. Special motorcoaches are used, all tour destinations and elements are intensely analyzed for suitability, and so on. Indeed, there are tour managers, some physically challenged themselves, who specialize in conducting such groups.

Illness and Accidents

Many people think that a tour, with its typically older passengers and its dependence on vehicles, is prey to all manner of accidents and medical emergencies. This is not true. Sickly people rarely take tours. And the most dangerous vehicle isn't a motorcoach or a plane but an automobile. Indeed, statistics show that trains and planes are ten times safer than cars, and motorcoaches are the safest of all: a bus fatality occurs only once in every two *billion* bus miles. (Injuries you may hear about that occur on buses almost always involve school buses, not touring motorcoaches.)

What if a medical emergency occurs? Ask whether anyone in the group has medical training. Apply your own medical knowledge (especially if you've had first-aid or CPR training) if there's no other choice. Contact local police if the situation is serious; they'll in turn summon a doctor or paramedic. (Do *not* use the motorcoach to transport the client to a medical facility unless there's no other choice.) Follow up by alerting your company, filling out a company accident/illness report (see Figure 8–2), and, if necessary, helping to set up separate arrangements for a client who is too ill to continue the tour (see Figure 8–3). Try to determine what portions of a tour will be refundable or can be changed (for example, the airline ticket). Again, make no promises and follow company procedure to the letter.

The motorcoach operator can be of enormous help when something goes wrong.
Courtesy of the National Tour Association

CLIENT ACCIDENT REPORT

ESCORT FILLING OUT THIS FORM: _____

TOUR AND DATE OF DEPARTURE: _____

CLIENT'S NAME: _____

CLIENT'S ADDRESS: _____

_____

CLIENT'S TELEPHONE NUMBER: (_____) _____

CLIENT'S INSURANCE COMPANY: _____

What is the nature of the claimed injury?

_____

_____

How did the accident and/or injury occur?

_____

_____

When did it occur?

_____

_____

How did you find out about it?

_____

_____

Did the client receive medical attention?   ☐ Yes   ☐ No

If yes, list the doctor and/or hospital, with address and telephone number.

_____

_____

What medical advice was given to the client?

_____

_____

If the client declines medical attention, please have the client sign the following:

"I do hereby decline the escort's offer to seek professional advice concerning my injury and/or illness."

Client's signature: _____ Date: _____Time: _____

Copyright © Delmar Publishers

Figure 8–2   **Sample client accident report**

Tour managers often wonder whether their actions in an emergency expose them to personal liability. Surely a tour director should neither diagnose an illness nor dispense medication of any sort. This must be left to a doctor. On the other hand, prudent action that a tour conductor takes in good faith is often protected by regional "Good Samaritan" laws. This statute from the state of Washington is typical: "Any person who, in good faith and not for compensation, renders emergency care at the scene of an emergency or who participates in transporting, not for compensation, therefrom an injured person or persons for emergency medical treatment shall not be liable for civil damages resulting from any act or omission in the rendering of such emergency care or in transporting such persons, other than acts or omissions constituting gross negligence or willful or wanton misconduct."

Death

No occurrence can be more disturbing—to tour manager and clients alike—than the death of a passenger. It happens rarely, but when it does, the tour conductor must take the following steps:

▼ Notify the local police immediately.

▼ Advise a consular official, if appropriate.

CLIENT CHANGE OF TOUR PLANS FORM

OBTAIN THE FOLLOWING INFORMATION FROM THOSE CLIENTS WHO

a. choose not to complete the tour
b. choose to extend their stay beyond tour's end
c. miss activities because of tardiness or illness/injury
d. are dismissed from the tour by the escort for inappropriate behavior

Client(s)	Missed Activities/ Destinations (with date)	Reason
1. Name _____	_____	_____
Street _____	_____	_____
City _____ State _____	_____	_____
Tel. no. (____)_____	_____	_____
2. Name _____	_____	_____
Street _____	_____	_____
City _____ State _____	_____	_____
Tel. no. (____) _____	_____	_____
3. Name _____	_____	_____
Street _____	_____	_____
City _____ State _____	_____	_____
Tel. no. (_____) _____	_____	_____
4. Name _____	_____	_____
Street _____	_____	_____
City _____ State _____	_____	_____
Tel. no. (_____) _____	_____	_____

Additional Comments: _____
_____
_____
_____
_____

Figure 8–3   **Sample client change of tour plans form**

▼ Remain with the deceased until police or consular reports have been completed and authorities have taken responsibility for the body. The tour may have to continue without you for a half day or so, under the leadership of the driver or the step-on guide. Make sure to be extra sensitive and sympathetic to the deceased's traveling companions.

▼ Call the tour company so it can inform the client's relatives and friends, and follow up with a letter of sympathy. (See Figure 8–4.)

▼ Do everything you can to comfort the rest of the group and get their minds back on the vacation.

Hotel Fires

Hotel fires occur very rarely. When they do happen, however, a firestorm of publicity sweeps through the media. Such publicity cannot help but put travelers on edge.

Many hotels and tour operators now give clients checklists of fire do's and don'ts. You may want to mention a few of these to a client group or to individuals who seem particularly nervous about the problem. Certainly as the tour manager, you should be well aware of these procedures.

▼ Make a mental map of hotel exits when you check into your room.

Dear

Our company wishes to extend its profoundest sympathies on the recent loss of your loved one. Such sad occurrences affect us all.

Our management wishes to reimburse you for your loved one's tour. Enclosed you will find a check for $

Again, please accept our condolences. Please feel free to contact us if we can be of assistance in any way.

With our deepest sympathy,

Figure 8–4   Example of a sympathy letter that would be sent to a deceased client's family

▼ Establish a set place (perhaps on the dresser or next to the lamp) for your room key or keycard.

▼ If there's a fire, do what you can to assist your tour members, unless such action would place you in inordinate jeopardy. Remember, firefighters are far more qualified to deal with a serious situation than you are.

▼ Before opening any door, feel it with the palm of your hand. If it's very hot, don't open it; stay in your room, for your exit path is probably blocked by fire or excessive heat.

▼ If the phone works, call for help for yourself and your group.

▼ Take exit stairways, not the elevator. Walk *down*, unless heavy smoke blocks your path. If this is the case, walk up to the roof.

▼ If the smoke is heavy, stay close to the floor where the air is breathable.

▼ Hang a bed sheet out the window to signal for help.

▼ Stuff wet towels and sheets in cracks around doors.

▼ Tie a wet towel around your nose and mouth.

▼ As a last resort, make the best exit possible. Above all, don't panic.

Most people assume that accidents occur with higher frequency on "adventure" tours, where the physical demands are greater. Diving, white-water rafting, and other such activities do have inherent dangers. Yet the general public may have a much "softer" idea of what an adventure tour might be. An ASTA poll revealed that the following places, most rather tame, are the most desirable sites for adventure travel:

▼ Yellowstone
▼ Alaska
▼ Florida
▼ Africa

▼ Costa Rica
▼ Colorado
▼ Mexico
▼ India

A Few Final Words

For you to anticipate every possible problem scenario would be a formidable, if not impossible, task. However, you'll soon learn that resourcefulness, sound judgment, and coolness of mind can tame just about any situation a tour manager is likely to encounter.

Summary

Unexpected occurrences continually reshape a tour. In dealing with challenging situations, a tour manager should rely on calm common sense, company advice, careful documentation, good preplanning, and confidence in other professionals. Physically challenged clients have become a small but important segment of the traveling public and are more easily accommodated on a tour than they once were. Theft and sickness are problems that can sometimes be averted by giving your clients good advice. Specific steps should be taken when cash, traveler's checks, credit cards, passports, driver's licenses, airline tickets, and valuables are lost. Particular strategies apply to lost or damaged luggage, transportation delays and cancellations, illness, accidents, client deaths, and fires.

■ ■ ■

QUESTIONS FOR DISCUSSION

1. What six principles should guide tour conductors in dealing with unexpected challenges?

2. What is a tour manual?

3. What are four problems with which consular officials can help you?

4. What is VAT? How can clients receive a refund when such a refund is available?

5. In countries where food or water may be contaminated, what must travelers do to avoid getting sick?

6. What must clients do if they lose their traveler's checks? Credit cards? Passports? Airline tickets?

7. What may you ask from airline officials if a flight has been delayed and the posted departure time has been changed? If the flight has been changed?

8. What steps must you take if a medical emergency occurs?

9. What steps must you take if a passenger passes away?

10. Give two precautionary habits hotel guests should develop that could come in handy in the event of a fire.

■ ■ ■

ACTIVITY 1

▼ Below are twelve events that occurred on real tours. For each case, write what you would have done. Remember, there's no one way to resolve each challenging situation.

CASE 1. You arrange a 6:45 A.M. wake-up call for your group. You yourself wake up at 7:15 A.M. and realize that there's been no wake-up call made to your room. On the schedule today is an 8:30 A.M. fifteen-minute transfer from the hotel to the airport, with a 10 A.M. domestic flight departure scheduled.

CASE 2. You're with your group at Orlando International Airport and are scheduled to leave for Chicago's O'Hare Airport at 11:30 A.M. At the gate, however, you're informed that the O'Hare controllers are holding your flight at Orlando and that you may be delayed as much as two hours. It's now noon and your travelers are hungry, but the 11:30 A.M. departure sign hasn't changed and the gate agent's story remains the same: a possible two-hour delay.

CASE 3. You've left Boston on the first leg of a seven-day motorcoach tour of Canada, destination Montreal. Fifty miles out, near Manchester, New Hampshire, passengers begin to scream, "The bus is crawling with roaches!"

CASE 4. It's October. You're escorting a Houston group of forty to New York City. You arrive at your Manhattan hotel, where you are informed that the World Series has gone to a seventh game. There hasn't been the expected guest check-out, and there aren't enough rooms for your tour.

CASE 5. You're guiding a summer motorcoach tour from San Diego to Yosemite. In the middle of the Mojave Desert at noon, the bus's air-conditioning breaks down. The coach has sealed windows—they don't open. You are hundreds of miles from any major city; immediate repairs are out of the question.

CASE 6. You're escorting forty-eight senior citizens on a motorcoach going from Jerusalem to Tel Aviv. You're halfway there. A passenger calls you over. Very calmly she tells you that Mildred, her traveling companion, who is seated beside her and appears to be sleeping next to the window, is dead. You feel Mildred's pulse; sure enough—she has no pulse. The person who called you over is fairly sure Mildred has been dead for a half hour at least.

CASE 7. A tour participant has an epileptic seizure on a plane. The next day the same client has another seizure on the motorcoach. What would you do in each case?

CASE 8. You arrive at a restaurant in Singapore. You tell your clients what the company has informed you: that the group will have full-menu choice and that the meal is included in the tour's cost. The restaurant manager, however, claims that the arrangement was that everyone was to be served chicken.

CASE 9. You're about to arrive at the last hotel on your fifteen-day tour of South America. A couple on your tour inform you politely, but with some anger, that they've had nothing but bad rooms on your tour: a view of a wall when everyone else had a balcony overlooking the ocean; a room with only a fold-out couch bed; a room that was next to dinging elevators and the ice machine. What, they ask, can you do for them?

CASE 10. You're a woman tour manager on your first San Francisco-to-Los Angeles tour. You've done plenty of advance research in preparation. Your driver is a veteran on this route. Unfortunately, he wants to do most of the talking on the microphone, and you feel that this is undermining your own position of authority. When the microphone isn't in use, the driver tends to leave it in his lap in a very strategic place.

CASE 11. You've arrived at London's Heathrow Airport with a group of twenty-four tour members. It's Sunday, 8 A.M. Your flight was delayed about an hour; your expected arrival time was 7:15 A.M. The scheduled transfer bus and the representative of the ground operator are nowhere to be found. You have the name of the company's manager and her office telephone number. You call, but it's Sunday and no one answers. Apparently the office is closed.

CASE 12. Your group arrives at a 1,400-room hotel in Mexico City. You hand out the keys, then the bellhops deliver luggage to the rooms. An hour later a client in room 679 calls you—her luggage has not been delivered. You check with the bell captain; his own checklist shows that every piece, including the "missing" one, was delivered.

■ ■ ■

PROFILE

Her name is Latvian, her upbringing is Brazilian, she lives in the United States and she sets up tours for German, Dutch, and French clients. How much more international can you be? "I guess I am pretty international," admits Gerseli Strelniek, "but I think that my international perspective really helps in planning tours."

Gerseli works for the Special Groups Department of Allied Tours, one of the largest inbound operators in America. There she creates one-of-a-kind, customized tours for specialized groups that are coming from outside the United States.

Her interest in the industry goes all the way back to high school, where she took classes in travel, and through college, where she received a B.A. in Communications with a specialty in travel. Her first job was with a local receptive tour operator, where she earned a tour guide license. She detoured from travel, however, for a while, doing market research for the Pirelli Company.

"When I came to the United States," she explains, "I wanted to brush up on my original interest, so I took travel courses at West Los Angeles College. Plenty had changed in the business during my years at Pirelli. I did find, however, that much of what I learned at Pirelli was directly applicable to travel."

What's the secret of putting together a group tour? "The most important thing," argues Gerseli, "is to carefully probe the needs of that group, to discover what they have in mind. You also must intimately know your hotels, attractions, and other suppliers, so you can recommend the right tour components to each particular group. You must be very familiar with the places that we typically send groups to. In fact, whenever my husband and I go on a trip, I insist that I want to see as many hotels as possible. It's become an obsession for me. It drives my husband crazy. Finally, you have to pull it all together for a great price. Most of our clients are very price sensitive."

Gerseli feels that her multi-cultural background helps her to better shape tours to the needs of each client. "When I came to the U.S., things like exchange rates really confused me. Even concepts of time. For example, northern European groups tend to want their tour to be fully thought out and set way ahead of time. Hardly any changes happen after that. On the other hand, Brazilians, Japanese, and groups from the Mediterranean tend to make changes right up to the last minute. These are the kinds of things that you can learn and understand only through experience."

"Tour planning is a tough job," admits Gerseli, "the hours are long and the details are endless, but having the opportunity to share interesting places and things with visitors from abroad—well, there's nothing more exciting."

9

Creating a Tour

Chapter Objectives

After reading this chapter, you should be able to:

▼ Justify the need to know how tours are planned.

▼ Identify the prime sources for researching a destination.

▼ Describe the principles behind a successful tour itinerary.

▼ Cost out and price a typical tour.

▼ Explain the many ways through which tours may be promoted.

"DO YOU THINK THERE'S SOMETHING WE OVERLOOKED IN THE BROCHURE?"

I f your career goal is tour planning, promotion, or operations, an understanding of how tours are created is essential. But if you wish to be a tour conductor, can you just skip this chapter?

Not at all. A tour conductor, like any professional, should have a clear understanding of the intricate decision-making that so intimately affects his or her job. Many tour managers find that they occasionally must restructure a tour while it's in progress or recommend changes when it's over. An astute knowledge of the tour-planning process makes the task easier. Many tour directors move on to office positions, where such knowledge is essential. Finally, persons who create and lead their own tours have no choice: they must possess a close and keen familiarity with tour-making from start to finish.

We've already examined many components of tour planning in other chapters. Now let's look at the larger picture, while filling in some of the details that have yet to be covered.

Marketing a Tour

Planning out a tour is, in certain ways, a unique undertaking. In other ways, however, it's no different from designing a new car or creating a breakfast cereal. Universal principles guide the process—principles tied to the science of marketing.

Marketing is a much misunderstood enterprise. Most people would say that marketing is the same thing as selling, when in reality selling is only a small (though significant) component of marketing. Marketing also encompasses such activities as needs assessment, research, product development, pricing, promotion, and distribution. A good catchall definition would be this: **marketing** is the process of transferring a product from its producer to consumers. In this case, the product is a tour, the producer is the tour operator, and the consumer is the traveler.

Assessing the Demand

Food, shelter, and clothing—these are the traditional survival needs of society. Travel isn't a need; it's a desire, a want that's bought with "discretionary" income (the money left over after paying for essentials). According to marketing principles, when such desire is driven by money, a **demand** is created.

Today's demand for travel is so huge that many experts predict that travel and tourism will soon

become the world's largest industry. Traveling has gone from being a once-in-a-lifetime luxury to something the average person feels he or she ought to do on a regular basis, like exercising or mowing the lawn (though presumably it's more fun). And as Chapter 1 pointed out, a great number of vacation travelers take advantage of tour packages, in one form or another, to get to their destination.

The Demand for Tours

Assessing the demand for tours in order to tailor them to would-be travelers requires a knowledge of not only why people take tours, but also why they *don't*. An NTA marketing study found three main consumer objections to touring:

▼ *A dislike of buses.* To counter the image of touring as a long journey on a smelly, uncomfortable vehicle, tour companies stress that many tours today are intermodal, and that the plush motorcoaches used are a far cry from the spartan city buses with which the public is familiar.

▼ *A dislike of passive, regimental "herding."* One response to those who find the thought of structured travel thoroughly distasteful has been the development of independent, freelance tour packages. To counter resistance to touring, many companies have dropped the word "tours" from their names and replaced it with more positive and inclusive ones, such as "vacations" or "holidays." Other tour operators have redesigned some or all of their tours to provide plenty of "free time" and relax the stereotypic "herding" that has traditionally marked touring.

▼ *The fear that one won't fit in with other people on a tour.* Selling affinity tours or targeting a very specific kind of traveler (the cultural explorer or adventure seeker, for example) is a good way of conquering this kind of resistance in the marketplace.

Market Research

Corporations often spend millions of dollars to identify untapped markets, likely customers, and purchase patterns. A marketing expert would probably counsel a tour company to ask itself such questions as: Does my target group like to take the type of tours I intend to offer? What level of structuring are they likely to want on a tour? Are there tours I could offer that "anti-tour" consumers might take? What is my typical client's "preferred value level"? (In other words, how much luxury does the client want, and how much is he or she willing to pay?)

The answers to such questions are usually arrived at through sophisticated and expensive surveys, tests, and focus groups. Yet tour operators rarely have the resources for such studies. Furthermore, the travel inclinations of consumers change unpredictably. For this reason, many tour operators feel that conventional research is of dubious worth to them. They tend to agree with industrialist Bernard Loomis, who argues that, "The trouble with research is that it tells you what people were thinking about yesterday, not tomorrow. It's like driving a car using a rear-view mirror."

Instead, tour operators are inclined to take the following marketing shortcuts:

They Pick Up Quickly on Trends. Good tour planners, like skilled tour leaders, read newspapers and magazines and follow other media in order to detect any new tendency or useful idea that can be translated into a tour.

The past decade, for example, has seen a huge increase in ecotourism: the desire to experience, protect, and manage nature's resources. Such places as Costa Rica, Alaska and Botswana responded to this demand by facilitating visits to their most naturally dramatic regions. And a number of tour operators addressed this same phenomenon by creating tours that focused on ecology. They were quick to recognize and respond to an important trend.

They Tap the Successful Ideas of Other Companies. Many tour operators have prospered by noting a competitor's early success, then adapting or improving on the idea. In the jungle of travel marketing, the tour planner who succeeds is the one who is alert to every new rustle in the thicket, every new snap of a selling vine.

They Survey Their Own Tour Participants. How much time does it take for a tour manager to distribute a questionnaire on board a coach? Not much. That questionnaire can both help profile the company's typical client and test the attractiveness of potential new tours. (See Figure 9–1.) One limitation is that the sample is "biased": these are a company's regular clients, not those new ones it may wish to attract through an atypical tour.

They Experiment Through Trial and Error. Let's say representatives of the East Overshoe Chamber of Commerce visit the office of Acme Tours. There are plenty of attractions and fine lodging in our area, the representatives argue, and we're about to unleash a national promotional campaign. So why not schedule a series of tours to our region for the coming season?

What does Acme Tours have to lose by scheduling this new tour, announcing it in Acme's general brochure, and seeing if it sells? Perhaps the cost of a quarter page of printing in its brochure and allied advertising, and that's all. If the tour appeals to the marketplace, Acme has a hit. If not, not much has been lost. This approach is, in truth, the way most tour companies judge the saleability of new tours.

Planning the Tour

Surveying and testing, trial and error, and awareness of trends and the competition can all lead a tour company to design a certain tour. In marketing, this step is called product development. Throughout this research and development phase, a tour company is ever mindful of the client who will pay to take the tour. In other words, the product—the tour—must match its intended market. As Dan Dipert, president of Dan Dipert Tours of Arlington, Texas, explains: "Every customer has different needs to be identified. For example, clients in the older retiree group generally want security. They want to travel with a group from their home town on an escorted tour with everything included. They'll balk at a tour that requires them to travel alone even part of the way.

Dipert adds that age isn't the only factor—regional traits must also be considered. "Southwesterners are well-to-do," observes Dipert, "but very cautious about how they spend money. We therefore design our tours for economy. Where deluxe tours stay in five-star hotels, we use four-star ones. Where some tours have hidden extra costs, we include almost everything—even tips for the driver and guide."

Tour Research

Once the tour planner has settled on a destination, he or she must gather information that will guide the itinerary-designing process. Which modes of transportation serve the area? Which hotels should be selected? Which routes should be followed? What attractions are must-sees? How much will each tour component cost? An arsenal of research tools awaits to help this process along.

CLIENT SURVEY

Dear Client: Could you take a few moments to complete this survey? Your comments will help us to evaluate this tour and determine which changes might be worth considering. Thanks for your input. And we sincerely hope that you had a wonderful tour vacation.

TOUR: _____ DEPARTURE DATE: _____

TOUR ESCORT'S NAME: _____

Item (if applicable)	Excellent	Very Good	Good	Poor	Comments
Attractions visited	☐	☐	☐	☐	_____
Driver's courtesy	☐	☐	☐	☐	_____
Driver's skill	☐	☐	☐	☐	_____
Escort's courtesy	☐	☐	☐	☐	_____
Escort's knowledge	☐	☐	☐	☐	_____
Escort's personality	☐	☐	☐	☐	_____
Escort's speaking ability	☐	☐	☐	☐	_____
Flights	☐	☐	☐	☐	_____
Hotels	☐	☐	☐	☐	_____
Motorcoach condition	☐	☐	☐	☐	_____
Motorcoach ride	☐	☐	☐	☐	_____
Restaurants	☐	☐	☐	☐	_____
Ship	☐	☐	☐	☐	_____
Shopping time	☐	☐	☐	☐	_____
Sightseeing	☐	☐	☐	☐	_____
Train	☐	☐	☐	☐	_____
Other _____	☐	☐	☐	☐	_____

Please fill out the following. It will be kept confidential:

Your age _____ Your sex _____ Your yearly income $ _____

Yearly expense on vacation travel (one person) $ _____

Your profession _____

The most you can imagine yourself paying for a tour package $ _____

Married ☐   Single ☐   Divorced ☐   Widowed ☐

In your opinion, what is the ideal number of days a tour should have? _____

Where will you probably go on the next tour you take? _____

Copyright © Delmar Publishers

Figure 9–1   **Sample client survey form**

Standard Guidebooks. These detailed publications, intended for the general public, have a wealth of information that both an escort and a tour operator can tap. *Fodor's, Birnbaum's, Frommer's,* and *Fielding's* are all excellent all-purpose guidebook series. Access, Baedeker, Mobil, and Michelin all publish attractive and useful texts. The American Automobile Association makes its guidebooks available free of charge or at a minimal cost to AAA members.

Industry Publications. Tour operators and, for that matter, most travel agencies stock specialized industry texts that can be immensely useful in tour design. We've already covered hotel-specific resources in Chapter 5. Other texts that tour planners consult include:

▼ *The Internet.* It's one of the most powerful research resources ever devised. You can easily find out about destinations through the many Web sites of tourist bureaus, tour operators, attractions, and other relevant sites.

▼ *The Weissmann Travel Reports* and the *World Travel Guide* give detailed information on virtually every destination in the world. They are *the* industry reference tools on travel geography.

▼ *Selling Destinations: Geography for the Travel Professional,* by this book's author, gives a 550-page

Industry publications often provide information that is hard to find elsewhere.
Courtesy of Cahners Travel Group

overview of the most popular worldwide destinations for tours.

Brochures. Most travel-related offices stock sample brochures from many tour companies. They can be a rich source of comparative information.

Maps and Atlases. To plan out a tour itinerary, it's essential to have a clearly presented, detailed atlas. Atlases contain not only maps but also statistics on rainfall patterns, water temperatures, and other information that you may need to research and describe a destination. As with many reference texts, you can buy them at a bookstore or consult them at your local library. Road maps, too, can be useful in planning out a motorcoach tour's routing. Perhaps the most sophisticated road maps of all are Triptiks. **Triptiks** are compact, flip-page documents custom-made by AAA for each of its members' itineraries. If you're planning a tour, Triptiks can be most convenient.

Tourist Bureaus. Never underestimate the willingness of tourist and convention bureaus—on the city, regional, state, or national level—to provide information over the phone, through correspondence, or by sending publications. (These tourist promotional organizations are often referred to as **CVBs**—Convention and Visitors' Bureaus—or **DMOs**—Destination Marketing Organizations.) Chambers of commerce can also be very cooperative.

AAA offers a broad selection of resources for travel research.
Courtesy of American Automobile Association

Computer Programs. Several computer programs provide extensive information on popular destinations. CD-ROM interactive programs provide the most flexible and entertaining explorations of the world's attractions. Some map programs even give door-to-door directions.

Friends and Family Who Live at the Destination. Want a fresh perspective on a place? Call people you know who live there. The majority of their ideas may be inappropriate, since your friends don't necessarily understand the requisites for a tour. On the other hand, they may come up with a restaurant, attraction, or new hotel that no one has yet used for a tour.

Many tourist bureaus think in predictable and tired patterns. To break away from the beaten tour planning path, give serious attention to the suggestions of locals.

On-Site Visits. There's little doubt: to visit an intended tour destination is the best method of research possible. You meet personally with your suppliers, perhaps ferret out things your competition knows nothing about, and gain a feeling for the place that's fresh and alive. When you finally sit down to fashion your tour, you'll find that your planning has the kind of direct, vital energy that firsthand knowledge generates. (See Figure 9–2.)

ANALYZING A DESTINATION

DESTINATION: _____

CLIMATE (excellent? favorable? somewhat negative? definite weakness?):

Winter: _____   Summer: _____

Spring: _____   Fall: _____

KEY ATTRACTIONS:	Excellent	Good	Fair	Not Good
1. _____	☐	☐	☐	☐
2. _____	☐	☐	☐	☐
3. _____	☐	☐	☐	☐
4. _____	☐	☐	☐	☐
5. _____	☐	☐	☐	☐

HOTELS INSPECTED:				
1. _____	☐	☐	☐	☐
2. _____	☐	☐	☐	☐
3. _____	☐	☐	☐	☐
4. _____	☐	☐	☐	☐
5. _____	☐	☐	☐	☐

DINING POSSIBILITIES:				
1. _____	☐	☐	☐	☐
2. _____	☐	☐	☐	☐
3. _____	☐	☐	☐	☐
4. _____	☐	☐	☐	☐
5. _____	☐	☐	☐	☐

EASE OF ACCESS TO DESTINATION:	☐	☐	☐	☐

Special activities: _____

Special events: _____

Appeal of area: _____

Comments: _____

_____

_____

Figure 9–2   **Analyzing a destination**

Itinerary Planning

Shaping a tour itinerary is a genuine art. Not every itinerary planner has mastered this skill. Awkward, ill-designed, or inept tours—the kind that sell poorly or bring complaints—pepper the brochures of some tour companies.

A sharp sense of who your clients are, what they want, and how their time should be managed all enhance the itinerary planning process. It's also important to mentally walk yourself through the tour: Would *you* like to get up at 5:30 A.M. to leave for the airport? Would *you* feel cheated if allowed only an hour at the Louvre museum? Would *you* feel frustrated if your tour to St. Louis, Missouri, never stopped at the Gateway Arch?

Each tour has its own particular demands. Certain general considerations, however, apply to most successful tour planning.

Determine What Your Intended Clients Want.

The ideal tour planner uses market research to fashion a tour in which all travel components match the customer's needs, expectations, interests, budget, and energy level.

Determine What Time of the Year Your Tours Should Ideally Depart.

Are your clients factory workers who generally get the first two weeks of July off? Then you might offer budget-conscious packages to the Caribbean. (Summer is off-season in the Caribbean.) Or are your customers people who can vacation at any time of the year—retirees, for example—but who are budget conscious? (Budget travelers, in marketing terms, are "price-sensitive.") A September departure to Acapulco or an October trip to St. Petersburg, Russia, may be attractive to this type of clientele, since rates to these destinations plummet during these low-season periods. Teachers and students travel during vacation periods, while people from farming communities favor the winter. Few people take tours around family holidays, such as Thanksgiving, Christmas, Easter, or Yom Kippur. On the other hand, tours, especially shorter ones, sell uncommonly well around "non-family" holidays; in the United States, those times would be Labor Day, Memorial Day, and the Fourth of July.

Determine What Day of the Week Your Tour Should Leave.

A favored pattern among working travelers is the Saturday-through-Saturday, eight-day configuration, because it requires only five days away from work and allows a day to recuperate. On the other hand, retired travelers can leave just about any day. Such flexibility would allow Tuesday, Wednesday, or Thursday departures and returns, since airfares for these days often price out better.

Determine How Many Days Your Tour Should Run.

Usually the itinerary determines how many days a particular tour will last. A tour of Washington, D.C., for example, justifies at least three but probably no more than six days. A Grand Tour of Europe, on the other hand, suggests a several-week-long itinerary, at least.

It's not just what the destination suggests, though. It's also what sells. Should that tour to Rio, for instance, be six, seven, or eight days long? Should it be nine days long and include side excursions to other attractions? An excellent clue to saleability when it comes to tour length is what other companies have found to be successful and settled upon. Another factor that determines a tour's length is its intended audience. Older, retired clients, for example, take longer, more expensive tours than do younger clients.

Choose the Appropriate Format for Your Itinerary.

Itineraries come in three types. In a **circle itinerary**, the tour begins in a certain city, circles out to other destinations and returns to the original city. For example, tour members might fly to Paris, motorcoach to Brussels, Amsterdam, Cologne, and Reims (with stays in each city) and return to Paris for their flight home. (Look at an atlas to better understand this.)

A **one-way itinerary** might instead go like this: The tour group flies into Paris, travels to Brussels and Amsterdam (with stays in each city), and flies home from Cologne. (The air portion—flying into Paris and out of Cologne—would be called an **"open-jaw" itinerary**.)

In a **hub-and-spoke itinerary**, the group would fly into Paris (the "hub") and stay there for the entire tour, taking day trips to nearby places (the "spokes"), but always returning back to Paris at the end of each day.

Each of these itinerary formats has its own strengths and weaknesses, based largely on the geography and economics of the destination. More about that later.

Choose Reliable and Well-Financed Suppliers.

Ground operators go out of business with alarming regularity. Hotels can go downhill fast and airlines can go bankrupt. Make sure that the people you're dealing with have sound track records. Imprudent supplier decisions—usually made to save money—can come back to mangle your tour.

Link Your Tour's Title and Itinerary to Only One Concept.

TWA Getaway Vacations, to cite an example, calls its tour of Italy "The Bellisimo" and its trip to several Italian, Spanish, and French cities "Mediterranean Magic." Good tour titles are simple, evocative, and direct. You might want to call your tour the "Argentina, Brazil, and Peru Vacation," but "South American Fiesta" will certainly conjure up far more intriguing and effective images in the buyer's mind. Remember that a tour is an *intangible*. It can't be seen or touched. It can be only experienced. Always strive to convey that experience in as exciting a way as possible.

Also, for some reason, travelers find it difficult to relate to an itinerary that visits more than one general area. For example, you might design a tour for Chicagoans that includes New York, Bermuda, and Paris (an easily arranged air route), but it probably won't sell.

Anchor the First and Last Days of Your Itinerary with Dramatic Destinations, Attractions, or Events.

Starting your tour of California with a first-day ride on San Francisco's cable cars and finishing it with a last-day visit to Disneyland or Universal Studios constitutes psychologically power-ful tour planning. It probably wouldn't work to begin it with a ride through Sonoma wine country and conclude it with a side excursion to Tijuana. Sonoma, though beautiful, won't play to the group's first-day energy. Tijuana will leave them with mixed feelings. Nothing influences a passenger's overall perception of a tour more fully than the first and last days. Dramatic attractions on these days and perhaps a reception meal and/or farewell party will help ensure client satisfaction.

Schedule Flights with Practical Client Considerations in Mind.

Maybe an 8 A.M. first-day airport departure seems reasonable to you, but how will it seem to those who must drive an hour to get there? Will they really like rising at 5 A.M. to get ready? A connecting flight from point A to point B may cost less than a non-stop flight, but it might produce more delays, missed flights, lost luggage, and other headaches. Or could the connection be turned into an attractive stopover (for example, Hawaii on the way back home from Hong Kong)? Such pragmatic considerations are essential in arranging tours.

Consider, too, the jet-lag factor. After a long flight, scheduling should adjust for the client's state of body and mind. Plan several interesting but untaxing activities for the arrival day (remember that the hotel may not have rooms ready for your group until later in the day) and get the group to bed early.

A visit to Kennedy Space Center might provide a dramatic finish to a tour's itinerary. *Courtesy of the National Tour Association*

Provide "Split" Itineraries for Groups that Warrant Them. A **split itinerary** is one in which part of the group does one thing while the other part does something else. It's more appropriate for affinity groups. For example, on a golf tour, you might schedule some sightseeing, shopping, or other entertainment for the non-golfers while their companions are hitting the greens.

Schedule as Few Hotel Changes as Possible. People hate packing and unpacking, and with good reason. You might want to schedule a group bound for, say, eastern Canada for two nights in Montreal, two in Quebec City, and two in Ottawa. It might work better to have them stay the entire time in Montreal and take day excursions to Ottawa and Quebec City. (Another example of the "hub and spoke" concept.) If you really wish to stay in several cities, fashion your itinerary in a logical manner. You might fly the group into Montreal, give them a day trip to Quebec City and continue on to Ottawa. Then either fly them out of Ottawa or continue on to Toronto and fly them home from there. (Both of these would be examples of one-way tour itineraries.) Limit the number of hotels you use through creative planning; avoid one-night stays whenever you can.

Schedule a General City Tour as One of Your First Tour Activities. When clients arrive in a new city for a multi-day stay, they need to be oriented to the city's layout, main attractions, and overall ambience. An early city tour lays the groundwork for your group's later in-depth explorations of a destination.

Keep the Number of Scheduled Activities to a Reasonable Number. Too many tour planners equate tour value with frantic activity that stretches from dawn to way past dusk. Although travelers want to be kept busy, they don't want to be driven into the ground. An itinerary must be "livable." Reasonable wake-up times, free blocks of time for shopping, or a couple of hours during the day to rest help pace out a group's day.

Choose Interesting Routings. Your motorcoach tour is going from Los Angeles to San Francisco. There are two options: the inland, boring Route 5, or the breathtaking, ocean-skirting Route 1. Unless speed is of the essence—a coastal highway routing takes more time and almost requires an overnight stay along the way—Route 1's scenic vistas will be well-appreciated.

Keep Motorcoach Rides to a Reasonable Length. What is too long for a bus trip? The absolute maximum distance any group should go on a single day is 600 miles—less if that travel is done on back roads instead of highways. A better distance would be around 350 miles. Rest stops, meal breaks, and brief attraction visits should punctuate motorcoach trips, for after about two hours of motorcoach riding, clients can get restless and tense. (On a city tour, that will happen after only forty-five minutes or so.) When developing an itinerary, you should spend time with a good detailed map. Figure out the mileage. Estimate, by the quality of the route, what speed the motorcoach will probably be able to go. Identify appropriate stop points along the way. Also be very wary of burning out clients with an unreasonably long trip.

Remember, too, that laws often wisely limit how long a motorcoach operator can drive. In the United States, drivers are allowed behind the wheel no longer than ten hours (though an additional five hours can be spent at rest stops, restaurants, etc.) and must be given eight hours per day to sleep.

Give Your Tour a Broad Variety of Features. Excessive predictability can lull a group into apathy. Schedule welcome and farewell parties. Vary the kinds of hotels you use: the first could be a bold resort property; the second, a large motor inn; the third, a grand old hotel. Alternate a cafeteria with formal sit-down dining, a hotel coffee shop with a restaurant that feature singing waiters or a dramatic view. Follow a day when passengers walk around a vast attraction with one during which they motor from place to place. Combine visits to historical places with events that are pure entertainment. And get clients to participate: listening to a tour leader talk about Prince Edward Island's mollusk industry is hardly as involving or memorable as taking off your shoes and socks, rolling up your pant legs, grabbing a bucket and shovel, and actually digging up your own clams.

Plot Out a Tour's Activities on a Calendar-like Chart. See Activity 3 for an example of such a chart. You should write things in pencil so you can change them easily. This approach helps you visualize the pacing and interactions of your tour's many events.

Determining a Tour's Cost and Price

No process is more intimidating than costing out and pricing a tour. The slightest error, uncorrected, can

A two-hour river cruise, narrated by the captain, might be an interesting break from the regular itinerary routine.
Courtesy of the National Tour Association

throw prices and profits deeply out of kilter. If you're a tour planner, it's a skill you *must* master.

The good news is this: even if you have trouble balancing your checkbook, even if you feel there's a hole in your head where the math-processing section of your brain should be, you *can* cost out a tour efficiently and correctly. First, though, you must give thought to the steps that come before the budget itself.

Negotiating with Suppliers

Dealing with suppliers and their sales representatives can be both fun and frustrating. On the one hand, watching each element fall into place as you plan a tour is a joy. On the other hand, suppliers can balk at your budgetary constraints or, through inefficiency, delay

your costing process. Each type of supplier presents its own set of costing concerns.

In Chapter 5, we examined hotel negotiations; in Chapter 6, airlines; and in Chapter 7, cruise lines and restaurants. In this chapter we'll focus on other suppliers.

Motorcoach Operators. Compared to airlines, motorcoach operators and local sightseeing companies are very obliging. They're often informal, family-like operations and usually are eager to give tour companies a sensible bid. Remember the following:

▼ Bus companies usually quote daily rates, although some may base charges on mileage or a combination of time and miles. The price quoted generally includes fuel, on-trip coach cleaning, and the driver's salary. Not included, as a rule, are tolls, parking fees, and the cost of a driver's hotel room (if it's not complimentary); the tour company will be billed for these charges later.

▼ Typically, local sightseeing companies (that also provide coaches) charge per half day or full day, though some do charge by the passenger.

▼ Request that the company supply its Interstate Commerce Commission (ICC) and Department of Transportation (DOT) numbers. This ensures that the company is operating legally. Ask for a Certificate of Insurance, too, to cover liability. Call the Federal Highway Administration at 1-800-832-5660 to verify their safety rating.

▼ There's often an enormous difference among bids from various bus lines in a given city, so get plenty of price estimates. Large, nationally known bus companies like Greyhound tend to charge rates that are higher than those of smaller local companies.

▼ Make sure to determine what kind and size of bus equipment the bid is for. Suggest the type of motorcoach you'd prefer.

▼ It's possible to request specific drivers, although companies with union contracts often cannot make any promises.

▼ If you schedule a trip in which a motorcoach starts in one city and finishes in another, you'll have to pay for the time it takes the driver to drive the coach back to the point of origin. Driving an empty bus back to its origin is called **deadheading**.

▼ Always reconfirm everything with motorcoach operators and sightseeing companies; their informality sometimes leads to oversights or outright mistakes.

Railroads. Public railroads, such as Amtrak, are quite predictable: expect a 10 percent discount but no more. Very little else is negotiable. Private companies—usually going short distances, but occasionally running long distance on tracks common to the public ones—are much more open to negotiating. Twenty to 30 percent off is not uncommon.

Ground Operators. Many of the recommendations made for motorcoach operators apply to ground operators. Don't forget that your arrangement with a ground operator calls for specialized personnel and services, such as guides or receptive representatives at the airport, and airport baggage handling. Often all admissions are paid for through the ground operator as well; they may be billed to you later or included in the operator's overall bid.

Miscellaneous Suppliers. Step-on guides are dealt with informally. Often the guide works independently; he or she may be compensated on an hourly, daily, or per-tour-member basis. Tour companies usually find out about step-on guides through tourist bureaus, chambers of commerce, or the tour operators' grapevine.

Attractions almost always provide discounted admission prices for groups and free admission for the tour manager. They like to be informed of your group's arrival in advance, although some of the larger attractions will extend a discounted price even to a group that arrives unannounced.

Completing the Budget

Once all quotations have been assembled, it's time to ascertain the cost of operating the tour and determine what your selling price will be. Many find this process to be daunting, the kind of thing best left to an accountant. If your tour is a complex one, it might be appropriate to assign the task to a bookkeeper or an accountant. For simpler tours, though, almost anyone can perform the necessary calculations. A sample tour-costing sheet is given in Figure 9–3; just about any tour could be plugged into this outline. Or you may wish to use any of a number of computer programs, such as that of Group Wizard, that facilitate the process.

Fixed vs. Variable Costs. Before starting, you must understand one critical thing: in any budgetary process, two kinds of costs exist. A **fixed cost** is one that never changes, no matter how many people are on your tour. For example, a particular motorcoach may cost $500 a day, no matter if twenty people or forty people are on it. Other examples of fixed costs are the daily salary of the tour manager, the price of a ground operator's services, and the amount you'll spend to publicize the tour.

A **variable cost** is one that changes according to how many people take your tour. For instance, if it costs $10 per person to visit a castle, then you'll have to spend $200 for twenty people. But if your tour is made up of forty people, the expense will be $400. In other words, because of variable costs, the overall cost to operate your tour increases as the number of passengers increases (of course, so does the profit). Other examples of variable tour costs would be expenditures for airline tickets, hotel rooms, and meals.

The Reasonable Number. Variable costs pose an accounting problem. How can you project your tour costs if they vary according to a number of passengers you can't predict? The trick is to estimate a *reasonable number* of passengers for your tour and budget your tour on a *per-person basis*.

Estimating a reasonable number will help you determine the per-client cost of your tour. For example, you may decide that for a forty-six-passenger coach, thirty-five would be an acceptable number of tour passengers. Forty-four would be great, but you can't count on that. Twenty-five might be the minimum number you'd accept; below that you might lose money. So you settle on thirty-five as a conservative, reasonable estimate of how many people will take your tour. (In reality, your reasonable number could be anything you decide upon.)

How will the reasonable number help you determine per-person costs? Simple. You take every fixed costs you have and divide it by the reasonable number. For instance, if your motorcoach costs $700 a day and your reasonable number is thirty-five, then your per-person cost will be $20.

Once you translate fixed costs to per-person expenses, you can mathematically mix them with variable costs. For example, if your coach cost is $20 per person and the airline ticket is $300 per person, then you can add these two figures together. As you cost out your tour, you'll add all the per-person costs together in the budget's right hand column.

```
┌─────────────────────────────────────────────────────────────────────┐
│ TOUR COSTING SHEET                                                    │
│                                                                       │
│ NAME OF TOUR: _____  Reasonable number (e.g.,30):  ◯   │
│ I.  Transportation                                                    │
│     A. Net airfare, per person:                        _____     │
│     B. Tax, fees on airfare, per person:               _____     │
│     C. Motorcoach cost: _____ + reasonable number ◯ =  _____ │
│        1. Parking fees: _____  + ◯ =               _____     │
│        2. Tolls: _____ + ◯ =                  _____     │
│     D. Transfer costs (e.g., bus, taxi): _____ + ◯ = _____ │
│     E. Ship or boat travel plus tax, per person:       _____     │
│     F. Train travel plus tax, per person:              _____     │
│     G. Miscellaneous transportation, per person:       _____     │
│     H. Tour conductor's transportation                                │
│        (if not comped): _____ + ◯ =             _____     │
│ II. Lodging                                                           │
│     A. Hotel (including taxes), noncommissionable                     │
│        Name       : per night room cost x no. of nights ÷ 2           │
│        1. _____ : _____ x _____ ÷ 2 =      _____     │
│        2. _____ : _____ x _____ ÷ 2 =      _____     │
│        3. _____ : _____ x _____ ÷ 2 =      _____     │
│        4. _____ : _____ x _____ ÷ 2 =      _____     │
│     B. Hotel costs, driver and escort,                                │
│        if applicable: _____ + ◯ =           _____     │
│     C. Luggage handling: number of times x average charge             │
│                         _____ x _____ =   _____     │
│ III. Meals (including tax and tip)                                    │
│     A. Restaurants                                                    │
│        Name                                                           │
│        1. _____ meal cost per person: _____  │
│        2. _____ meal cost per person: _____  │
│           [etc.]                                                      │
│     B. Reception party: _____ + ◯ =          _____     │
│     C. Farewell party: _____ + ◯ =           _____     │
│     D. Meals for driver and escort (if not comped): _____ + ◯ = ____│
└─────────────────────────────────────────────────────────────────────┘
```

Figure 9–3   **Tour costing sheet**

The Reason for Per-Person Costing. Why figure things out on a per-person basis? After all, many accountants would make the right-hand column a total tour cost column. In other words, they would enter a $700 motorcoach cost and a $10,500 ($300 x 35 PAX) air transportation cost, thus projecting overall company expenses if the group has thirty-five people. This system works too. But it requires large computations and figures that carry less meaning to the amateur budgeter than per-person figures. (Another system is to compute all fixed costs at the budget's beginning and all variable costs in the second part, then mesh them together at the end, but this really confuses the amateur.) So rely on the system given here. It's the one least likely to produce mistakes on the part of a non-accountant.

By now you may be scared or confused or have a headache. (If not, great!) Put this section aside, then come back and review it. Try Activity 4 at the end of

IV. Sightseeing
    A. City sightseeing tours
       Name of city
       1. _____   cost per person: _____
       2. _____   cost per person: _____
       3. _____   cost per person: _____
       4. _____   cost per person: _____
    B. Step-on guide salary (overall fee basis)
       Name   : cost
       1. _____ : _____ ÷ ◯ = _____
       2. _____ : _____ ÷ ◯ = _____
    C. Attraction admissions
       Name of attraction
       1. _____   cost per person: _____
       2. _____   cost per person: _____
       3. _____   cost per person: _____
       4. _____   cost per person: _____
       5. _____   cost per person: _____
       6. _____   cost per person: _____
V. General
    A. Estimated supply costs
       (total for this tour): _____ ÷ ◯ = _____
    B. Estimated advertising costs
       (total for this tour): _____ ÷ ◯ = _____
    C. Estimated office overhead
       (total for this tour): _____ ÷ ◯ = _____
    D. Escort's salary for tour: _____ ÷ ◯ = _____
    E. Miscellaneous costs: _____ ÷ ◯ = _____
          SUBTOTAL (cost to operate this tour, per person):   _____

TO DETERMINE SELLING PRICE, USE THE FOLLOWING FORMULA:

Subtotal   ÷   (1.00 − profit margin, expressed as a decimal) = sales price

_____ ÷ (1.00 − . _____) = _____

Copyright © Delmar Publishers

Figure 9–3   **Tour costing sheet (continued)**

this chapter. You'll find it easier than you think. Be wary of making the following errors:

▼ Confusing fixed and variable costs. For example, if you fail to divide your motorcoach cost by a projected number of passengers, you'll write a mammoth per-person coach cost in your right-hand column. This will throw your final total completely off.

▼ Forgetting to divide the room cost by two. If a room costs $100, then it costs $50 *per person*, since two people will be in the room. Tours are always costed on a double-occupancy basis.

▼ Forgetting that a five-day tour spends only *four nights in hotels*.

▼ Forgetting that luggage moves *twice* at any hotel—once in, once out. So if luggage handling is $2 per

Consultants Bruce Beckham and Richard Douglass have put together an amusing list of brochure clichés—and what they really mean:

▼ Options galore—(*Nothing's included*)
▼ Off the beaten path—(*People have stopped coming here*)
▼ Pre-registered rooms—(*They're already occupied*)
▼ A choice of menu dinner is served—(*It was our choice and it's chicken*)
▼ Explore on your own—(*Pay for it yourself*)
▼ Relax in your room—(*There's nothing to do*)
▼ Too numerous to mention—(*The writer's never been there*)
▼ The crisp mountain air whets your appetite for a hearty breakfast—(*You're going to freeze because the restaurant is outside the hotel*)

piece, then for each hotel stay you must multiply $2 x 2.

▼ Forgetting to factor in the fixed cost of the tour manager's salary and expenses.
▼ Forgetting taxes on various services.

Determining the Sales Price

Once you total up all your per-person costs, you have a figure that represents what it will cost you to operate your tour, per person. You can multiply this number by 35 to determine what the tour will cost the company if thirty-five people take it. (The geometric progressions involved in calculating a total cost if you have more or less than thirty-five are beyond the mathematical scope of this chapter.)

However, this figure doesn't include any profit margin at all. How do you factor in profit? First, determine what you'd like your profit to be. (Twenty or 30 percent is common for public tours, 30 to 40 percent for special, individually planned departures.) Remember, too, that you may wish to add a few percentage points as a safety margin to cover errors, inflationary increases, foreign currency fluctuations, and minor unanticipated costs. Then use the following simple equation:

Final per-person tour cost ÷ (1.00 − profit margin, expressed as a decimal) = sales price

For example, if the profit margin was to be 20 percent (expressed as .20), you might have:

$635 ÷ (1.00 − .20) = $635 ÷ .80 = $793.75

And that's it! The price at the bottom, $793.75, will give the company 20 percent profit if thirty-five (or whatever reasonable number you decided upon) people go on the tour. (Again, there are some geometric progressions involved: fewer than thirty-five people will reduce the profit percentage to below 20 percent, more than thirty-five will increase it past 20 percent.) You may wish to round off the sales price, as many sellers do. Thus, you would advertise the tour as costing not $793.75, but $798 or $799.

And now relax. The math is over.

Promotion

You've designed a tour. You've determined its cost and selling price. Now you must somehow let the public know about your tour—you must promote it. One way is through publicity. The other is through advertising. What's the difference? **Publicity** is information that is disseminated at no cost to the tour company. Some examples include free articles in newspapers, promotional presentations to clubs (assuming no one is paid to do them), and announcements in newsletters. **Advertising**, on the other hand, is promotional information for which the tour operator must pay.

Promotional Channels

The means by which tours can be promoted are many: brochures, fliers, postcards, press releases, print media, faxes, e-mail, Web sites, radio, and TV—the list is nearly endless. Tour promotional material can be *direct-mailed* to clients, distributed via travel agencies or associations, plastered on billboards, and announced through web site promotions. The promotion can be targeted to specialized clients (say, in a "tour night" event) or *broadly marketed* to the general public (in a newspaper ad, for example). News of tours can especially be spread along that most powerful of promotional channels: word-of-mouth.

Any number of fine books exist that can guide you in determining which marketing channels to follow, some traditional, some thoroughly original.

The Cost of Advertising

Advertising can be very expensive. Novices are often shocked to discover how much even a small ad in a large-circulation newspaper can cost. Four strategies can help control advertising expenses:

Look for Co-op Money. When a supplier provides advertising support, called **co-op money**, in return you're expected to mention that supplier in your advertising. You may have noticed that tour companies often print in their brochures the logos of the airlines that will transport their group. This probably indicates that the airline has absorbed some of the brochure printing costs.

Ask for Shells. In the tour business, a **shell** is a preprinted brochure with photos, illustrations, and graphics but no text. (In some parts of the country, shells are called **slicks**.) The tour operator buys the shells from a supplier or a tourist bureau for a very small fee; sometimes they're made available free of charge. The tour company then prints its own name, itinerary, prices, and the like, in the shell's blank spaces.

When Placing Ads or Using Direct Mail, Target the People Who Are Most Likely to Take Your Tour. If you've designed a tour for astronomy buffs, for instance, you would do best to advertise in an astronomy magazine or to buy the magazine's mailing list and send your brochures to its subscribers. That would be far more efficient and cost-effective than placing an ad in general newspapers or mailing the brochure to everyone in your town.

Don't Spend Additional Advertising Money Based on Promised Sign-ups. Until you have a client's deposit, you don't have a booking. You may speak at a promotional meeting and have thirty people tell you afterwards that they're definitely going. You could decide to spend additional money on your promotional campaign to get the remaining passengers, since you're already well on the way to a full tour. But are you? Perhaps only one or two of the thirty people will actually send in a deposit. Never make plans based on promises. Count only actual deposits as firm bookings. (Even then, assume that 20 percent of these bookings will be canceled before departure; this is the reason some tour companies require nonrefundable deposits and why all maintain "stand-by" lists.)

Brochure Design

A striking, professional-looking brochure can help ensure that your tour will be a sales success. Conversely, a poorly planned one can undermine your entire promotional campaign. When designing your brochure, keep the following points in mind:

Study the Brochures of Other Companies. Pick out the things you like. Avoid those you don't. Make a list of the items (for instance, enrollment forms, terms, and conditions) that must be included.

Follow the KISS Principle. In the advertising world, the KISS principle stands for "Keep It Simple, Stupid!" Potential clients reject cluttered, complicated brochures and flowery, poorly written prose. Edit out anything that is not absolutely necessary. When in doubt, throw it out.

Give Your Brochure a Professional Look. Clients estimate the skillfulness of your tour operations based on the professionalism of your advertising. Creating a polished brochure has become relatively easy. Desktop publishing has drastically lowered the cost of producing fine-looking copy, and shells provide an inexpensive way to bring full-color gloss to your brochures.

Make It Visual. Because of the impact of video on our daily lives, people today *read* less but *look* more. An all-prose, black-and-white, no-photo brochure looks dull in comparison to everything else in the marketplace. Older consumers do tolerate extended prose sections in promotional pieces, but even they are influenced by our increasingly visual society.

What Prose You Do Use Should Be Visually Organized, Intimate, and to the Point. Examine some of the professional sales pieces you get in the mail. You'll notice several common patterns. First, skilled writers today often use bullet points, numbers,

Good brochure design is integral to selling the tour product.
Courtesy of the National Tour Association

short paragraphs, quick sentences, and plenty of blank white space to make the layout visually pleasing and easily digested. Second, they make frequent use of the words "you," "us," and "we," as well as questions and imperative verbs, to link the reader with the seller in a very personal way. Third, they create what is called a **double path**. Key words and phrases are underlined, italicized, or boldfaced. This permits a hurried reader to pay attention to only key concepts and still get the message. Readers with more time can still follow the traditional reading path and read every word.

Think Out the Brochure's Detach-and-Mail Portion. Make sure the client will be supplying all the data you need. Don't put on the back of the detach-and-mail portion any information that the client will need later on (for example, your company's address). Establish deposit rules and deadlines that mesh with your own supplier and operation deadlines.

Be Careful About Legal Terms and Conditions. It may be necessary to hire a lawyer to look at your brochure's "terms and conditions" section. Since most tour operators use similar language in this section, study theirs carefully.

Consider Clever Ways to Supplement or Even Replace Brochures. Many small tour companies use a well-presented single sheet of paper as a low-cost alternative to a brochure. One Hawaiian tour operator attached little announcements to pineapples and

shipped them to high-probability clients. An Asian company sent out ads inside fortune cookies. In a society flooded with mailings, faxes, e-mail, and brochures, a little imagination goes a long way.

Getting the Tour Product Out and Back

The distribution end of a tour is an essential step in travel marketing. Since every tour dictates a different strategy and the size of a tour operator shapes its distribution system, we can only review a few basic principles here.

Create a Well-Organized Sales Tracking System. Whether you use a computer or a filing system to track bookings, make sure the information is extremely well organized and easily accessible.

Design Forms that Are Orderly and Efficient. Everything—reservation forms, responses to inquiries, and confirmation letters—should be concise, clear, and functional. (See Figure 9–4.)

Acknowledge All Inquiries Promptly. Delay in responding is very likely to dampen clients' enthusiasm or drive them to a competitor. Swift confirmations of deposits and timely mailings of final tour documents are also a must, if only to deflect calls from clients who are anxious about information.

TOUR RESERVATION FORM

NAME OF CLIENT(S): _____

PHONE NUMBER:

Business: (__) _____

ADDRESS: _____

Home: (__) _____

_____

_____

_____

NAME OF TOUR: _____

DEPARTURE DATE: _____

ACCOMMODATIONS: ☐ SINGLE ☐ TWIN ☐ TRIPLE ☐ QUAD

COST

Land portion: _____ (pp) x _____ = _____

Air portion: _____ (pp) x _____ = _____

Other portions: _____ (pp) x _____ = _____

_____ (pp) x _____ = _____

Single supplement (if applicable) _____

TOTAL PACKAGE: _____

Confirmed by: _____ Date: _____

Option date: _____ Deposit sent on: _____ Amount: _____

Final payment date: _____ F.P. sent on: _____ Amount __ _____

Form of payment: _____

Documents needed: ☐ Passport ☐ Visas ☐ Tourist cards

Date documents received from client: _____

Date documents given or sent to client: _____

Airline ticket number(s): _____

_____

Notes:

Copyright © Delmar Publishers

Figure 9–4 **Tour reservation form**

Assume Deposits, Bookings, and Final Payments Will Arrive Very Near the Deadline You Set. Suppose your brochure says that all deposits must be received by May 1. It's April 20 and you have received so few deposits/bookings that you're considering canceling your tour. Should you worry? Maybe. But you probably will receive most of the deposits on April 29 and 30. That's the pattern for even successful tours: some bookings will occur when you first announce the trip, then you'll receive almost no deposits until a few days before the deadline date. (See Figure 9–5.) Of course, you may *not* receive such a concentration of bookings around the deadline, so you may indeed have to cancel the tour. Just don't do it prematurely.

What if you *do* have to cancel a tour? Always try to propose an alternative to your customer. That way you won't lose the business. For example, you may have to cancel your August 7 departure, but a few seats are left on the August 14 tour. Why not offer that date to those on the canceled departure? There's a good chance that at least some of your clients will be able to change their vacation time.

Travel Agents and the Internet

E-commerce has dramatically reshaped the way travel products are distributed. The Internet has become an important vehicle for consumers to book and buy such

Figure 9–5   Typical timeline to operate a single tour

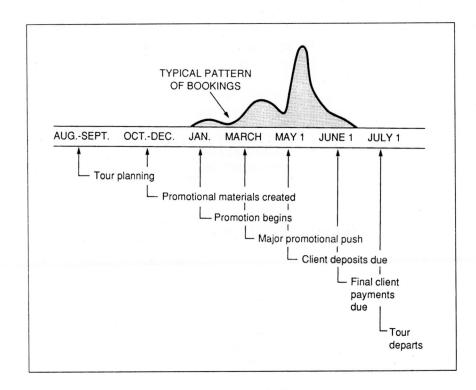

simple commodities as airline tickets, car rentals and, to some extent, hotel stays.

On the other hand, consumers seem reluctant to book tours on the Internet. The reason: tours (and cruises) are complex travel experiences. People do use the Internet to *research* tours, but they don't feel comfortable *buying* a tour there. Instead, they feel a need for an expert travel agent to validate their conclusions and guide their purchase. For the foreseeable future, travel agents will be the primary channel for distributing conventional per-capita tours. There are a few exceptions: niche tour products (e.g., eco/adventure tours), incentive tours, and customized tours. Such group departures often result from a direct relationship between the tour operator and the consumer, with no "middle man," such as a travel agent. (However, many travel agencies do plan out and operate their own customized tours. In such instances they *are* the tour operator.)

Following Up the Tour

Operating the tour itself is a critical portion of your marketing scheme. Information on this phase appears throughout this book. But what must be done afterwards, rapid, effective follow-up, is often the most neglected aspect of a marketing plan.

Distribute "Tour Assessment" Forms at the Trip's End. These forms provide vital feedback on your clients' needs and satisfaction levels, as well as an assessment of the tour manager's performance. Analyze them diligently; they may offer important clues on what you should concentrate on for future tour design.

Have New Tours Ready for Clients to Think About Even Before the Current Tour Ends. Presenting a brochure publicizing a new, exciting tour, especially if the clients are happy with the trip they're on, is a powerful sales strategy. Even a brief mention of other tours by the tour conductor works well. This promotion must be done in a low-key fashion, however, to avoid sounding too pushy.

Add Your Clients' Names to a Mailing List Immediately Upon a Tour's Completion. The most valuable asset a tour operator can possess is a mailing list of satisfied customers. Good tours build client loyalty. Targeting your mailings and announcements of promotional events to these loyal clients ensures a high probability of future bookings.

Send a Follow-up Thank-You Letter to Tour Participants. Everyone likes to feel that he or she is not forgotten after a sale has been closed or a product delivered. A good follow-up letter shows that you're committed to the client beyond a single tour and that he or she is part of a family of travelers for whom you will continue to design new, exciting trips.

Marketing to Groups

Marketing to pre-formed affinity groups (such as ski clubs, Rotary groups, or church societies) requires many of the same strategies we've discussed in this chapter. Here are a few special ideas that you need to consider in order to serve their needs:

▼ **Find a "pied piper."** A **pied piper** is a member of a group, club, or other organization who shows leadership skills, is openly enthusiastic, and would love a free trip in return for helping you to promote a tour to his or her group. A pied piper can serve as a powerful ally in getting an organization's members to sign up for your tour.

▼ **Research the organization.** Knowing the group's makeup will help you tailor your tour to their needs.

▼ **Stage a presentation.** Giving a small speech at one of the organization's meetings, perhaps enhanced by a video or slides and reinforced by the pied piper, is an efficient way to inform and motivate any group. You might even get sign-ups that very night.

▼ **Follow up with "waves" of promotional material.** As the organization's members begin to "talk up" your tour concept, more and more will be ready to buy. You must have flyers and brochures out there, however, to remind them that it's time to act.

▼ **Schedule a pre-departure meeting.** About two weeks before your special group leaves, invite them to a presentation where they can ask any last-minute questions and where you can distribute tour documents to them.

Summary

Tour managers should have a sense of how tours are marketed. The demand for tours is affected by many factors, most of which tour companies determine through marketing shortcuts. In researching a destination, it's necessary to refer to guidebooks, industry resources, maps, atlases, and tourist bureau publications, as well as to conduct on-site visits and consult friends who live there. Many strategies can be used to ensure good tour planning. To determine a tour's cost and price, you must negotiate with suppliers and work out a budget. Promotion, made up of advertising and publicity, and good follow-up are also vital to tour marketing, whether you are selling to individuals or to pre-formed groups.

■ ■ ■

QUESTIONS FOR DISCUSSION

1. State four reasons a tour manager should know something about tour planning.

2. What four marketing shortcuts do tour operators often take?

3. List six general sources of destination information.

4. Give eight strategies for effective itinerary planning.

5. State the formula used to determine a tour's selling price.

6. Give four strategies for keeping advertising costs down.

7. What eight considerations should guide brochure design?

8. In what four ways can distribution of a tour be well managed?

9. List four ways to follow up on a tour.

10. List five steps to consider when marketing to groups.

■ ■ ■

ACTIVITY 1

▼ Complete the crossword puzzle using the appropriate words from the list:

AAA	fixed costs	open jaw	Tijuana Taxi
advertising	fuel	PAX	tolls
atlas	head hunting	pied piper	Triptik
CVB	marketing	publicity	variable costs
deadheading	Montezuma's Revenge	reasonable number	World Travel Guide
demand	need	sales	
double path	OAG	split itinerary	

Across

6. This cost would probably not be included in a motorcoach operator's bid

7. Not the maximum number of people on a tour or the minimum, but a good goal

10. An abbreviation for "passengers"

11. Something created when desire is driven by money

12. A reference book containing information on the world's destinations

13. A compact, flip-page map from AAA

14. Promotion that costs money

Down

1. Promotion that costs a tour operator nothing

2. Costs that never change, no matter how many people take a tour

3. An air itinerary in which passengers fly into one city and out of a different one

4. Costs that change according to how many people take a tour

5. Driving an empty bus

8. The process of transferring a product from producer to consumer

9. A book containing maps and statistics

■ ■ ■

ACTIVITY 2

▼ What others do in order to market tours often yields clues on how to market, or not market, a tour. Examine the travel section of your city's Sunday newspaper, then answer the following:

1. Which newspaper did you use? Which date?

2. How many ads are there that feature escorted tours? Independent tours? How many ads, total, are there for all forms of transportation? What can you conclude from your figures?

3. Select one ad that caught your eye immediately and that you consider to be an example of highly effective advertising. List all the factors that made that ad so effective.

4. Select one ad that you feel is a *bad* example of advertising. List all the factors that work against the ad being effective.

■ ■ ■

ACTIVITY 3

▼ You're starting to plan a seven-day tour of Paris for a local church society. Your group will depart from New York City. Your flight leaves New York at 9 P.M. on Sunday, July 12, and arrives in Paris at 10 A.M. the next day. The return flight leaves Paris at 4 P.M. on Saturday and arrives at New York's Kennedy Airport at 6 P.M. the same day.

Plot your rough itinerary on the following chart. Include flight departures and arrivals and the following activities in whichever order you deem best: arrival at hotel; departure from hotel; half day at the Louvre museum; full-day trip to Versailles Palace and Chartres Cathedral; three-hour, general sightseeing tour; full-day, in-depth sightseeing tour of major attractions in the Right Bank area; half-day, in-depth sightseeing tour of Left Bank attractions; half day for shopping; half day of free time; evening dinner cruise on the Seine River; evening farewell dinner at a Paris nightclub.

Sunday, July 12	Monday, July 13	Tuesday, July 14	Wednesday, July 15	Thursday, July 16	Friday, July 17	Saturday, July 18

■ ■ ■

ACTIVITY 4

▼ Study the following tour description and review the discussion of costing in the chapter. Then cost out the tour in the blank area provided below. Give the sales price at the bottom of the page.

You're operating a three-day senior citizens bus tour from Riverside, California, to San Diego. It leaves Friday morning and returns Sunday evening. Your reasonable number of passengers is thirty.

The bus will cost $1,200, all inclusive. Your group will stay at the Del Coronado Hotel, where you've been quoted a nightly rate of $130, double occupancy, noncomissionable, tax included. The escort's and driver's rooms are free. The bellhops charge $2 for each piece of luggage they move; they don't charge for the escort's and driver's baggage. Each client is limited to one piece of luggage.

Two breakfasts are provided at $22 each, tax and tip included. Driver and escort meals are comp. There will also be one dinner in the hotel's Crown Room, at $32 per person, tax and tip included—again, no charge for driver and escort.

You must also cost in admission to Sea World ($22 per client), the San Diego Zoo ($18 per client), and the Reuben Fleet Museum ($8 per client)—no charge on any of these for driver and escort. A step-on guide will give a half-day San Diego tour. The guide charges your company $90 for the service.

Supplies, advertising, and overhead are estimated at $20 per person. The escort's full salary is $240. For an ideal number of thirty passengers, the profit is to be set at 20 percent of the sales price.

There are no additional costs associated with this tour. What should be its sales price to the public?

PROFILE

When your name is Julia Roberts, you have to be ready for people to joke about that *other* Julia Roberts. And when you work as a tour guide at Warner Bros. Studios, you also have to be a good sport about posing for photographs—including next to Bugs Bunny.

Julia is one of about a dozen guides who take people on behind-the-scenes tours of the famous Burbank lot. Less publicized and commercialized than the more famous Universal Studios down the street, the Warner Bros. tour is billed as a "real" tour. Unlike the theme park experience at Universal, Warner's guides take very small groups of visitors in golf carts right onto sets, into music scoring sessions, through prop rooms and across the studio's vast backlot.

"Just about every tour is different," explains Julia. "Each guide has a unique approach to the tour, plus we change it from day to day, according to what's going on at the lot."

Julia's background positioned her well for the job. A business and theater major at the University of California, Riverside, she did plenty of public speaking and was a performer in the singing group, the Young Americans. "In many ways, to give a tour is to give a performance, especially when it's a movie studio tour. But you also have a huge responsibility to be accurate, to know your movies and TV shows, both past and present. Because many movie buffs take our tour. They know which films were shot here. That's why the first thing I did when I got the job was to rent and watch *Casablanca*."

Julia feels two other elements are vital to tour guiding: "Enthusiasm and interaction. They keep those on your tour really involved. I try to ask them as many questions as they ask me."

Of course the energy level really escalates among visitors to the studio when a celebrity is sighted. "We try to follow 'star etiquette' and not overly disturb them." Julia did, unfortunately, once run over George Clooney's basketball with her golf cart.

"What's really exciting," Julia remarks, "is to realize that this film you're watching being made could become a classic." As the author of this book, I know what Julia means. In 1977 I took the Warner Bros. tour for the first time. We watched the sound effects being created for a little science-fiction movie. It had an odd name: *Star Wars*.

10

Getting the Job . . . and Keeping It

Chapter Objectives

After reading this chapter, you should be able to:

▼ Chart out the tour industry's hiring patterns.

▼ Prepare a professional resume.

▼ Conduct yourself well in a job interview.

▼ Identify the potential on-job challenges to a tour manager's ethical standards.

"I DON'T KNOW WHAT IT IS, BUT THERE'S JUST SOMETHING I LIKE ABOUT YOU."

If you're already a tour manager, then congratulations! You've passed one of tour conducting's most formidable hurdles: getting the job in the first place. Major tour operators receive as many as five hundred escort job inquiries a year. From that sizable pool of applicants, the average tour company may hire only a dozen full-time tour directors. A recent poll indicates that the chances of landing a full-time tour-conducting position are one in twenty-three; of getting a part-time job, one in fourteen.

If you're not yet a tour manager, those odds may seem daunting. Then again, if you want to be a tour leader, you aren't the type to discourage easily. Indeed, you love such challenges. This chapter will supply tools to improve the odds that you not only get the position you want, but keep it. If your goal is some other job in the tour industry, the guidelines we'll be giving you will be just as valuable.

Tour Manager Hiring Patterns

Most tour operators try to keep their tours rolling all year long and their tour managers working as much as possible. Some companies see only minor seasonal fluctuations in their tour operations over a twelve-month period. The majority, however, operate most of their tours from June through September, with additional brief peaks during the pre-holiday and holiday periods. In southern hemisphere countries, tourism peaks from January through March. It's the same for companies that specialize in sun destinations, such as the Caribbean or Mexico—the high season occurs during the winter months. A few select tour managers can bank on year-round employment. Most, though, work only portions of the year and like it that way.

This pattern has strong implications for any person looking for a tour-management position. You should, for example, send out cover letters and resumes around January, just before most employers start thinking about the summer "bulge" of touring and hiring that lies ahead. Then perhaps in early March you might follow up this initial contact with a phone call to the person who supervises tour managers at each company, since he or she probably does the hiring, too.

Research the company in advance and show you know what makes it unique. If your resume grabs the company's attention, you'll probably be asked to fill out an employment application form (see Figure 10–1) and be invited to an interview. If you pass that hurdle, you'll attend the company's escort training session in the spring. Remember that companies hire additional tour directors during their high season in emergency situations—if a few escorts quit or the number of tours is greater than projected. (See Figure 10–2.) So if you didn't get hired in the first round, a call to the director of

Tours to family destinations peak during summer and major holidays.
Courtesy of Marriott International

APPLICATION FOR EMPLOYMENT

TYPE OR PRINT CLEARLY

PERSONAL INFORMATION

DATE _____   SOCIAL SECURITY NUMBER _____

NAME _____
    LAST   FIRST   MIDDLE

PRESENT ADDRESS _____
    STREET   CITY   STATE   ZIP CODE

PERMANENT ADDRESS _____
    STREET   CITY   STATE   ZIP CODE

PHONE NO. _____

ARE YOU LEGALLY ELIGIBLE FOR EMPLOYMENT IN THE USA?   YES____ NO____   (IF YES, VERIFICATION WILL BE REQUIRED)
ARE YOU EMPLOYED NOW?

EMPLOYMENT DESIRED

POSITION _____   DATE YOU CAN START _____   SALARY DESIRED _____

ARE YOU EMPLOYED NOW? _____   IF SO MAY WE INQUIRE OF YOUR PRESENT EMPLOYER _____

*The Age Discrimination in Employment Act of 1967 prohibits discrimination on the basis of age with respect to individuals who are 40 years of age or older.

EDUCATION	NAME AND LOCATION OF SCHOOL	DEGREE OR CERTIFICATE	SUBJECTS STUDIED
HIGH SCHOOL			
UNIVERSITY OR COLLEGE			
TRADE, BUSINESS, OR CORRESPONDENCE SCHOOL			

DO YOU HAVE ANY EXPERIENCES, SKILLS, OR QUALIFICATIONS THAT WILL BE OF SPECIAL BENEFIT IN THE POSITION FOR WHICH YOU ARE APPLYING? _____

WHAT FOREIGN LANGUAGES DO YOU SPEAK FLUENTLY? _____

READ? _____   WRITE? _____

WHAT PROFESSIONAL ORGANIZATIONS DO YOU BELONG TO? _____

Please attach a one-page explanation of travel experience and previous travel-related jobs.

CONTINUED ON OTHER SIDE

Figure 10–1   **Sample job application form**

tour managers a little later in the season might well yield results.

If you're interested in other positions at a tour company, seasonality isn't really an issue. Keep checking the classified ads in your local newspaper or occasionally call the company to find out if anything will be opening. Some tour operators post their job listings on their Web sites.

Selecting Tour Companies

How do you find out which companies operate tours and therefore presumably hire tour conductors and other tour-related personnel? One way is to obtain a list of tour-operator members from one of the industry's premier professional organizations, the National Tour Association (P.O. Box 3071, Lexington, KY 40596) or the United States Tour Operators Association (342 Madison Avenue, Suite 1522, New York, NY 10173). A list of major tour operators appears in the back of this book. You might also peruse a tour agency's brochures, research the Internet, or check the Yellow Pages to identify companies that operate in your area.

Of course, be selective. Being selective means being well informed about the companies you contact and whether you're what they want. Do you wish to work for an intermodal company, for an incentive house, or

WORK EXPERIENCE

List all present and past employment, including part-time or seasonal, beginning with the most recent.

Employer	Employment Dates and Salary	Describe the work you did in detail	Reason for leaving
Name_____ Address_____ City_____ State_____ Phone_____Supervisor_____	From: _____ To: _____ Salary _____		
Name_____ Address_____ City_____ State_____ Phone_____Supervisor_____	From: _____ To: _____ Salary _____		
Name_____ Address_____ City_____ State_____ Phone_____Supervisor_____	From: _____ To: _____ Salary_____		
Name_____ Address_____ City_____ State_____ Phone_____Supervisor_____	From: _____ To: _____ Salary_____		

REFERENCES: GIVE BELOW THE NAMES OF THREE PERSONS NOT RELATED TO YOU, WHOM YOU HAVE KNOWN AT LEAST ONE YEAR.

	NAME	ADDRESS	BUSINESS	YEARS ACQUAINTED
1				
2				
3				

IN CASE OF EMERGENCY NOTIFY _____
                                        NAME

_____   _____
ADDRESS   PHONE NO.

I AUTHORIZE INVESTIGATION OF ALL STATEMENTS CONTAINED IN THIS APPLICATION. I UNDERSTAND THAT MISREPRESENTATION OR OMISSION OF FACTS CALLED FOR IS CAUSE FOR DISMISSAL. FURTHER, I UNDERSTAND AND AGREE THAT MY EMPLOYMENT IS FOR NO DEFINITE PERIOD AND MAY, REGARDLESS OF THE DATE OF PAYMENT OF MY WAGES AND SALARY, BE TERMINATED AT ANY TIME WITHOUT ANY PREVIOUS NOTICE.

DATE _____ SIGNATURE _____

***Figure 10–1* Sample job application form (continued)**

for a motorcoach operator? Do you have foreign language skills and would you, therefore, prefer to escort for an outbound operator or an inbounder who deals primarily with foreign tourists? Would your ties at home prohibit you from working as a tour manager for a company that runs long overseas trips? Are you willing to move to another city where a company that interests you is based? Or does that company have major tours operating where you live?

In other words, you need to first gather as much information about each tour operator as possible. An excellent way to do this is to obtain company sales brochures and study them for clues. This will also help you exclude those companies that operate mostly independent tours, not escorted ones (unless, of course, you wish a non-escort position). Telephoning the company and asking pertinent questions may likewise prove worthwhile. (For example, some tour operators only consider employing people who already live in the area where the company is located.)

Be sure to find out whether the company you're applying to is one that concentrates on a narrow market segment. Some specialize in adventure trips, others focus on groups going to the Tournament of Roses Parade, still others target school groups, and some design tours for specific ethnic groups. Such a company might be right down your alley—or it might be a complete dead end.

Figure 10–2 **Tour operations patterns (conventional company)**

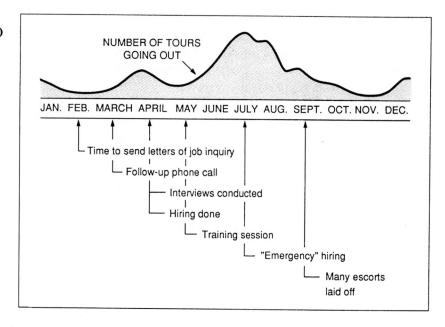

If you wish to be a tour manager, you must be willing to work your way up through the industry. The prime tour operators prefer that applicants have at least some tour-related experience. A typical pattern is for a person to first work as a city guide for a local sightseeing operation, then take part-time employment with a smaller tour company, and finally move on to an escort position with a major tour firm or with an incentive house. At each step you may decide that particular level is actually what you want.

Another path to tour conducting is to take an office position with a tour company. Sometimes tour operators draw new escorts from their own operational ranks. More significantly, many tour operators find

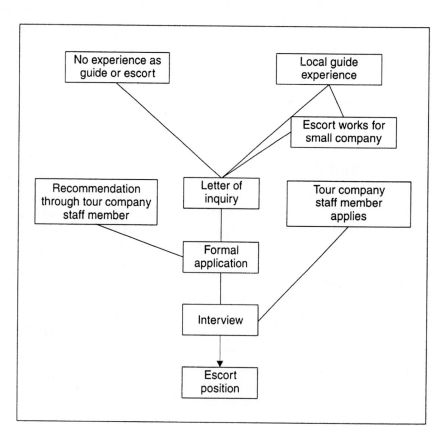

Figure 10–3 **Patterns for securing escort jobs**

escorts through recommendations from their own staff. If you know someone at a company, by all means have that person bring you to the attention of the director of tour managers. This is also a powerful strategy if you want a non-escort position at the company.

Information and contacts are useful, however, only if you take a hard look at yourself. Matching your skills, attitudes, and life situation with a tour company is the best way to maximize your job-hunting success. (See Figure 10–3.)

A Tour Company's Hiring Criteria

Tour companies have clear-cut patterns regarding what they look for in would-be tour leaders. As noted in Chapter 1, hiring personnel seek people with outgoing personalities, superior organizational skills, a solid sense of ethics, good decision-making abilities, and a love of people, places, and travel. Different companies stress different traits, of course. But overall, there's a consensus about what makes a fine tour manager. As for other job positions, tour operators generally favor applicants who give evidence of reliability, initiative, and solid communications skills. They're more open to hiring individuals with limited or no tour-related experience for entry-level positions.

Tour operators focus on three sources of information about applicants: the resume, the cover letter, and the interview. Job seekers who polish their resume-writing and interview skills will have a special advantage when applying for an escort job.

The Resume Format

A good **resume** is a concise, well-organized summary of what you have to offer. By forcing you to identify your marketable skills, it helps you organize your job search. It also assists you in discussing your assets while being interviewed and serves to remind employers of your availability.

Many resume formats exist. The one most popular among tour operators is the *job-targeted reverse chronological*. This resume is written specifically for a tour-related position and lists work history in reverse chronological order. (See Figure 10–4 for an example.)

Your resume should be brief—one page, if possible. It should look professional, and list all of the following information:

- ▼ *Essential Data.* Give your name, address, and phone number.

- ▼ *Job Objective.* State your desire for a specific position (e.g., tour manager) in a single phrase or sentence.

- ▼ *Work Experience.* Begin with your most recent experience (including summer jobs) and work backwards. List the years you held each job and official job titles. Emphasize any experience that was travel industry-related or in some way similar to the job you seek and its demands. (For example, nursing, teaching, or acting experience is good training for tour conducting.) You may wish to leave out any experience that doesn't really reflect your ability to do the job. (For instance, carpentry, astronomy, or stock brokering would not strengthen a tour management application.) Don't forget to mention how well you did in each position and what you achieved.

- ▼ *Education.* List schools, degrees, certificates, and special training, also in reverse chronological order. List your high school only if you didn't attend college. If you took any classes or training sessions in tour conducting, you should list these first or underline them. Cite things like scholarships and notable extra-curricular activities.

- ▼ *Special Skills.* Do you speak a foreign language? Do you have experience in driving motorcoaches? Do you have CPR training? If so, mention it here.

- ▼ *Personal Data.* Limit this section to items that would grab the reader's attention or have a direct bearing on the position you seek. Have you traveled extensively? Have you taken any tours? Do you belong to a public-speaking society? These are the things that will interest your potential employer.

- ▼ *References.* If you have room, give names, titles, addresses, and business phone numbers of persons who have consented to be references—be sure you get permission from them in advance. If there's no room, state, "References available upon request."

Resume Do's and Don'ts

- ▼ **Do** limit your resume to one page, if possible.

- ▼ **Do** start sentences with impressive action verbs, such as "designed," "achieved," and "conducted."

64 Escort Way
Superior, Wisconsin 54600
(715) 555-4360
February 1, 2000

Ms. Jane Doe
Director of Escort Services
Acme Tours
220 Vesey Street
New York, New York 10285

Dear Ms. Doe:

   Like many letters you must receive, this one is for an escorting position with your company. I believe, though, that my particular skills would be of special interest to Acme Tours. I've guided groups for several years now and am fluent in both French and German. I've also taught, acted, and designed a major corporation's client relations program.

   I'll be in New York soon. Might an interview with you be possible? I'll call in a week or so to find out if we may meet during my stay.

   Attached is my résumé for your reference. Thank you in advance for considering this request.

                                        Very sincerely,

                                        Robin Latour

Attachment

Figure 10–5   **Sample cover letter**

any tour-related courses you have taken, and give it to the interviewer if the subject of your prior training comes up. Allow the interviewer to guide the conversation—this way your responses won't sound like bragging but will serve to underscore your self-confidence. Don't speak badly about former jobs and employers. The interviewer may conclude that you'll do the same thing someday to him or her.

Ask Questions. These should come toward the end of an interview, although a few peppered throughout the process can be effective. Questions demonstrate your interest, show you're not self-centered, and give you clues about what the company is looking for.

Be Yourself. Acting the way you think someone wants you to act often leads to false, anxious behavior, useless digressions, and inattentiveness. Don't worry if you're a little tense—interviewers expect this and make allowances for mildly nervous behavior.

Follow Up with a Thank-You Note. In Chapter 9, you learned that follow-up is an important step in a marketing and sales campaign. It's just as important when you're trying to sell *yourself*. A brief thank-you note reminds the interviewer of your wish for employment and shows you are a diplomatic and considerate person, just what a tour manager should be. (See Figure 10–6.)

64 Escort Way
Superior, Wisconsin 54600
March 15, 2000

Ms. Jane Doe
Director of Escort Services
Acme Tours
220 Vesey Street
New York, New York 10285

Dear Ms. Doe:

This is to express my thanks for the opportunity to interview with you last week. I would also like to reaffirm my desire to be considered for a position as a tour manager with Acme Tours. Enclosed is the application you requested. If you need any additional information, please feel free to contact me at any time. My phone number is (715) 555-4360.

Very sincerely,

Robin Latour

Enclosure

Figure 10–6   **Sample thank-you note**

How Tour Managers Keep Their Jobs

If you land a non-escort position with a tour operator, you can expect a long career, possibly with significant advancement opportunities, as long as you perform well and your company continues to succeed. But if you become a tour manager, your odds of long-lasting success are less secure. One out of two tour directors quits or loses his or her job within six months. For some it's a blessing in disguise—the job's demands turn out to be just too much, or the fit of personality to profession is not a suitable one.

Sometimes, though, the job is lost because the tour director copes poorly with an overwhelming and unexpected onslaught of hard-to-resist temptations. What is or isn't proper as far as tour managing goes? In a field with few ethical landmarks and in an era with hazy codes of conduct, it's sometimes hard to figure out the difference between a kickback and a commission, between deserved perks and disguised pilfering. A clearheaded, unequivocal sense of integrity is essential in tour conducting, where the rules are ambiguous and the temptations frequent.

Company Loyalty and Job Pride

Usually tour managers know exactly where to put their loyalties: into the efficient and effective operation of a tour. Sometimes, though, loyalties become mixed,

Tour operators favor escorts who reflect favorably on their company. *Courtesy of the National Tour Association*

even conflicting. Should your first loyalty be to the company? To the clients? To co-workers? For example, suppose you found out that another tour conductor was having an affair with a passenger and that it was distracting him or her from escort duties. Would you talk to the person about it? Would you leave well enough alone? Would you report the tour conductor to the company?

No universal principles can be applied to each unique situation. But career-related standards, especially those related to company loyalty and pride in one's job, are clear-cut. For instance, tour managers discover that they can easily cut corners as they perform their job. Why not leave out that little portion of the itinerary and finish a tour early? Why not sleep in the back of the bus rather than socialize with the passengers? The reason: a tour manager's duty is, above all, to his or her tour members. To deprive them of deserved services is inexcusable. A professional ought to give 100 percent to a job at all times. Anything less is a betrayal of client, company, and self.

Another easy temptation is to view tour members as enemies or fools. This problem plagues many other service areas; the sarcastic waiter, the arrogant hotel manager, and the hostile Motor Vehicles Department clerk have become stock characters in books, plays, and films. To be curt with passengers; to snap at them; to ignore, avoid, or mock them—these are the bad habits

a tour manager must avoid no matter what the mood or situation.

A tour manager must likewise avoid bad-mouthing clients, competitors, colleagues, or company. Gossip, ridicule, and innuendo have a way of circling back to their point of origin. A tour leader's critical or disdainful comments can spread through a tour group like a plague, more swiftly than you ever imagined. The classic story is of the tour conductor who sits on an empty motorcoach while the group is visiting some attraction. He or she spends this time in conversation with the driver, laughing at the tour members. Suddenly the driver glances in his rear-view mirror and begins making peculiar warning signals to the tour director. The tour director doesn't understand but looks back. There in the seventh row is a passenger who stayed on the coach. How long do you think it will take that client to tell others about what has transpired or to write to the tour company about this tour manager's attitude?

Liaisons with Clients and Colleagues

The story is almost a cliche: an actor on a distant location has an affair with an actress, who happens to be married to the studio chief, who in turn . . . Well, you know the plot. Of such stuff gossip magazines are made.

But there's a kernel of truth in such tales. For when people go for a week or two to a faraway place, they often leave their morals at home. The implication for a tour conductor, who is already a sort of star to forty clients, is clear: a liaison with a client can happen swiftly and with uncommon ease. Single or married, male or female, twenty years old or sixty—it doesn't matter; almost every tour director will someday be given the opportunity for an easy fling.

But on-tour affairs are fraught with peril. Will the situation become known to the other passengers? If it does, it will surely upset some of them. Will it lead to a neglect of duties? If a tour manager makes a wrong decision, it will be blamed on any on-going social distraction. What will happen after the tour? Will the home office get a curiously perfumed letter addressed to the tour director? Will a sexual harassment suit be filed? Will word of the affair get back to one's spouse? To cite religious, ethical, and medical objections isn't even necessary; having affairs with clients in any business is just plain stupid.

The same can be said about liaisons with colleagues: at first it may be fascinating, but in the end it's usually uncomfortable, embarrassing, or bitterly nettlesome. There's nothing wrong with socializing with one's peers, but when it goes beyond that, the complications begin.

An awful loneliness can beset tour managers on the road. Chapter 4 gives strategies for overcoming such feelings. Certainly it can happen that a tour director meets someone during the course of a tour who becomes very special. If it's a client, perhaps it would be acceptable to get together with the person after the tour's end. If it's someone at the destination, it might be okay if no conflicts of interest exist. The object of this chapter isn't to moralize; moral systems are best left to each individual. Your overriding business ethic, though, should be to do nothing that could corrode the quality of your tour, or even anything that might be *perceived* as detrimental to your on-job performance.

The Question of Money

You might think that a tour director's greatest temptation is sex. Think again. For many tour managers, it's money.

Appeals to a tour conductor's greed are endless. The most obvious, though, are kickbacks, schemes to boost tips, and pilfering from the tour company.

Kickbacks. Usually, after only a few weeks on the job, a tour manager becomes acquainted with a myriad of methods to make extra cash. Here the peer grapevine works only too well. If a tour stops at a certain souvenir

stand, 10 percent of total purchases will end up in the tour leader's pocket. If a certain extra boat ride is arranged, 10 percent of the ticket price will be returned as a "commission." If breakfast is set up in an out-of-the-way Las Vegas restaurant, a $20 bill may be stuffed into the tour manager's pocket. If a Hong Kong tailor shop or a gem store is the stop, commissions could approach thousands of dollars.

Certain commissions seem justifiable. Some tour operators sanction escort commissions for extra sightseeing trips; they may even require that the tour manager divide this money with the home office. What happens in this case is that the standard 10 percent commission that would flow back to the tour company is divided with the tour leader to provide him or her with a sales incentive. Also, a commission-gift, such as a case of oranges from a Florida fruit stand, seems acceptable, since it's not much different from a free meal at a restaurant. Like any gift or comp, however, it should not be overdone.

The following considerations should guide you:

▼ *Avoid any kickbacks that come from suppliers who charge your clients more than the going rate.* A jewelry store that slips you a 10 percent commission but charges your client 10 percent more than every other jewelry shop in town is fleecing your clients. So, too, are you.

▼ *Don't steer a group to a store or unplanned attraction at the expense of the official itinerary.* Clients aren't naïve—they resent it when a tour becomes a series of unexpected buying stops.

▼ *Never take a kickback from a supplier when the company is paying.* The one exception is when the tour operator has sanctioned the commissioned activity.

▼ *Be completely informed about your company's commission policies.* Check the company tour manual. If it forbids some or all commissions, don't even think about sneaking around the rules. If found out, you'll probably be fired.

▼ *Make sure to split acceptable commissions with the motorcoach driver.* This is an unwritten but firm rule, especially on a motorcoach tour where the same driver is with you for several days. A three-way split may be warranted if a step-on guide is involved. On the other hand, you must resist a driver's or guide's efforts to steer a group beyond what you or the company deems appropriate.

▼ *When a restaurant comps your meal, be reasonable about what you order.* This is not the time to order appetizers, soup, salad, the most expensive entree, and dessert. Always leave a tip, even if the meal is free.

Tip-Boosting Schemes. Gratuities are part and parcel of tour conducting (though a few companies and most incentive companies prohibit them). The usual procedure is for a company to announce in its brochure that "tips for escort and driver are not included in the tour price. If you wish to show your appreciation for a job well done, a gratuity of $3 per person per day is customary." Other companies add that "such appreciation should be extended on a voluntary, individual basis and not as a group," thus discouraging awkward group "pass the hat" collections. Still others provide clients with special preprinted envelopes, much like those in the cruise industry, in which they can place their gratuity and hand to the driver and tour leader at tour's end.

Gratuities can be a substantial portion of a tour manager's remuneration. Tips reflect an escort's performance: usually, the better the tour directors do their jobs, the better their gratuities will be. (By the way, clients tend to tip more per day on a short tour than on a long one.)

Occasionally, tour conductors use sly ways to enhance their tips. If a company permits group collections, a driver or tour leader may manipulate one persuasive, cooperative passenger into getting a group tip rolling (and suggesting a dollar amount). A certain tour director, in order to augment a group's generosity, was notorious for telling passengers that his birthday happened to be taking place during the tour. He did this every tour, every week. When clients from different departures began comparing notes, his scam came to an end. So did his job.

Pilfering. One disquieting poll discovered that 68 percent of all workers in the United States steal supplies from their work. There's no reason to believe that the touring business is any different. Some tour managers steal travel bags, sell off unused tickets, make claims for phony expenses, and bury unauthorized personal charges in the hotel bill. One tour conductor once cashed company checks, which he then lost on the blackjack tables of Atlantic City. When discovered, he claimed that he had "loaned" the money to himself.

When a tour manager signs on for a job, he or she agrees, *de facto*, that the salary is acceptable and the perks well defined. To go beyond these agreed-upon boundaries is clearly unprofessional, unethical, and foolish.

Alcohol and Drugs

What reason do alcohol- or drug-dependent people give for their substance-abuse problems? Ask any therapist or health care professional and they'll tell you that one of the most common reasons they hear is "to get away from problems."

Pleasant Holidays, an operator of independent tours, has 300 employees at its headquarters and 1,700 worldwide. *Courtesy of Pleasant Holidays*

Whether this is the real reason or an excuse doesn't matter. Tour management is a career replete with "problems." To ease the challenge of dealing with forty clients or to dampen the loneliness of the road, some tour managers resort to the false relief that alcohol or drugs can bring.

If you think substance abuse has become a problem for you, don't even hesitate: see a doctor or other professional *immediately*.

After reading the above, you may conclude that tour conductors are a sleazy bunch, but rest assured that the complete opposite is true. The vast majority of tour managers are loyal, ethical, and thoroughly brilliant at giving the traveling public a splendid and superior vacation experience.

Some Final Words

If your goal is to serve in a clerical, administrative, or sales-related position at a tour company, know that you'll be involved in one of the most creative and exciting segments of the travel industry. If you wish to be a tour manager, this book should prepare you well. On the job you'll continue to learn and grow. Remember that someday, somewhere, someone will take out a photo album, show it to a friend, point out a certain picture, and say, "And that was our tour manager. That escort really did make our trip!"

Summary

A would-be tour manager should begin a job search in early spring when tour operators gear up for the high tour season ahead. Someone who is looking for a non-escort position can apply at any time. A resume should list essential data, work experience, education, special skills, personal information, and references. It should be accompanied by a brief, striking cover letter.

At an interview, an applicant should present a professional appearance, exhibit knowledge of the company, be on time, ask good questions, and be natural. Afterwards, the applicant should follow up with a thank-you note.

To keep a job, a tour manager must be loyal to the needs of both client and company. He or she should avoid entangling liaisons, improper monetary schemes, drugs, and alcohol abuse.

■ ■ ■

QUESTIONS FOR DISCUSSION

1. When does the tour season usually peak? At which two times of the year are companies most likely to hire tour managers?

2. What three sources of applicant information do tour operators pay close attention to?

3. Name the seven sections of a good resume.

4. List six "do's" for effective resumes.

5. What elements make for a successful cover letter?

6. Indicate seven strategies that you should follow as part of the interview process.

7. What three bad habits must a tour manager avoid with regard to loyalty to company, clients, job, and self?

8. Give four reasons why on-tour affairs are a bad idea.

9. Three temptations exist when it comes to money and tours. What are they?

10. List five considerations that should guide you when dealing with kickbacks or commissions.

■ ■ ■

ACTIVITY 1

▼ Complete the outlined resume below. Enter no more than three items in any given section. Use the reverse-chronological format.

Essential data:

Job objective:

Work experience:

Education:

Special skills:

Personal data:

■ ■ ■

ACTIVITY 2

▼ If you were being interviewed for a position as a tour conductor, how would you answer the following questions? Answer each question with a maximum of three sentences.

1. Why do you want to be a tour manager?

2. Do you realize how much work tour conducting is?

3. What is it about your previous work experience that you think makes you qualified?

4. What do you think would be the hardest thing about escorting for you?

5. What previous job did you like most? Why? Which one did you like least? Why?

6. Do you see tour managing as a short-term or a long-term career?

7. What was your favorite vacation trip? Why?

8. Don't you think your friends and family will object to your being away so much?

■ ■ ■

ACTIVITY 3

▼ Describe what you would do in each of the following situations.

CASE 1: You're on a city tour. Most of your group seems tired and bored. Only a few minor attractions remain to be pointed out. It's 4 P.M. You're supposed to tour until 4:45 P.M., but you could cut the tour short and return to the hotel.

Your strategy:

CASE 2: You're conducting a tour in Florida, with clients from all parts of the country. No activities are planned for tomorrow evening. A representative from a land development company comes to you and offers to provide dinner for your whole group, free of charge, the next evening if the group is willing to listen to a sales pitch for buying Florida land.

Your strategy:

CASE 3: It's the last tour of the season. You've been conducting the same tour all summer. Your group is about to board a harbor cruise boat (something your company has set up for your groups to do every week). The owner of the company, who has become somewhat of a friend, asks you to join him while your group is on the cruise. You agree, since the guide on the boat tends to your group and your presence on the large boat is rarely noticed anyway. The owner takes you to a clothing store. He says, "Buy anything you want. It's my way of showing my thanks."

Your strategy:

CASE 4: It's 2 A.M. There's a knock on your hotel room door. You open it. A very attractive passenger who is on your tour is standing there, smiling. The passenger is naked.

Your strategy:

CASE 5: You're a trip director for an incentive tour to Seoul, South Korea. The group insists on visiting a specific electronics store, which you know gives commissions to the tour conductor. You stop there. The manager tells you that of course she'll give you 10 percent of all your clients' purchases as a commission.

Your strategy:

CASE 6: You and your colleague are escorting two busloads of clients on a return from a Mexico tour. You've crossed the border and were subjected to only a minor inspection. Both groups are in a restaurant, dining. You go out to the motorcoach to get something out of the underneath luggage compartment. You open the compartment of the other tour conductor's coach by mistake. It's filled with a dozen television sets.

Your strategy:

■ ■ ■

ACTIVITY 4

Your name is Y. Lee Coyote. ACME Tours has asked you to serve as one of their tour conductors this summer. They ask you to sign the contract given below.

▼ Read the contract carefully, then answer the questions that follow.

Sample Agreement Between a Tour Operator and a Tour Manager

This professional services agreement is entered into by and between *ACME Tours,* a company incorporated in the State of Delaware and based in New York City, hereafter referred to as the Tour Operator, and *Y. Lee Coyote,* an independent contractor operating his business based in Burbank, California, hereafter referred to as the Tour Conductor. This agreement will be in effect from June 1, 2001, to September 4, 2001.

The Tour Conductor shall travel with ACME's pre-formed groups as specified in ACME's tour itinerary and shall perform, to his best efforts, all typical tour conducting functions, including but not limited to the management and coordination of the group's activities at airports, hotels, cruise ships, trains, restaurants, attractions, motorcoaches and other such locations, as specified in the tour departure's itinerary, as well as give sightseeing commentary, as needed. As an independent contractor, the Tour Conductor reserves the right to exercise his judgment with regard to commentary content, routings, scheduling, problem resolution, and the like, provided that such judgments are consistent with the passengers' expectations, such expectations being the result of the Tour Operator's tour itinerary and promotional materials, as well as the Tour Operator's expectations with regard to the tour's costs, legal requirements, and the like.

The Tour Operator shall treat the Tour Conductor's expenses as part of the group's normal expenses. As a result, the Tour Operator shall pay for any and all transportation, accommodation, dining, baggage handling, and similar expenses that would normally be included as part of a passenger's paid-for tour package and that are incurred by the Tour Conductor, including "repositioning" travel costs to get the Tour Conductor to the tour's starting point and from the tour's end point. The Tour Operator shall also pay the Tour Conductor $120 per calendar day for his rendered services, beginning with the first day he meets his group through the last day he will be with the group.

Both parties to this agreement acknowledge that the Tour Conductor, as a self-employed independent contractor, reserves the right to accept or refuse each assignment offered by the Tour Operator during the duration of this agreement, according to his circumstances and schedule. The Tour Conductor also reserves the right to accept assignments from other tour operators. Once a tour management assignment is offered and accepted by the Tour Conductor, he must not accept any other assignment from another company for the same time period unless the Tour Operator cancels the tour or releases, in writing, the Tour Conductor from his agreed-upon assignment. The Tour Conductor agrees to not accept commissions, fees, and the like from hotels, restaurants, attractions, stores, and other suppliers who provide components to the tour's itinerary, since such fees or commissions may compromise the relationship, stated or implied, between the Tour Operator and the passengers and/or suppliers.

The Tour Conductor represents and warrants that he is an independent contractor for purposes of federal, state, and local employment taxes. The Tour Conductor agrees that ACME Tours is not responsible to collect or withhold any federal, state, or local employment taxes, including, but not limited to, income tax withholding and social security contributions, for the Tour Conductor. Any and all taxes, interest, or penalties, including, but not limited to, any federal, state, or local withholding or employment taxes imposed, assessed, or levied as a result of this Agreement shall be paid or withheld by the Tour Conductor upon demand by the Tour Operator.

The Tour Conductor also acknowledges that, as an independent contractor, he is in no manner entitled to health insurance coverage, profit-sharing plans, health plans, unemployment benefits, paid sick leave, paid vacation leave, overtime pay, or other such benefits which the Tour Operator may provide its employees.

This Agreement shall be governed by and construed in accordance with the laws of the State of New York. The Tour Conductor hereby consents and submits to the jurisdiction of the courts in the State of New York in all questions and controversies arising out of this Agreement. This Agreement constitutes the entire agreement between the parties.

Executed on the dates set forth below to be effective as of the date first above written by the Tour Operator and the Tour Conductor.

for ACME Tours

Date:_____

Print name: _____

Date:_____

Address: _____

SS#: _____

1. If another company asks you to conduct a tour for the week of July 4 at a rate of $150, can you accept the assignment?

2. Can you accept gratuities from passengers?

3. Will ACME reimburse you for phone calls that you make to reconfirm restaurant or hotel reservations?

4. Will ACME withhold social security from your paycheck?

5. How far in advance must ACME inform you that a tour you've been booked to conduct has been canceled?

6. Your tour arrives in Boston. Will you or a step-on guide give the city tour?

7. The itinerary shows no rest stop scheduled during a three-hour motorcoach ride. Can you schedule one?

8. Can you set up a nightclub tour for your passengers on an evening when ACME has not scheduled anything?

9. You go to a restaurant where the passengers must pay for their meal—the lunch is not included in the tour package price. Will ACME reimburse you for the cost of your meal?

10. You travel on June 15 from Burbank to New York City. You will meet the group on June 16 for a seven-day tour of New England. But on the morning of June 16, you wake up sick and cannot take the group. Will you still be paid for the New England tour? Will you be paid for your June 15 travel day?

■ ■ ■

Useful Addresses

American Association of Retired Persons
(AARP)
601 E St., NW
Washington, DC 20049
(202) 872-4700

American Bus Association (ABA)
1100 New York Ave., NW, Suite 1050
Washington, DC 20005-3934
(202) 842-1645

American Hotel and Motel Association
(AHMA)
1201 New York Ave., NW, #600
Washington, DC 20005-3931
(202) 289-3100

American Society of Travel Agents (ASTA)
1101 King St.
Alexandria, VA 22314
(703) 739-2782

Association of American Railroads
American Railroads Bldg.
50 F St., NW, F13
Washington, DC 20001
(202) 639-2100

Council on Hotel, Restaurant and Institutional
Education
1200 17th St., NW
Washington, DC 20036-3097
(202) 331-5990

Cruise Lines International Association
500 5th Ave., Suite 1407
New York, NY 10110
(212) 921-0066

Culturgrams Series
1305 N. Research Way
Orem, UT 84097-6200
(801) 705-4250

Group Wizard: Group Management Software
FST Systems
319 W. Church St.
Elmira, NY 14901
(607) 732-4781

Institute of Certified Travel Agents (ICTA)
P.O. Box 812059
Wellesley, MA 02181-0012
(781) 237-0280

International Association of Amusement Parks
and Attractions
1448 Duke St.
Alexandria, VA 22314
(703) 836-4800

International Association of Tour Managers
65 Charnes Dr.
East Haven, CT 06513-1225
(203) 466-0425

International Tour Management Institute (ITMI)
625 Market St., Suite 810
San Francisco, CA 94105
(415) 957-9489

National Tour Association (NTA)
P.O. Box 3071
Lexington, KY 40596
(606) 226-4444

Society for Advancement of Travel for the
Handicapped (SATH)
347 Fifth Ave., Suite 610
New York, NY 10016
(212) 447-7284

Society of Incentive & Travel Executives (SITE)
21 W. 38th St., 10th Fl.
New York, NY 10018-5584
(212) 575-0910

Society of Travel and Tourism Educators
c/o Tomkins Cortland Community College
Box 139
Dryden, NY 13053
(607) 884-8211

United Motorcoach Association
113 S. West St.
Alexandria, VA 22314
(703) 838-2929

United States Tour Operators Association (USTOA)
342 Madison Ave., Suite 1522
New York, NY 10173
(212) 599-6599

B

Tour Operators

This is a list of North America major tour operators. The information is up-to-date, as of printing. However, addresses and phone numbers change frequently.

AAT King's Australian Tours
9430 Topanga Canyon Blvd.
Chatsworth, CA 91311
(818) 700-2732

Abercrombie & Kent International
1520 Kensington Rd.
Oak Brook, IL 60523-2141
(630) 954-2944

African Travel
1100 E. Broadway
Glendale, CA 91205
(818) 507-7893

AHI International
6400 Shafer Ct., Suite 200
Rosemont, IL 60018
(847) 384-4500

Air France Holidays
440 Franklin Turnpike
Mahwah, NJ 07430-2211
(201) 934-3500

All About Tours
12168 SW Garden Pl.
Tigard, OR 97223
(503) 598-0100

Ambassador Programs
S110 Ferrell St.
Spokane, WA 99202
(509) 534-6200

American Student Travel
16225 Park Ten Pl., Suite 450
Houston, TX 77084
(281) 647-7000

Americantours International
6053 W. Century Blvd.
Los Angeles, CA 90045
(310) 641-9953

Anderson Coach & Tour
One Anderson Plaza
Greenville, PA 16125
(724) 588-8310

Apple Vacations
7 Campus Blvd.
Newtown Square, PA 19073
(610) 359-6500

ATA Vacations
7337 W. Washington St.
Indianapolis, IN 46251-0609
(317) 240-7115

ATS Tours & Islands in the Sun
2381 Rosecrans Ave., Suite 325
El Segundo, CA 90245
(310) 643-0044

Australian Pacific Tours
4805 Lankershim Blvd., Suite 620
North Hollywood, CA 91602
(818) 755-6392

Blue Sky Tours
10832 Prospect Ave., NE
Albuquerque, NM 87112
(505) 293-0696

Brendan Tours
15137 Califa St.
Van Nuys, CA 91411
(818) 785-9696

Brennan Tours
1402 3rd Ave., Suite 717
Seattle, WA 98101-2118
(206) 622-9155

Brian Moore International Tours
1208 VFW Pkwy., Suite 202
Boston, MA 02132
(617) 469-3300

CanAm Tours
3768 Bathurst St., Suite 307
North York, ON M3H 3M6
Canada
(416) 630-3499

Caravan Tours
401 N. Michigan Ave.
Chicago, IL 60611
(312) 321-9800

Celtic International Tours
1860 Western Ave.
Albany, NY 12203
(518) 862-0042

Central Holidays
P.O. Box 1664
Englewood Cliffs, NJ 07632
(201) 228-5200

Certified Vacations Group
P.O. Box 1525
Ft. Lauderdale, FL 33301
(954) 522-1440

Chi-Am Tours
98 Bowery St.
New York, NY 10013
(212) 334-3600

China Travel Service
575 Sutter St., Lower Fl.
San Francisco, CA 94102
(415) 398-6627

CIE Tours International
P.O. Box 501
Cedar Knolls, NJ 07927-0501
(973) 292-3899

CIT Tours
15 W. 44th St., 10th Fl.
New York, NY 10036
(212) 730-2121

Classic Custom Vacations
One N. First St., Third Fl.
San Jose, CA 95113-1215
(408) 287-4550

Collette Tours
162 Middle St.
Pawtucket, RI 02860
(401) 728-3805

Contiki Holidays
3300 E. Katella Ave.
Anaheim, CA 92806-6046
(714) 935-0808

Cumberland Tours
P.O. Box 50590
Nashville, TN 37205
(615) 352-4169

Dan Dipert Tours
P.O. Box 580
Arlington, TX 76004
(817) 543-3720

DER Travel Service
9501 W. Devon Ave.
Rosemont, IL 60018
(847) 430-0000

Donatello Tours
14 E. 60th St.
New York, NY 10022
(212) 755-5000

Educational Field Studies
14325 Willard Rd., Suite 102
Chantilly, VA 20151
(703) 631-7078

Educational Travel Services
5725 Imperial Lakes Blvd.
Mulberry, FL 33860
(941) 644-2456

FreeGateTourism
585 Stewart Ave., Suite 310
Garden City, NY 11530
(516) 222-0855

Friendly Holidays
1983 Marcus Ave., Suite C-130
Lake Success, NY 11042
(516) 358-1320

Gate 1
101 Limekiln Pike
Glenside, PA 19038
(215) 572-7676

General Tours
53 Summer St.
Keene, NH 03431
(603) 357-5033

Global Leisure Travel
100 W. Harrison, Suite 350
Seattle, WA 98119-4123
(206) 216-2905

Global Vacation Group
1420 New York Ave., NW, Suite 550
Washington, DC 20005
(202) 347-1800

Globetrotters MTI
2211 Butterfield Rd.
Downers Grove, IL 60515
(630) 271-6000

Globus & Cosmos
5301 S. Federal Circle
Littleton, CO 80123-2980
(303) 703-7000

GOGO Worldwide Vacations
69 Spring St.
Ramsey, NJ 07430
(201) 934-3500

HMHF Fun Vacations
29566 Northwestern Hwy.
Southfield, MI 48034
(248) 827-4050

Holland America Line-Westours
300 Elliott Ave. W.
Seattle, WA 98119-1422
(206) 281-3535 / (206) 286-3442

Homeric Tours
55 E. 59th St.
New York, NY 10022
(212) 753-1100

Insight Vacations
745 Atlantic Ave., Suite 720
Boston, MA 02111
(617) 482-2000

Intrav
7711 Bonhomme Ave.
St. Louis, MO 63105-1961
(314) 727-0500

Isram World of Travel
630 Third Ave.
New York, NY 10017-6780
(212) 661-1193

IST Cultural Tours
225 W. 34th St.
New York, NY 10122
(212) 563-1202

Japan & Orient Tours
4025 Camino del Rio S., Suite 200
San Diego, CA 92108-1719
(619) 282-3131

Jetset Tours
5120 W. Goldleaf Circle, Suite 310
Los Angeles, CA 90045-1268
(323) 290-5800

Kailani Hawaii Tours
P.O. Box 9751
Bellingham, WA 98226
(360) 752-4505

Kingdom Vacations
22 S. River St.
Plains, PA 18705
(570) 824-5800

Lakeland Tours
2000 Holiday Dr.
Charlottesville, VA 22901
(804) 982-8600

The Leisure Company
111 W. Rio Salado Pkwy.
Tempe, AZ 85281
(480) 693-7580

Lindblad Special Expeditions
720 Fifth Ave., 6th Fl.
New York, NY 10019
(212) 765-7740

The Mark Travel Corp.
8907 N. Port Washington Rd.
Milwaukee, WI 53217
(414) 228-7472

Maupintour
1421 Research Park Dr., Suite 300
Lawrence, KS 66049-3858
(785) 331-1000

Mayflower Tours
P.O. Box 490
Downers Grove, IL 60515-3597
(630) 435-8500

MLT
5130 County Rd. 101
Minnetonka, MN 55345-4172
(612) 470-7777

Mountain Vacations
12075 E. 45th Ave., Suite 220
Denver, CO 80239
(303) 214-7000

Newmans South Pacific Vacations
6033 W. Century Blvd., Suite 1270
Los Angeles, CA 90045
(310) 348-8282

Nippon Express Travel USA
720 Market St., 6th Fl.
San Francisco, CA 94102
(415) 434-4060

Pacific Bestour
228 Rivervale Rd.
Rivervale, NJ 07675
(201) 664-8778

Pacific Delight Tours
204 E. 42nd St., Suite 1908
New York, NY 10017-5706
(212) 818-1781

Paragon Tours
P.O. Box 499
Swansea, MA 02777
(508) 379-1976

Parker Tours
255 Executive Dr., Suite LL110
Plainview, NY 11803
(516) 349-0575

Peter Pan Tours
P.O. Box 1776
Springfield, MA 01102-1776
(413) 781-2900

Pleasant Holidays
2404 Townsgate Rd.
Westlake Village, CA 91361
(818) 991-3390

Pleasure Break Vacations
3701 Algonquin Rd., Suite 900
Rolling Meadows, IL 60008
(847) 670-6301

Presley Tours
P.O. Box 5B
Makanda, IL 62958-0058
(618) 549-0704

Princess Tours
2815 Second Ave., Suite 400
Seattle, WA 98121
(206) 336-6000

Rail Europe Group
500 Mamaroneck Ave., Suite 314
Harrison, NY 10528
(914) 682-2999

Rebel Tours
25050 Ave. Kearny #215
Valencia, CA 91355
(805) 294-0871

Regina Tours
401 South St., Suite 4B
Chardon, OH 44024
(440) 286-9141

Runaway Tours
120 Montgomery St., Suite 800
San Francisco, CA 94104
(415) 788-0224

Sunburst Holidays
4779 Broadway
New York, NY 10034
(212) 567-2050

Sunmakers Travel
100 W. Harrison, Suite 350
Seattle, WA 98119-4123
(206) 216-2900

Sunny Land Tours
166 Main St.
Hackensack, NJ 07601
(201) 487-2150

Tauck World Discovery
P.O. Box 5027
Westport, CT 06881-5027
(203) 226-6911

Tourlite International
551 Fifth Ave.
New York, NY 10176
(212) 599-3355

Trafalgar Tours
11 E. 26th St., Suite 1300
New York, NY 10010
(212) 689-8977

Travcoa
2350 SE Bristol St.
Newport Beach, CA 92660
(949) 476-2800

Travel Bound
599 Broadway
New York, NY 10012
(212) 334-1350

Travel Impressions
465 Smith St.
Farmingdale, NY 11735
(516) 845-8000

Travel Industry Partners
2601 S. Bayshore Dr.
Miami, FL 33133
(305) 860-2556

Uniworld
16000 Ventura Blvd., Suite 200
Encino, CA 91436
(818) 382-7820

Vacationland
690 Market St., Suite 222
San Francisco, CA 94104
(415) 788-0503

Your Man Tours
8831 Aviation Blvd.
Inglewood, CA 90301
(310) 649-3820

Glossary

AC Abbreviation for air-conditioning.

ACTIVITIES DIRECTOR See Cruise Director.

ADD-ONS Optional tour features that are not included in the tour price; also called Optionals.

ADJOINING ROOMS Two rooms located next to each other, usually with no door connecting them.

ADVENTURE TOUR A tour designed around some adventurous activity such as raft riding, hiking, or ballooning.

ADVERTISING Promotion for which the tour operator must pay.

AFFINITY TOURS Tours for groups having something in common, usually made up of individuals who are all members of the same organization.

AFT The back of a ship; also called the Stern.

ALL-EXPENSE TOUR See All-inclusive Tour.

ALL-INCLUSIVE TOUR A tour that offers most of its features (lodging, meals, transportation, admissions, etc.) for a single, inclusive price; also called All-expense Tour or Inclusive Tour.

ATTRACTION The facilities, activities, locations, or sights that a tour visits, such as a monument, museum, or natural wonder.

BAGGAGE HANDLER See Porter.

BEEFEATERS On-site guides at the Tower of London who are world-class authorities on its history.

BELL CAPTAIN The person in charge of luggage at a hotel.

BOARDING PASS The document that allows you to pass through the gate area and onto a plane or ship.

BOW The front of a ship.

CABIN See Stateroom.

CAR MANAGER A step-on guide particular to railroading.

CAROUSEL A type of baggage claim device that is circular in shape.

CARRIER Any company that transports passengers, such as airlines, bus lines, cruise lines, and railroads.

CHARTER To hire a vehicle and/or offer a tour for exclusive use by one company, organization, or group.

CHECK-IN COUNTER The place in an airline terminal, usually near the entrance, where clients check in for a flight.

CHIEF PURSER The person who is in charge of all passenger ship services and financial functions, including shore excursions.

CHIEF STEWARD The person who is in charge of meals and housekeeping on a ship.

CIRCLE ITINERARY An itinerary where the tour begins in a certain city, circles out to other destinations and returns to the original city.

CITY GUIDE Someone who points out and comments on the highlights of a city, usually from a motorcoach, mini-bus, or van.

CITY TOUR A sightseeing trip through a city, usually lasting a day or a half day, during which a guide points out that city's highlights.

COMMISSION (1) A percentage paid to a seller for the sale of an item or service; (2) a kickback.

COMMISSIONABLE Denotes that a percentage of the ticket price or hotel rate, not including taxes, will be paid back to the tour company.

COMPLIMENTARY (COMP) Free of charge.

CONNECTING FLIGHT A flight that requires a passenger to change planes as part of the itinerary.

CONNECTING ROOMS Two rooms that are connected to each other by a door.

CONTINENTAL BREAKFAST A breakfast usually consisting of coffee and rolls.

CONVENTION & VISITORS BUREAU (CVB) An organization that promotes tourism to an area and provides information.

CONVENTION PLANNER See Meeting Planner.

CO-OP MONEY Advertising support provided to a tour operator by a supplier.

COUCHETTE A bunk in a sleeping compartment on a train that sleeps four to six people but has no toilet or sink.

COUPON A piece of paper or cardlike item in a client's air ticket that represents a single flight; see also Voucher.

CRUISE DIRECTOR The person who is, in essence, the head tour manager for an entire ship; also known as the Social Director or Activities Director.

CUSTOMIZED TOUR A tour created by a tour operator specifically for a pre-formed affinity group.

CUSTOMS (1) The procedures by which government agents inspect goods and baggage entering a country in order to check for contraband and to assess any duty or tax due; (2) the behavior patterns of a group or society.

DEADHEADING (1) Making a trip or a segment of a trip without passengers; (2) driving an empty bus somewhere.

DECK One of the floors of a ship.

DECK STEWARD The person who manages deck facilities, including drink service, on a ship.

DEMAND According to marketing principles, desire backed by money.

DESTINATION MARKETING ORGANIZATION (DMO) See Convention & Visitors Bureau.

DIRECT FLIGHT A flight that stops one or more times on the way to a destination, but usually does not require passengers to change planes.

DOCENT Someone who works, free of charge, as a guide at a museum.

DOMESTIC FLIGHT Air travel within the boundaries of one country.

DOUBLE DOUBLE A room with two double beds.

DOUBLE PATH A promotion technique where key words and phrases are highlighted, permitting readers to get the message by merely scanning the article.

DRIVER-GUIDE A guide who does double duty by driving a vehicle while narrating.

DUTY-FREE SHOP A store within an international terminal where passengers leaving on international trips can purchase goods on which import taxes have not been levied.

ETHNOCENTRISM The belief that one's own nationality or ethnic group is superior to all others.

EXCHANGE ORDER See Voucher.

FAMILIARIZATION TRIP (FAM) A tour to acquaint travel agents, tour managers, etc., with a particular destination. Fams are usually offered free of charge or at a greatly reduced rate.

FEEDBACK The irritating whine that occurs when a microphone is in a direct line with a loudspeaker.

FIXED COST Cost that never changes, no matter how many people are on the tour.

FLIGHT ATTENDANT A person who tends to passenger needs on an aircraft; also called Steward or Stewardess.

FLIGHT CREW Pilots, flight engineers, and flight attendants.

FLIGHTSEEING A short trip, either by small aircraft or helicopter, over a scenic place.

FOLIO A hotel master bill listing all group charges.

FREELANCE TOUR See Independent Tour.

FRONT DESK Area in a hotel's lobby where guests check in or a tour manager checks in a group.

GATE AREA The place in an airport from where a flight leaves.

GROUND OPERATOR A type of inbound tour operator who specializes in serving other tour companies' arriving groups in a limited geographic area; also known as Land Operator or Receptive Operator.

GROUP DESK A division of an airline's reservations department that takes care of group reservations.

GROUP RATE See Tour Rate.

GROUPS MANAGER A "one-stop" serviceperson who facilitates all logistic matters on a ship.

GUIDESPEAK A commentary provided to passengers on a tour.

HUB-AND-SPOKE ITINERARY An itinerary where the group is based in one city and stays there for the entire tour, taking day trips to nearby places, but always returning back to the base city at the end of the day.

IMMIGRATION The process by which a government official verifies a person's passport, visa, or birth certificate.

INBOUND TOUR OPERATOR A subcategory of tour operator that specializes mostly in groups arriving in a specific city, area, or country from another place.

INCENTIVE HOUSE A company that approaches a corporation with an overall strategy to boost sales, services, or efficiency by providing some sort of reward to its most productive employees.

INCIDENTALS Purchases or expenditures made by a client that are not included in the purchase price of a tour or of a hotel stay and must be paid by the client.

INCLUSIVE TOUR See All-inclusive Tour.

INDEPENDENT TOUR An unescorted tour; for one price the client receives air travel, a hotel room, attraction admissions, and, typically, a car rental; also called a Freelance Tour.

INSIDE STATEROOM On a ship, a room that has no view.

INTERMODAL OPERATOR A company that combines several forms of transportation, such as plane, motorcoach, ship, and rail, to create a diversified and efficient tour package.

ITINERARY A listing of a tour's day-to-day activities.

JET LAG A physical condition caused by the disruption of a person's "body clock" by long flights over many time zones.

KICKBACK An amount of money paid to a tour manager, driver, etc., for bringing a group to an establishment such as an attraction, restaurant, or souvenir shop.

LAND OPERATOR See Ground Operator.

LOCATOR MAP A map of an area of a city, showing locations of attractions and hotels.

MAITRE D' The person in charge of the dining room on a ship or of a restaurant.

MANIFEST An official list of all passengers on a flight.

MARKETING The process of transferring a product from its producer to consumers.

MEET-AND-GREET Meeting passengers when they arrive in a city, assisting them with luggage, and directing them onward.

MEETING PLANNER A person who plans conventions and business meetings.

MIC Abbreviation for microphone; also spelled Mike.

MOTORCOACH A large, comfortable, well-powered bus that can transport groups and their luggage over long distances.

MOTORCOACH OPERATOR A company that creates tours in which group members are transported via motorcoach to their destination and back.

MYSTERY TOUR A tour in which the destination and itinerary are kept secret to the client until he or she joins the tour.

NARRATION See Guidespeak.

NET See Noncommissionable

NONCOMMISSIONABLE Denotes that no percentage of the ticket price or hotel rate will come back to the tour company; also called Net.

NONSTOP FLIGHT A flight that does not stop on the way to its destination.

ON-SITE GUIDE Someone who conducts tours of one or several hours' duration at a specific building, attraction, or limited area.

ONE-WAY ITINERARY An itinerary where the tour begins in one city and ends in another city.

OPEN-JAW ITINERARY An air itinerary in which passengers fly into one city and depart from a different one.

OPTIONALS See Add-ons.

OUTBOUND OPERATOR A company that takes groups from a given city or country to another city or country.

OUTSIDE STATEROOM On a ship, a room that has a porthole or window.

OVERRIDE A commission over and above the typical 10 percent base.

P.A. A public address system.

PASSENGER SERVICE REP (PSR) An airline or cruise line employee who answers questions and handles special needs.

PAX Industry abbreviation for Passengers.

PER-CAPITA TOUR See Public Tour.

PER DIEM SALARY A set amount per day paid to a tour manager.

PERSONAL GUIDE See Private Guide.

PIED PIPER A member of a group, club, or other organization who helps promote a tour to the group, usually in return for a free trip.

PODIUM The desk at an airline gate at which gate attendants work.

PORT The left side of a ship (while facing the bow).

PORTER A person who handles luggage at an airport, train station, etc.; also called Skycap or Baggage Handler.

PRIVATE GUIDE A guide who takes a very small number of people on their own exclusive tour; also called Personal Guide.

PROPERTY Industry term for hotel.

PUBLIC TOUR A tour offered by a tour operator to the general public; also called Per-capita Tour.

PUBLICITY Promotional information that is disseminated at no cost to the tour company.

RACK RATE The regular, official rate that a hotel charges for a room.

RECEPTIVE OPERATOR See Ground Operator.

RESUME A concise, well-organized summary of what a person has to offer a potential employer.

RHETORIC The art and science of public speaking.

ROOM STEWARD The person who is in charge of passengers' rooms on a ship.

ROOMETTE See Sleeper.

ROUTINE A general procedure used on all tours.

SECURITY GATE The gatelike area at an airport where passengers and their carry-ons are checked for weapons and illegal devices.

SHELLS Preprinted brochures with photos, illustrations, and graphics but no text; also called Slicks.

SHORE EXCURSION A tour upon arrival at a port destination that a passenger on a ship can purchase.

SKYCAP See Porter.

SLEEPER Small sleeping room on a train; also called Roomette or Wagon-lit.

SLEEPER SEAT A seat that reclines to an almost horizontal position, permitting a passenger to sleep.

SLICKS See Shells.

SOCIAL DIRECTOR See Cruise Director.

SPECIALIZED GUIDE A guide whose expertise or skills are highly unique and who has in-depth knowledge of a specific activity or place.

SPLIT ITINERARY An itinerary in which part of the group does one thing while the other part does something else.

SPOT TIME The time at which a tour manager must report for duty.

STARBOARD The right side of a ship (while facing the bow).

STATEROOM A sleeping room on a ship; also called a cabin.

STATION See Terminal.

STEP-ON GUIDE A freelance guide who comes aboard a motorcoach to give an informed overview of the city to be toured.

STEREOTYPING The tendency to believe that an unvarying pattern or manner marks all members of a group.

STERN See Aft.

STEWARD For cruises, see Chief Steward, Room Steward, and Deck Steward. For airlines, see Flight Attendant.

STEWARDESS See Flight Attendant.

STUDENT-STUDY EDUCATIONAL TOUR A tour designed around some educational activity, such as studying Renaissance art.

SUITE A large, luxurious room on a ship.

SUPPLIER A company that provides services to tour operators.

TABLE CAPTAIN A person who oversees a group of tables within a ship's dining room.

TERMINAL A building where clients report for trips via train, plane, etc.; also called a Depot or a Station.

TOUR BROKER See Tour Operator.

TOUR COMMENTARY See Guidespeak.

TOUR COMPANY See Tour Operator.

TOUR CONDUCTOR See Tour Manager.

TOUR COURIER See Tour Manager.

TOUR DIRECTOR See Tour Manager.

TOUR ESCORT See Tour Manager.

TOUR GUIDE Someone who takes people on sightseeing excursions of limited duration.

TOUR LEADER See Tour Manager.

TOUR MANAGER A person who manages a group's movements over a multi-day tour; also called a Tour Conductor, Tour Courier, Tour Escort, Tour Director, or Tour Leader.

TOUR MANUAL A compendium of facts about a company's rules, regulations, and official procedures.

TOUR MENU A menu that limits group clients to two or three entree choices.

TOUR OPERATOR A company that contracts with hotels, restaurants, attractions, airlines, motorcoach operators, and other transportation companies to create a multi-day tour "package"; also called a Tour Company, Tour Packager, Tour Broker, or Wholesaler.

TOUR ORDER See Voucher.

TOUR PACKAGER See Tour Operator.

TOUR RATE A special rate charged by a hotel to tours; also called Group Rate.

TRAINING TOUR A tour composed entirely of new tour managers.

TRANSFER The movement of a group from an airport to a hotel, or vice versa, usually by means of a motorcoach.

TRIP DIRECTOR A tour manager for an incentive company. Larger companies reserve this title for the person who directs all personnel and activities for a particular incentive trip.

TRIPTIK A compact flip-page document that AAA tailor makes for a member's itinerary.

VALUE ADDED TAX (VAT) A type of sales tax levied on merchandise sold in many countries.

VARIABLE COST A cost that changes according to how many people take a tour.

VOUCHER A document that is exchanged for goods or services, substantiating that payment will be or has already been made; also called an Exchange Order, Tour Order, or Coupon.

WAGON-LIT See Sleeper.

WHOLESALER See Tour Operator.

Bibliography

Bravos, Brook Shannon. *Cruise Hosting.* Sausalito, CA: Travel Time Publishing, 1992.

Bryant, Carl, Isaac Reynolds, and Teresa Poole. *Travel Selling Skills.* Albany, NY: Delmar Publishers, 1993.

Burke, James, and Barry Resnick. *Marketing and Selling the Travel Product.* Albany, NY: Delmar Publishers, 2000.

Dervaes, Claudine. *The Travel Dictionary.* Tampa, FL: Solitaire Publishing, 1998.

deSouto, Martha Sarbey. *Group Travel.* Albany, NY: Delmar Publishers, 1993.

Fay, Betsy. *Essentials of Tour Management.* Englewood Cliffs, NJ: Prentice-Hall, 1992.

Fielder, Anita. *Managing Group Tours.* Holland, MI: Shoreline Creations, 1995.

Klender, Jeane S. A *Coach Full of Fun.* Washington, DC: American Bus Association, 1995.

Kwortnik, Rob, and Marc Mancini. *Essentials of Travel Packaging: Creating, Marketing and Managing the Travel Product.* Lexington, KY: National Tour Association, 1997.

Mancini, Marc. Cruising: *A Guide to the Cruise Line Industry.* Albany, NY: Delmar Publishers, 2000.

Mancini, Marc. Selling Destinations: Geography for the *Travel Professional.* Albany, NY: Delmar Publishers, 1999.

Pond, Kathleen Lingle. *The Professional Guide.* New York, NY: Van Nostrand Reinhold, 1993.

Poynter, James M. *Tour Design, Marketing, and Management.* Englewood Cliffs, NJ: Regents/Prentice Hall, 1993.

Reilly, Robert. *Handbook of Professional Tour Management.* Albany, NY: Delmar Publishers, 1991.

Webster, Susan. *Group Travel Operating Procedures.* New York, NY: Van Nostrand Reinhold, 1993.

Regularly Updated Publications

Hotel and Travel Index. Riverton, NJ: Cahners Travel Group.

OAG Business Travel Planner. Oakbrook, IL: OAG Worldwide.

Official Cruise Guide. Riverton, NJ: Cahners Travel Group.

Official Hotel Guide. Riverton, NJ: Cahners Travel Group.

Star Service. Riverton, NJ: Cahners Travel Group.

Travel Agent Official Travel Industry Directory. New York, NY: Advanstar Communications.

Weissmann Travel Reports. Austin, TX: Weissmann Travel Reports.

World Travel Guide. Roanoke, VA: SFC Travel Publications.

Index

CPSIA information can be obtained
at www.ICGtesting.com
Printed in the USA
FFOW03n1523070715
14980FF

9 780766 814196